What if I told you that so-called "b[...] was not really "biblical"? What if [...] and womanhood" was in fact an artificial constru[...] [...]ban, affluent, middle-class culture in the post-World War II era with its weird marriage of consumerism and patriarchy. Curious? Well, if you're up to it, follow Aimee Byrd down the rabbit hole, and she will deconstruct every mistruth that you've been sold about the Bible and women, and then she'll give you a more biblical and genuinely Christian account of men, women, and ministry. But be warned! Once you go down this trail, there is no going back; you won't view marriage or ministry the same way ever again. This book could provide the gender reset that evangelical churches have needed for a long time. No, not a dour and dismal descent into liberalism but the beginning of a true recovery of the biblical vision of women as partners in the church of Christ and the gospel. Byrd is bringing down the #GenderReformation to crush "biblical manhood" under the weight of its interpretive incredulity, its pastoral irresponsibility, its refusal to listen to female voices, and its captivity to culture.

REV. DR. MICHAEL F. BIRD, academic dean and lecturer
in theology at Ridley College, Melbourne, Australia

The biblical-manhood-and-womanhood movement has generated more heat than light because it has failed to recognize that its own pet theories of manhood and womanhood derive more from black-and-white TV of the 1950s—think of Timmy's mom and dad in *Lassie*—than from the Bible. What makes this obvious are the many studies on what it was like to be a man or a woman in the time of Barak and Deborah, Ruth and David, or the Syrophoenician woman and Jesus, or Priscilla and Paul in their Greco-Roman world. We now know that the so-called manhood-and-womanhood movement is a set of cultural ideas imposed on the Bible itself. Byrd offers here enduring wisdom and wit about how we as Christians ought to relate to one another as "coed colaborers."

SCOT MCKNIGHT, professor of New Testament,
Northern Seminary

With a deep reverence for Scripture and a sincere search for truth, Aimee Byrd peels back the layers of culturally informed teachings on gender that keep both women and men from flourishing in Christ and in relationship with each other. This is the book that Christians who have been misled by popular notions of biblical manhood and womanhood—but who still believe that maleness and femaleness are meaningful categories in the church, home, and society—have been waiting for.

KATELYN BEATY, author, *A Woman's Place*

Aimee Byrd has written a book that will impact the church-and-gender conversation for years to come. *Recovering from Biblical Manhood and Womanhood* doesn't only expose the emptiness of so-called "biblical manhood and womanhood" teaching, it presents a vision of true Christian complementarity defined by empowered women, sibling love, and union with Christ. Saturated in Scripture and rooted in a strong theological tradition, this is the book that Aimee has been working toward for years. I thank God that it's here.

MARCOS ORTEGA, assistant pastor, Goodwill Church (EPC), founder of Reformed Margins and cohost of the Family Discussion podcast

I am not a prophet nor the son of a prophet, but I have a prediction. Many people who haven't read Aimee Byrd's book will praise her for positions she does not hold and criticize her for things she does not believe. But let's hope I'm wrong. Why? Because it would be wonderful if all of us might listen attentively to a sister who is calling *all* believers—women and men—to grow in their love of Scripture even as she asks us to recognize our blind spots and problematic assumptions. Here is an author who cares deeply that our worship is biblical, trinitarian, and consistently leading to and promoting a holy communion of the saints.

KELLY M. KAPIC, author of *The God Who Gives: How the Trinity Shapes the Christian Story*

After years of vigorous and insightful interaction, egalitarians and complementarians today have too often retreated to their own tribes, even setting up requirements for membership unlike any in the history of the church. Fortunately, there are also several recent writers who defy simplistic categorization or labeling, who are calling on the church to consider new and healthy directions with respect to just what the Bible does and doesn't teach about being faithful Christian women and men. Aimee Byrd is one of these writers, and people from every perspective on the topic can learn much from her study of Scripture and of history as well as her personal experience.

CRAIG L. BLOMBERG, distinguished professor
of New Testament, Denver Seminary

If there is a slippery subject in the church today, it's "biblical manhood and womanhood." We're confused by the disagreements, constricted by the "rules," and seemingly helpless to discern what's true. This is why Aimee Byrd's book is so important. Wading through the cultural murkiness, Byrd returns us to Scripture with theological rigor. I celebrate her strong voice and urgent plea to recover a better vision—for the good of the family and the church.

JEN POLLOCK MICHEL, award-winning author of
Surprised by Paradox and *Keeping Place*

RECOVERING FROM BIBLICAL MANHOOD & WOMANHOOD

*How the Church Needs to
Rediscover Her Purpose*

AIMEE BYRD

ZONDERVAN
REFLECTIVE

ZONDERVAN REFLECTIVE

Recovering from Biblical Manhood and Womanhood
Copyright © 2020 by Aimee Byrd

Requests for information should be addressed to:
Zondervan, *3900 Sparks Dr. SE, Grand Rapids, Michigan 49546*

ISBN 978-0-310-10871-9 (softcover)

ISBN 978-0-310-10873-3 (audio)

ISBN 978-0-310-10872-6 (ebook)

Cover design: Darren Welch Design
Cover photos: © Srdjan Jovic / Shutterstock; © duncan1890 / iStock
Interior design: Kait Lamphere

Printed in the United States of America

HB 11.09.2023

To my husband, Matt, who never
cared for yellow wallpaper.

CONTENTS

ACKNOWLEDGMENTS

This project has morphed and narrowed its focus as it hit different roadblocks along the way. In its infancy, the book was guided by several people who helped me to corral my ideas into the work that lies before you. I'm thankful for Bob Brady and Jonathan Master at the Alliance of Confessing Evangelicals for meeting with me as I began developing my vision. I'm thankful for the speaking opportunities that I've had, beginning with Fourth Presbyterian Church in Philadelphia, to share my work going into this and to engage with both laypeople and church leaders. Thanks to Mike Allen and Kelly Kapic for introducing me to an editor whom they thought would be a good fit as I was continuing to shape the book. That leads me to Katya Covrett, who took the time to call me, ask good questions, and point out that maybe the road block needs to be addressed more directly.

Some sections of the book are taken from talks I gave. Particularly, I'd like to thank the Alliance of Confessing Evangelicals for the permission to use material from my time at the Women at the Feet of Jesus conference, as well as *Modern Reformation* for the permission to include an article I wrote for them, "Silence of the Women." Also, I deeply appreciate the feedback from the many men and women who have attended the church retreats and conferences where I've tested out material for the book.

Special thanks are in order to my elder and friend, Dave Myers, who read through my chapters in their beginning stages, offering much insight. Of course, the opinions in the book are my own and do not represent my church or my session. Also, thanks to my friend Anna Anderson for our enriching talks over lunch and for sharing articles and research. And to my husband Matt, who has never read Virginia Woolf, but instinctively knew this woman would need some money (which really translates into time) and a room of my own to get cracking.[1] Your support drives my motivation to explore, discover, and share my work. As I write about peeling wallpaper as a theme in the book, I can't help but remember our first townhouse and how hard it was for us to peel off all that ugly wallpaper together. We had no idea what a metaphor that was!

1. "A woman must have money and a room of her own if she is to write" (Virginia Woolf, *A Room of One's Own* [New York: Harvest, 1989], 4).

THE INTRODUCTION THAT YOU MAY NOT SKIP!

The Church's Yellow Wallpaper

Charlotte Perkins Gilman's doctor drove her mad. His prescription for her unknown condition did, anyway. Gilman's condition was, in her own words, a "severe and continuous nervous breakdown tending to melancholia and beyond."[1] Gilman was showing signs of severe postpartum depression. But in the nineteenth century these symptoms were not often diagnosed properly and were easily labeled as "neurasthenia," a fashionable diagnosis for the privileged class that looked to blame all anxious symptoms on "the accelerating pace of modern life."[2]

Gilman finally sought relief from one of the best-known specialists in nervous diseases of her time, Dr. S. Weir Mitchell. What was his terrible prescription that pushed Gilman "so near the border line of utter mental ruin that [she] could see over"?[3] Believing that her problem was too much mental and social activity, Dr. Mitchell prescribed

---

1. Charlotte Perkins Gilman, "Why I Wrote *The Yellow Wallpaper*," The Forerunner, www.nlm.nih.gov/exhibition/theliteratureofprescription/education/materials/WhyIWrote YellowWallPaper.pdf.

2. Nitsuh Abebe, "America's New 'Anxiety' Disorder," First Words, *New York Times Magazine*, April 18, 2017, www.nytimes.com/2017/04/18/magazine/americas-new-anxiety -disorder.html?ref=todayspaper.

3. Gilman, "Why I Wrote *The Yellow Wallpaper*."

rest therapy: abstention from any mental, social, or physical activity. From her 1887 visit, Gilman describes doctor's orders: "[He] sent me home with solemn advice to 'live a domestic a life as far as possible,' to 'have but two hours' intellectual life a day,' and 'never to touch pen, brush or pencil again as long as I lived.'"[4] This is the opposite of what Gilman thought would help her, but he was the expert, after all. And she wanted to get better. So she obeyed the doctor's orders. Instead of getting better, she got much worse.

Something else about Dr. Mitchell and his expertise on neurasthenia: the prescribed cure was very different for men who were suffering the condition than it was for women:

> The underlying notion of neurasthenia—that nervous energy gets depleted because people's bodies weren't built for modern life— provided an easy way to reinforce traditional gender roles. When men spent too much time indoors, when they couldn't keep up with the pace of their work, or had money problems, they were susceptible to neurasthenia. Women were susceptible when they were too socially active, or spent too much time outside the home.
>
> For men, the frontier held the cure. Doctors would often send male neurasthenics westward to ride horses, rope cattle, do push-ups, and slap each other's butts until the sheer manliness of it all restored their nervous energy.[5]

The culture of the time was steeped in Victorian-era values and ideals of what it means to be a man and a woman. Still relying on ancient Greek assumptions, society maintained that women's brains were considered inferior to men's, incapable of contributing at the same intellectual and social level. This culture seeped all the way down to medical diagnoses. Since women weren't even given the right to vote until 1920, poor Charlotte Perkins Gilman didn't have much of a voice

4. Gilman, "Why I Wrote *The Yellow Wallpaper*."

5. Julie Beck, "'Americanitis': The Disease of Living Too Fast," *Atlantic*, March 11, 2016, www.theatlantic.com/health/archive/2016/03/the-history-of-neurasthenia-or-americanitis -health-happiness-and-culture/473253/.

when it came to her own diagnosis and treatment. She was to trust in this diagnosis from a medical authority. And it plunged her into deeper depression and madness.

TAKING CREATIVE ACTION

Somehow Gilman still had the strength of mind to quit this bogus "rest therapy" and regained her mental and physical health. Her now infamous nineteenth-century novella, *The Yellow Wallpaper*, is a brilliant and disturbing exploration of the effects patriarchal attitudes and constrictions have on female psychosynthesis.[6] The woman narrating the story also suffers from a form of postpartum depression and is prescribed the rest cure by her loving doctor, who happens to be her husband. He takes her rest therapy seriously, renting a remote estate house for the summer that has been long vacant and unattended.

In the beginning of the story, the woman admits to the reader that she is defiantly writing in secret. Her concern—one that she would never voice to her husband—is that maybe the fact that he is a physician is the very reason she can't seem to get better. She expresses to her husband her desire to be in a different bedroom, but he disagrees. Instead, she is in a room she thinks used to be a nursery of some sort, but it sounds more like a house prison with its barred windows, gnawed-at furniture, nailed-down bedstead, and extremely disturbing yellow wallpaper that is ripped in various spots. She wants to work, to socialize, and maybe be stimulated by change rather than be subjected to repetitive mundanity. She repeats herself in defeat, "But what is one to do?"[7] She is helpless. Voiceless.

The husband, John, is away at work most of the time while her sister-in-law, Jenny, strictly monitors her "therapy." A foil to our narrator, Jenny "is a perfect and enthusiastic housekeeper, and hopes for

---

6. I snagged this great word from a review posted by "bookeros," "The Yellow Wallpaper by Charlotte Perkins Gilman: Review," *Guardian*, November 25, 2014, www.theguardian.com/childrens-books-site/2014/nov/25/review-yellow-wallpaper-charlotte-perkins-gilman.

7. Charlotte Perkins Gilman, *The Yellow Wallpaper* (1892; repr., Middletown, DE: n.p., 2017), 3.

no better profession."[8] Following the stream-of-consciousness writing of the narrator's journal-like entries, the reader joins her downward spiral from sanity. The narrator becomes completely fixated on the yellow wallpaper and convinced that there is a woman trapped inside of its smothering pattern. At the end, her voice changes to that of the woman in the wallpaper whom she's set out to free. John, who thought she was getting better, returns to find her creeping around the room in a mad state, saying, "I've got out at last . . . in spite of you and Jane. And I've pulled off most of the paper, so you can't put me back!"[9] John faints at the sight, and she continues to creep in her path, stepping right over him. The end.

DO YOU SEE WHAT I SEE?

The Yellow Wallpaper is one of those stories that you want to start over from the beginning and reread right away. It unsettles you, and you want more answers. As the woman strips away the yellow wallpaper in her madness, Gilman unveils its disturbing reality to the reader. I keep using the word *disturbing* because there is no better word. I first read *The Yellow Wallpaper* on a plane. And that is how I felt when I closed it: disturbed. As we deplaned, a woman rushed up to me from behind and said, "Excuse me, I have to ask, are you a professor?" *Well, that was an odd question.* I said no and asked, "Why did you think that? Is it because I was reading *The Yellow Wallpaper*?" I was still flustered from reading it and hoped this woman could relate to the experience. She said, "Well, yes, that and your smart shoes!" *I'll give her that; the shoes did make me look smart.* After she confirmed that she had read the book, I had to find out if she was affected like me. So I threw it out there, in more of a whisper: "Did you identify with her in an ominous way?" She affirmed in a whisper of her own, "Yes!"

I've never been subjected to rest therapy, and I am in a healthy marriage to a husband who values my intellectual contributions both inside

---

8. Gilman, *Yellow Wallpaper*, 10.
9. Gilman, *Yellow Wallpaper*, 27.

and outside the home. I don't live in the Victorian era, my husband isn't stuck in it, I've never suffered from depression or anxiety, and I am not under any kind of oppression like the woman who narrates the story. (I do, however, have a sister-in-law named Jenny.) But I was left with the question, *Is the woman in this story crazy for what she saw in the yellow wallpaper, or is everyone else crazy for not seeing it?* Because in reading it more than one hundred years after its publication, I too see the lingering yellow wallpaper. Much of it is ripped off, of course—thanks to the woman who was behind it. She was trapped in the traditional patriarchal structures of family, medicine, and society that the yellow wallpaper in her confined room represented for her. Gilman explained, "I wrote *The Yellow Wallpaper*, with its embellishments and additions to carry out the ideal (I never had hallucinations or objections to my mural decorations) and sent a copy to the physician who so nearly drove me mad. He never acknowledged it."[10] He didn't acknowledge it to Gilman, and yet years later she learned that he quit prescribing his rest therapy after she sent him that copy of her book. Dr. Mitchell wasn't going to admit to seeing the yellow wallpaper, but he did change his treatment.

The narrator's husband, John, thinks she is silly for being so bothered by the yellow wallpaper. He discourages her from thinking or talking about it. She describes him as loving and practical, even as the reader can see how he speaks to her in a condescending and patronizing way. He treats her more like a fragile child than his wife. Still, John thinks he is doing the right thing in caring for her this way. He doesn't see the truth.

And neither does Jane. Did you catch that name in the quote from above? As the narrator shifts personalities and identifies as the woman who is finally free from the wallpaper, she tells John that it's "in spite of [him] and Jane."[11] Well, who's Jane? It's the first time we see this name, and it's at the very end of the book. *She* is Jane! At least Jane is a placeholder name for the personality of the original voice in the narration. John and Jane—we might as well slap the last name Doe at the end—are placeholders for us! Throughout the story, Jane uses

---

10. Gilman, "Why I Wrote *The Yellow Wallpaper*."
11. Gilman, *Yellow Wallpaper*, 27.

self-deprecating language while promoting the goodness and leadership of her husband. But really she's calling us to read between the lines. She writes things like, "He is very careful and loving, and hardly lets me stir without special direction. I have a scheduled prescription for each hour of the day; he takes all care from me, and so I feel basely ungrateful not to value it more."[12] The reader already sees the problem, but Jane doesn't. She's participating in her own oppression. It's enough to drive you crazy. But at the end, she doesn't identify as Jane anymore. She's rejecting the confinement of her personhood that John and Jane have both participated in. She has ripped as much of the yellow wallpaper off the wall as she could.

And John faints to see it all. His wife has gone mad. Does he see that it's from his rest therapy? Does he see the problem now with the yellow wallpaper?

THEN AND NOW

As an emancipated woman living in the twenty-first century, why am I so fixated on this yellow wallpaper? Why have I titled the introduction to my book "The Church's Yellow Wallpaper"? Am I saying that we are no better than the 1800's? Surely we are. Or are we? I see the yellow wallpaper as a result of the fall. And that is something that we will always have to peel back. Like John and Jane, we want to do what is right but often get sucked into cultural stereotypes that confine us without our even noticing it.

We keep going through the motions and perpetuating a false remedy to the detriment of the health of God's church. We don't see the vestiges of yellow wallpaper around us. Like the hideous wallpaper Jane describes, we create a pattern that's "dull enough to confuse the eye in following" and "pronounced enough to constantly irritate and provoke study." Sometimes our witness to the watching world is that we "destroy [ourselves] in unheard of contradictions."[13]

---

12. Gilman, *Yellow Wallpaper*, 4.
13. Gilman, *Yellow Wallpaper*, 5.

Jane wasn't the only one who was confined by and hurting from the stereotypes of the time. So was John! Diminishing her womanhood did not enhance his manhood. It stunted it. Sure, he didn't see the rest therapy and the assumptions behind it as diminishing Jane's womanhood. But by stereotyping her and her symptoms, that's what it did. It diminished her personhood. So did his patronizing behavior. He missed the gift of her contributions to the marriage, household, and society as his partner and ally.

This isn't a man-bashing book. And this isn't a woman-empowerment book. This is a book that appeals to the reader to look at the yellow wallpaper in the church and to do something about it. Today the church's yellow wallpaper manifests itself in much of the current teaching on so-called "biblical manhood and womanhood." Gilman had her doctor in mind when she wrote her novella. She intended to open his eyes to this problem. But he refused to acknowledge her. I too hope to get the attention of a specific audience—church leaders, the ones entrusted with shepherding God's people, the ones who can prescribe a better approach, the ones who can lead the way forward to a richer culture in God's household. One of our biggest challenges is to actually see this yellow wallpaper's scrawling patterns that are stifling the force of the biblical message and strangling the church's witness and growth. Don't we want to rip those away and reveal the beauty and unity in God's Word?

We often don't see the yellow wallpaper because it was established as a hedge against real threats to God's people. I believe that is the case with a lot of the teaching on biblical manhood and womanhood. The church needed to equip her people to critically engage with the sexual revolution and its message of promiscuity, abortion, and gender fluidity. God made man and woman; he instituted marriage to be a unity between one man and one woman; sex is a fruit of this unifying bond; and life is a gift from God. Men and women are not androgynous. Gender is not fluid. And when God created Eve, Adam had to sacrifice for her. Although God can create from nothing, he put Adam to sleep and used one of his ribs in creating Eve. Adam saw that unlike all the other creatures God made, she was suitable for him.

And the man said:

> This one, at last, is bone of my bone
> and flesh of my flesh;
> this one will be called "woman,"
> for she was taken from man. (Gen. 2:23)

Man and woman are very much alike. And yet they are also distinct. In wanting to highlight this distinction and to contrast the self-serving messages of the sexual revolution, some evangelical leaders began writing about "biblical manhood and biblical womanhood." One honorable goal was to uphold the value of the family and the sacrifices both men and women make to responsibly love and serve their families.

When I married back in 1997, I embraced this teaching. I married fresh out of college at a mere twenty-one years old. My husband and I found a church, and I was eager to be the perfect Christian wife. So I began reading books from trusted authorities in the church on this matter. The one that is considered the manual for Christian biblical manhood and womanhood is titled *Recovering Biblical Manhood and Womanhood*.[14] I remember my young, impressionable self learning, underlining, and later even quoting from this book. I wanted to be a *biblical* woman, a good wife and mom.

But I was also confused by some of what I read. Was it my own sinful proclivity, or were some of the distinctives being taught in the book taking things too far? As a young wife, I gave the benefit of the doubt to the authors, who were much more educated and experienced than I. But here I am, no longer a "young" wife, finding myself tripping over some of the teachings in that same book as they have been further amplified and applied. I've noticed more and more strange teachings on femininity and biblical womanhood in the last handful of years.[15]

---

14. John Piper and Wayne Grudem, eds., *Recovering Biblical Manhood and Womanhood* (1991; repr., Wheaton, IL: Crossway, 2006).

15. For example, see Aimee Byrd, "Sanctified Testosterone?" *Housewife Theologian*, Mortification of Spin, April 21, 2016, www.alliancenet.org/mos/housewife-theologian/sanctified-testosterone#.WxU7bVMvwyk.

Every now and then I decide to publicly respond on my blog. I do this because I know there are many young, impressionable women, like I was, who want to be good Christian wives. And even though the teaching may have good intentions behind it, it is damaging. And it is separating men and women into some of the same *Yellow Wallpaper* stereotypes from the nineteenth century. This is not good for the family, and it is not good for God's church.

Unfortunately, like for Gilman, the men who could do something about it did not acknowledge the questions and critique from me or from the handful of other women who tried to address them.[16] Even when I exposed on my blog that an errant view of the Trinity was being taught and applied to reinforce so-called biblical manhood and womanhood, and a massive debate ensued involving professors, pastors, and laypeople through blog posts, magazine articles, conferences, academic journals, and books, the leaders teaching this errant doctrine never acknowledged or interacted with me. I invited a respectable man to write about it, and suddenly everyone had to pay attention.[17] Leaders were shuffled around as a result, but many of the main concerns were not dealt with.[18] Don't let the furniture shuffling distract you from the yellow wallpaper in the background.

So, one must ask, what is biblical manhood and womanhood? It sounds good, but what is it? Here is how it is defined in the book calling us to recover biblical manhood and womanhood:

> At the heart of mature masculinity is a sense of benevolent responsibility to lead, provide for and protect women in ways appropriate to a man's differing relationships.

---

16. I discuss this in further detail in chapter 4.

17. See Kate Shellnut, "The Complementarian Women behind the Trinity Tussel," *Christianity Today*, August 22, 2016, www.christianitytoday.com/ct/2016/september/behind-trinity-tussle.html.

18. The Council on Biblical Manhood and Womanhood has never retracted their previous teaching on eternal subordination of the Son, none of the popular books teaching it by their leaders have been retracted, nor have they retracted all their conference and journal material that teaches ESS.

At the heart of mature femininity is a freeing disposition to affirm, receive, and nurture strength and leadership from worthy men in ways appropriate to a woman's differing relationships.[19]

These definitions appear to say that all men lead all women. A man needs to be leading a woman, many women, to be mature in his masculinity. A woman's function is to affirm a man's, many men's, strength and leadership. This plays out in the oddest scenarios in the book and in other related teachings. For example, if the mailman comes to the door and a woman answers, he needs to be thinking about how his leadership is affirmed as a man in their interaction.[20] Or if a man is lost driving in a neighborhood and the only person he can find outside is a woman, the book considers how he can ask for directions from her without his masculinity suffering.[21] Another scenario questions how muscular a woman can be and still expect her husband to want to care for her.[22] Do you see the yellow wallpaper here? Manhood and womanhood are viewed through a filter of authority and submission, strength and neediness, and "to the degree that a woman's influence over a man is personal and directive it will generally offend a man's good, God-given sense of responsibility and leadership, and thus controvert God's created order."[23] *Will it?* Is God's created order that delicate, that a man needs to be careful about whether a woman giving him driving directions is doing it in a personal and directive manner? Do women need to so manipulate their words to be careful not to damage the male psyche if they have something they could teach a man? Does male leadership define my femininity? Is that how a woman is an image-bearer of God?

The pattern in the wallpaper is *pronounced enough to constantly irritate and provoke study.* This kind of teaching chokes the growth of God's people. Certainly plenty of Christians disagree with this extreme

---

19. John Piper, "A Vision of Biblical Complementarity," in *Recovering Biblical Manhood and Womanhood*, ed. Piper and Grudem, 35–36 (capitalized in the original).

20. See John Piper, "Should Women Be Police Officers?," *Ask Pastor John*, Desiring God, August 13, 2015, www.desiringgod.org/interviews/should-women-be-police-officers.

21. Piper, "Vision of Biblical Complementarity," 50.

22. Piper, "Vision of Biblical Complementarity," 50–51.

23. Piper, "Vision of Biblical Complementarity," 51.

of so-called manhood and womanhood. And yet it goes unchallenged and continues to cover the walls in many evangelical churches. It is also showcased in more nuanced ways that are *dull enough to confuse the eye in following*. And that is what I hope to address in this book.

A RESTORATION PROJECT

The old estate that John and Jane looked to for respite in *The Yellow Wallpaper* reminded me of a discovery from my teenage years. My friend Sarah and I took a lot of walks. We made many discoveries. One day we found ourselves off the beaten path in Burkittsville, Maryland. If you are familiar with the infamous horror film *The Blair Witch Project*, you will recognize the name of this small town. My mom lived right beside that town. On that short walk, Sarah and I noticed the eeriness of Burkittsville just a few years before that movie released in 1999. We were ahead of our time like that. As we were walking, Sarah noticed "something cool" down the hill in the woods a little ways. We wandered down to find an old, derelict church. It was both creepy and cool at the same time. The main level was just the size of a small sanctuary, with a modest basement below. It had obviously been abandoned for a while, and yet everything seemed set up for worship. There was still a dusty, old Bible open on the podium (we later took that). The empty pews looked sad to us. We imagined who could have worshiped there and what happened in their lives. This was one of our better discoveries. As a matter of fact, we decided to take my younger brother Luke there with Sarah's cousin Dusty for a second look. They were intrigued as well.

My teenage memory is a bit foggy, but maybe the third time we revisited this mysterious church we realized that we were not its only patrons. All of the pews were knocked over, and there was satanic graffiti on the walls. A few of us were brave enough to check out the basement when a loud noise came from nowhere. Needless to say, we burned the rubber on the bottom of our shoes getting out of there! It then became the place to go at night when we wanted to give our friends a good scare. My brother and his buddies would challenge each other to see who could stay inside the longest.

That empty church invited teenagers like us by the opportunity it lent. I doubt there ever was actual satanic activity there, just some delinquent teenagers trying to scare people. Satan usually works in far subtler ways. But we know his more offensive symbols. Whoever painted them on the church walls was making a statement. They were bold in doing so because the church was neglected and there was no one to stop them.

How did a house of worship come to this—a spot where teenagers like to go to scare one another? It reminded me of what Jesus said: "When an unclean spirit comes out of a person, it roams through waterless places looking for rest but doesn't find any. Then it says, 'I'll go back to my house that I came from.' Returning, it finds the house vacant, swept, and put in order. Then it goes and brings with it seven other spirits more evil than itself, and they enter and settle down there. As a result, that person's last condition is worse than the first. That's how it will also be with this evil generation" (Matt. 12:43–45).

This was an abandoned church. It is a metaphor to me of some important implications of the gospel that have been abandoned in the church today. Christians want to be a moral people. But morality can sometimes be culturally constructed. Without even realizing it, we can pick up traditions from secular society to decorate our good works. Everything may appear swept and in order. But if we rely on our own efforts for righteousness, if we do our own cleaning, our adversary will see that as an open invitation. What we may think is full of goodness, he finds as an empty space.

We know how to identify obvious sinful behaviors stemming from the sexual revolution and keep them out of the church. But can we identify the yellow wallpaper that has been in the background all along? Can we remove it? Do we let the Bible that is in plain sight guide us all? What furniture do we keep and restore, and what needs to be cleared away? Let's let Christ rearrange our furniture. Let it be his house. Although, if we let him, he does more than rearrange—he completely takes over, transforms, and sanctifies. Just think of how merciful our God is, turning our sinful bodies into temples of his Holy Spirit. And this being the case, then God himself is the Lord of our souls. Who can separate us from his love?

That mysterious structure Sarah and I found looked like a church. But it was empty and abandoned. Sometimes we can look like good Christians, but our insides are full of spiritual cobwebs. Are we just trying to be good Christians, displaying to others our moral superiority and sparkling bootstraps, or are we repentant sinners, ransomed by grace and persevering in the life of faith and obedience? If we are in union with Christ, then our house is full indeed. When we go to the riches in his Word, we don't find a masculine and a feminine version, but one Bible to guide us all. We don't find that our ultimate goal is biblical manhood or biblical womanhood but complete, glorified resurrection to live eternally with our Lord and Savior Jesus Christ. We don't find a command anywhere in Scripture for all women to submit to all men. We don't find directions for women to function as masculinity affirmers. We find that men and women are called together in the same mission: eternal communion with the triune God.

PEEL AND REVEAL

This book presents an alternative to all the resources marketed on biblical womanhood and biblical manhood today, focusing on the reciprocity of the male and female voices in Scripture, the covenantal aspect to Bible reading and interpretation, and bearing the fruit of that in our church life. Sometimes we know there is restoration to be done but we don't do the necessary renovating because we are afraid of what we will uncover. If we start peeling off the wallpaper, maybe part of the wall will come off with it. After all, it's been there a long time.

We are good at distracting ourselves from the church's yellow wallpaper by continuing to debate who's in charge. While evangelicalism dukes it out about who can be church officers, the rest of the 98 percent of us need to be well equipped to see where we fit in God's household and why that matters. Until both men and women grow in their understanding of their relationship to Scripture, there will continue to be tension between the sexes in the church. The yellow wallpaper will remain. Do men and women benefit equally from God's Word? Are they equally responsible in sharpening one another in the faith and passing it down to the next generation? When Jane began peeling off the yellow wallpaper, there was just the ugly wall of an old house behind it. Metaphorically speaking though, she revealed the patriarchal systems of her time that affected women's psychosynthesis.

In part 1, I hope to show more subtle vestiges of the yellow wallpaper in the church and how they are separating God's people and stunting our growth. If we peel this yellow wallpaper back to see what is really in Scripture, we reveal the reciprocity of both men's and women's voices that are coactive in teaching one another through God's Word. Isn't this what the leaders in the church want for God's people? Let's discuss what that looks like for the edification of his church.

Interconnected patterns in the yellow wallpaper exist that affect our relationship to Scripture, how we read it, and what our responsibility is in the church. Part 2 peels back the parts of the pattern that steered us off from the church's mission. As we've been taught to focus on aiming for biblical manhood and womanhood, we have missed the bigger picture of Christlikeness to which we are called. And we have lost aim of what the church is for: preparing us for eternal communion with the triune God. We have taken discipleship out of the church, further separating God's people by culturally constructed gender paradigms. Ironically, while the debate continues about who can lead God's church, functional ministers have risen up in parachurch organizations, taking the place of local church officers in leading God's people. But these functional ministers are not charged with shepherding the souls of all the people in their parachurch ministry in the way a pastor or church officer is. They do not have the same accountability and responsibility before God. Why has this happened? What are God's people learning? What is the role of worship and congregational life in discipleship anymore? If we peel back this pattern, we can reveal Scripture's message that the church is the school of Christ[24] and then appreciate and use parachurch ministries in their proper place.

---

24. This is a term borrowed from Scott Swain and Michael Allen, *Reformed Catholicity: The Promise of Retrieval for Theology and Biblical Interpretation* (Grand Rapids: Baker Academic, 2015).

While we are collectively separating men and women in the church in some stereotypical and unnecessary ways, an individualistic pattern in the yellow wallpaper affects the way we interpret Scripture. In the chapters that follow, we will see that the troubling teaching of biblical manhood and womanhood has thrived under popular Biblicist interpretive methods. And Biblicist interpretive methods ironically flourish in our individualistic culture that works against the values of family and community that the biblical manhood and womanhood movement is trying to uphold. If we peel back these Biblicist trends in the church today, we can reveal that we do not read God's Word alone; we read it within our interpretive covenant communities,[25] namely, in conjunction with continual, ordinary preaching of the Word and faithful discipleship in our churches. We will also peel back the connecting pattern that confines the intellectual stimulation and contribution of women, reducing our reading to "quiet time" and pretty devotionals, to retrieve true integral community where men and women are both contributing as whole, fruitful persons.

Finally, in part 3 we peel back the gender tropes of manhood and womanhood that have been imposed on the church, to reveal a household of brothers and sisters in Christ. We will look at the early church to disclose the great honor and responsibility of every believer as we are headed to the new heavens and the new earth to reign with our Lord and Savior Jesus Christ. We will end with a theme from the beginning of the book, where Paul authorizes Phoebe to deliver a treasure of the church—the book of Romans—as a tradent of the faith. Since every believer has this same "baton," this same honor and responsibility to communicate God's Word to others, we hold that in common with our brothers and sisters in the faith.

This book shouldn't end by leaving us disturbed as *The Yellow Wallpaper* does. It doesn't merely draw attention to a tragic problem. It should not leave us going mad. In peeling away the troubling yellow wallpaper, we reveal the glorious beauty of God's church, Christ's bride,

---

25. Another term I borrowed from Scott Swain, *Trinity, Revelation, and Reading* (New York: T&T Clark, 2011).

whom he is sanctifying, cleansing by his Word, and preparing for glory to be holy and blameless (Eph. 5:26–27). Thus this book is not merely a critique but also an invitation to recover the beauty and participate more fully in it.

PART 1

RECOVERING THE WAY WE READ SCRIPTURE

CHAPTER 1

WHY MEN AND WOMEN DON'T READ SEPARATE BIBLES

How many Bibles are in your house? How many new study Bibles have you seen released in the last few years that have piqued your interest? It's funny, the Bible is the most popular book ever, but you rarely see someone reading it in public. We know most households have Bibles, and yet many are embarrassed to be seen with one. Executive director of LifeWay Research, Scott McConnell, laments that despite the Bible's popularity, the majority of people aren't reading it much at all. "Most Americans don't know first-hand the overall story of the Bible—because they rarely pick it up. . . . Even among worship attendees less than half read the Bible daily. The only time most Americans hear from the Bible is when someone else is reading it."[1]

That doesn't stop us from buying more and more Bibles. Even the *Washington Post* is talking about it: The Bible business is booming. Forty million Bibles are sold annually—from study Bibles to family Bibles to pocket Bibles. That's not even counting foreign markets. As journalist Daniel Radosh observed, "The familiar

---

1. Bob Smietana, "Americans Are Fond of the Bible, Don't Actually Read It," Lifeway Research, April 25, 2017, https://lifewayresearch.com/2017/04/25/lifeway-research-americans-are-fond-of-the-bible-dont-actually-read-it/.

observation that the Bible is the best-selling book of all time obscures a more startling fact: The Bible is the best-selling book of the year, every year."[2]

And yet Charles Spurgeon's rebuke back in the nineteenth century, "There is dust enough on some of your Bibles to write 'Damnation' with your fingers,"[3] is still pertinent today. We just have more Bibles to gather dust while the new ones hold so much promise.

Bibles are a lucrative source of profit for publishing houses. They are reliable bestsellers! This can be both good news and bad news. The good news is obvious. We love to hear that 88 percent of households own a Bible, or three.[4] But while it is also good to have different translations and study Bibles to choose from, we are going to look at a shift in popular marketing that makes some of our Bibles more about us than the One the whole Bible is about.

Also, think about the many customized resources that supplement our Bible reading. How many devotionals and other books do you have to help you with time in the Word? There is a lot out there. Some are fantastic resources, while many others are troubling. We need to learn how to be discerning in picking good study aids or devotional material. One discerning question to ask is whether they connect us with Christ's body or isolate us. Is the one Bible that God's people are to be united under now separating and cutting us off from the community of faith? Could it be that fewer Christians are reading their Bibles because it has become more of an isolating experience than it was designed for?

---

2. Daniel Silliman, "The Most Popular Bible of the Year Is Probably Not What You Think It Is," Acts of Faith, *Washington Post*, August 28, 2015, www.washingtonpost.com/news/acts-of-faith/wp/2015/08/28/the-most-popular-bible-of-the-year-is-probably-not-what-you-think-it-is/?utm_term=.77681b68d831. Quoted from Daniel Radosh, "The Good Book Business," Annuls of Publishing, *New Yorker*, December 10, 2006, www.newyorker.com/magazine/2006/12/18/the-good-book-business.

3. Charles H. Spurgeon, "The Bible," in *Spurgeon's Sermons*, vol. 1 (Grand Rapids: Baker, 1996), 33.

4. American Bible Society, "The State of the Bible 2015," Barna Group, www.americanbible.org/uploads/content/State_of_the_Bible_2015_report.pdf.

QUIET TIME IN PINK AND BLUE?

The current selection of Bibles can be quite overwhelming. You have your women's Bibles, your *Sportsman's Bible*, your *Lifehacks Bible*, your *Couple's Devotional Bible*, your *American Patriot's Bible*—and even art-journaling Bibles now. Our time reading Scripture has become customized, individualized, and privatized. If we follow the help that is marketed to us in many Christian bookstores, we'll read Scripture that relates to our particular roles, according to our particular tastes, and—special bonus for women—it will all be very pretty. All we need is the perfect mug showcasing a Scripture verse to place beside our Bible so we can snap that perfect devotion shot for Instagram. Quiet-time selfies are all the rage these days.

But you don't often see men posting pictures of their quiet time, do you? That makes me wonder about how men and women view their devotional, private reading time differently. Why do women want to publicize their devotional time; and why do they want to make it look like a magazine shot? How does this affect the way they read or study God's Word? It's easy to get caught up in the life-as-performance mind-set that is prevalent on social media, blending time in God's Word with market-able beauty. If the aesthetics are good, then our sanctification must be on point. And this sanctification is distinctly feminine. Women's Bibles these days are published in beautiful colors, often with overt feminine designs on the cover. Married men: which is more horrifying to you, holding your wife's purse for her or holding your wife's Bible?

While I note this strange trend of women posting pictures of their quiet times on social media, I do want to commend women for the amount of Bible reading they are doing. According to a 2017 Barna Research study, Christian women are more engaged with the Bible than men. Sixty percent of Christian women affirm that Scripture is the inspired Word of God and read it four or more times a week, compared to 40 percent of Christian men.[5] Lifeway Research affirms

5. Barna Research, "State of the Bible 2017: Top Findings," Research Releases in Culture & Media, Barna, April 4, 2017, www.barna.com/research/state-bible-2017-top-findings/.

that 39 percent of men admit to skipping Bible reading all together, compared to 31 percent of women.[6] I doubt it's because their Bibles are prettier, but the publishers are target marketing to women all the same, as we are the likelier buyers.

Even before the explosion of the women's genre in the Christian publishing industry, I imagine the Zondervan brothers picked up on a trend of women readers as they were selling paperbacks out of the trunks of their cars. The first official book that Zondervan published in 1938 was Abraham Kuyper's *The Women of the Old Testament.*[7] This was a time when religious books were mainly written by pastors and professors, which gave readers a good idea of the author's qualifications and denominational distinctives. But unfortunately, even while the first Zondervan book suggests they sensed a strong base of women readers, the books written before the establishment of Christian trade publishers had an androcentric, or male-centered, perspective.

HEARING THE WOMAN'S VOICE

There is, of course, nothing at all wrong with reading the androcentric perspective, but there were barely any female voices to reciprocate male authorship when it came to religious books. Maybe this explains the popularity of the few female leaders in American church history, such as Anne Hutchinson and Aimee Semple McPherson, among both men and women. It's easy to see the doctrinal errors these women were tangled up in and write them off. But it's important to look at the possible reasons for their broad influence and success.

I often wonder if Anne Hutchinson's theological education had been invested in at the same level as men's if things would have turned out differently. Her story is fascinating. In Anne we see a woman who thirsted for God's Word and the implications it had on her own life. Anne and her husband, William, painstakingly decided to follow

---

6. Smietana, "Americans Are Fond of the Bible."

7. See James E. Ruark, *The House of Zondervan: Celebrating 75 Years*, rev. ed. (Grand Rapids, Zondervan: 2006), 24–26.

their Puritan pastor, John Cotton, from England to Massachusetts in the New World. Shortly after she gave birth to her fourteenth child, Anne's remaining family left behind most of their possessions and set sail for an excruciating eight- to ten-week voyage on the *Griffin*. It was the summer of 1634, and Anne was forty-three years old.

Once a part of this new community, Anne didn't settle for quiet time. She wanted to engage theologically. After hearing the Word preached on Sunday morning, she wanted to discuss it with others. Unfortunately, she got the message from her preacher, whom she admired, that he didn't want to be bothered with all her questions and insights.[8] So she opened her home on Sunday afternoons for a women's discussion group. The church already separated the women from the men in the congregational seating, so this further separation of the women was natural. Anne's biographer Selmar Williams explains how this opportunity was attractive to many women who were "frustrated by the intellectual stagnation that was their lot as outsiders."[9] Finally, these women could talk theology and its implications on their lives.

Anne's group grew rapidly as the "godly magistrates and elders of the church... winked at... her practice."[10] Rather than recognizing the theological vigor and influence Anne had and investing in her for the good of the whole church, they left her unshepherded to continue in these women's meetings. She wasn't taken seriously—until men began to take an interest as well. "After two years in Massachusetts, [Anne] had the strongest constituency of any leader in the whole colony, and her Boston disciples were starting to spread the word to the other thirteen towns."[11] Things were getting out of hand, and those who once winked at Anne's practices now wanted to put an end to her. After persevering through a kangaroo court trial in 1638, Anne was excommunicated from her church and banished from the Massachusetts Bay Colony,

---

8. See Selmar R. Williams, *Divine Rebel* (New York: Holt, Rinehart, and Winston, 1981), 95.

9. Williams, *Divine Rebel*, 96.

10. Williams, *Divine Rebel*, 96.

11. Williams, *Divine Rebel*, 121.

"denounced as [a] liar, leper, and the Devil's helper."[12] That was the end
of that kind of thing. Extra measures were taken to make sure that no
women would carry the kind of influence Anne had.

Anne's theology was fraught with real problems. But we will never
know what the outcome could have been if she had been taken seriously
in the beginning and invested in and shepherded well by her elders. Do
you see the yellow wallpaper? Maybe she could have grown to be an ally
to the church, helping the elders relate better to the women, offering a
reciprocal female voice to the dominant male voice, and uniting men
and women under the ministry of the Word. Instead, it didn't matter
where her theology led, as long as she was harmlessly teaching women.
But as her influence grew and reached even the men, she then became
a threat to their authority. Her excommunication sent a warning
message to squash any thought of female contribution. And the whole
church suffered for it.

Over time the passing of women's rights followed by the explosion
of technology led to many women's authors gaining footing. If women
didn't have a voice in the church, at least they could speak and write
outside it—in the parachurch. Acquiring a base of readers from radio
and social media platforms became easier. In the mid-1990s, more and
more women authored Christian trade books. As technology exploded,
so did the woman's voice. We now have our own genre in Christian
publishing and broadcasting. Women seem eager to have a multitude
of resources to read through the lens of the female perspective and
experience. This genre of women's Bible studies and Christian books
has become extremely profitable. We therefore need to think more
critically about navigating through these resources and how they shape
our reading of Scripture and discipleship in the covenant community
of our local churches. The need for male and female reciprocity has not
gone away. Do we see any parallels to the living space in Anne's house,
where many women, separated from the men, contributed without
good training in the Word?

---

12. Williams, *Divine Rebel*, 184.

Let us pause and ask: As more is available to us online and in print, how do these teachings affect women in our private time in the Word, in our service in the church, and in our everyday living? How do all these separate resources affect men? Our answers should start with how we view God's Word. Liberal radical feminists like to regard our canon of Scripture as a "hopelessly patriarchal construction."[13] Conservative evangelicals usually balk at this accusation, but I wonder if the way we market customized devotions to women sends that same message.

Is the Bible, God's Word, so male-centered and authored that women need to create our own resources to help us relate to it? Were women involved in the process of canonical selection, or was it the more powerful men who were able to throw together the authoritative message they wanted for the church? Is all of Scripture androcentric, or is there a female voice in Scripture? And should we be learning from women now? Sadly, when confronted with these questions, many will simply dismiss them (at best) or be quick to remind you of Anne's slippery slope (or worse).

I had a rather discouraging conversation with an older woman in the faith, one whom I thought I could look up to, about all the bad theology that is marketed to Christian women and women's ministries. She shared that she wasn't so sure women should be doing *any* teaching or Bible studies but should be content to learn from our pastors and husbands. That, she said, would solve the problem of poor theology taught by women. But what about the troubling teaching imparted by men? Is this really the answer? Is this biblical?

SEGREGATING GOD'S WORD?

We've come a long way since Anne Hutchinson's day. But almost four hundred years later, I can't help but compare the separate seating

---

13. See Allyson Jule and Bettina Tata Peterson, eds., *Being Feminist, Being Christian: Essays from Academia* (New York: Palgrave Macmillan, 2006), 148. Richard Bauckham added the "hopelessly" in *Gospel Women: Studies of the Named Women in the Gospel* (Grand Rapids: Eerdmans, 2002), xix.

arrangement in her church to the separate Bibles marketed to men and women today. Is there yellow wallpaper on our Bibles? How do separate Bibles for men and women shape the way we read Scripture? How is a woman's Bible different from a man's Bible? Is it just the pretty cover? Well, let's start there. Since I consider myself counter-culturally capable,[14] I will go ahead and admit that no matter how I'm advised against it, I do in fact judge a book by its cover. And I find these fluffy "women covers" just as embarrassing to hold as the men would. Don't get me wrong; I like pretty things. But I find froufrou covers for women insulting—especially on God's Word. The Bible isn't an accessory that decorates my Instagram feed or bookshelf. While the amazing grace of God is a beautiful thing, there's also a lot of downright ugly in Scripture, isn't there? Sin is horrifying. And Scripture gives us the uncut version. Is the pretty cover supposed to soften this? It seems to cheapen the whole message in Scripture. I find it all very condescending. I want to read my Bible just as seriously as the men. The pretty cover on the women's Bible already begins to send a message that women will approach Scripture less seriously than men. I'm judging the cover as I see the cover judging the readers by their gender.

You might say, if both men and women are reading God's Word, what difference does it make if one version has a pretty cover or if it's marketed to each sex differently? Some people like pretty covers; so what's the big deal? Well, let's peel back the pretty cover and see if there are any other differences. What does the man's version offer that the woman's version doesn't? Taking a look at one of the more theological attempts at this approach, the *ESV Women's Devotional Bible*[15] has some similar topics of study to the countering *ESV Men's Devotional Bible*,[16] as well as some topics that cater more to the experiences of the targeted gender. Both have articles on the Bible, marriage, singleness, and parenting, although customized for the corresponding gender. Here are some articles exclusive to the distinct Bibles:

---

14. I first saw this expression used on Twitter. See, Twitter can be good sometimes.
15. *ESV Women's Devotional Bible* (Wheaton, IL: Crossway, 2014).
16. *ESV Men's Devotional Bible* (Wheaton, IL: Crossway, 2015).

ESV Women's Devotional Bible	ESV Men's Devotional Bible
The Church and Women at Risk	Leadership
Eating Disorders and Other Self-Destructive Behaviors	A Man's Inner Life (and Why Regard Self-Control as the One Essential Ingredient to Biblical Manhood?)
Missional Living	Life in the Local Church
Emotional Health	Calling
Forgiveness, Healing, and Shame	Pornography
	A Man's Work

Do you see a difference in themes here? The titles of these articles reflect the cultural stereotypes and gender tropes of "manhood" and "womanhood." The specific articles targeted to the women's Bible predominantly address weakness and victimhood while the men's are about leadership and agency. The ones that do address a man's weakness are focused on how they victimize women. It is good to address those things, and I am glad they do. But do women have nothing to learn about leadership, self-control, calling, and life in the local church? Do men not need to learn about forgiveness, emotional health, and missional living? Why isn't pornography labeled as a "self-destructive behavior" in the article's title as in the title addressing the women's weaknesses, and are men the only gender prone to lust, or women to eating disorders? Why is it positive to use an expression such as "A Man's Work," while the authors would be cautious to title an article "A Woman's Work"?

Many of the articles written for these women's and the men's Bibles are well-written truths. I am enriched by most of the contributors. However, that is exactly why I am so bothered by the underlying message of manhood and womanhood present in the two publications. Some articles address women as graciously invited to join God as "agents of truth and joy"[17] while others frame a woman's agency as a

---

17. Devotion by Gloria Furman, "Missional Living," in *ESV Women's Devotional Bible*, 1588.

"channel of blessing for [her] husband."[18] In the latter devotion we are taught that a strong woman is a negative description, associated with the sin of "continually express[ing] disapproval" of her husband.[19] Why would a man's strength be associated with leadership and a woman's strength as disrespect? This article in the *ESV Women's Devotional Bible* tells us "God made man's ego unique" and "placed that precious ego in your care." We also learn that "God has given your man a task to complete in life." Women are to serve their man's ego and support the man's task if they want to be "cherished" by him.[20] Do you see the yellow wallpaper here? Does God only call men to be strong? Do women have a task to join God as "agents of truth and joy," or is their agency directed toward coddling the male ego and supporting her husband's "God-given call on his life"?[21] Shouldn't we encourage both men and women not to have fragile egos and to look to the Lord for strength as we jointly serve one another under the mission of God?

A subtle message about manhood and womanhood is revealed even in the contributors of these two devotional Bibles. A mixture of men and women contribute to the *ESV Women's Devotional Bible*. Women obviously are going to be able to write from experience in womanhood as they contribute with a goal to be specifically relevant to women. But most of the Bible isn't directed specifically to women, and there is a benefit in women learning from both male and female church workers, Bible teachers, scholars, and Christian authors. However, this is not the approach taken in the *ESV Men's Devotional Bible*, which has only male contributors. The unspoken message is that while women benefit from learning from both sexes, men cannot be taught or enriched by women church workers, Bible teachers, scholars, and Christian authors. Why is that? In Scripture itself, we see men learning plenty from women. What does excluding female contributions to the *ESV Men's Devotional Bible* say about biblical manhood and womanhood? Doesn't it reinforce the idea that the Bible is a patriarchal construction?

---

18. Devotion by Jani Ortland, "The Godly Wife" in *ESV Women's Study Bible*, 1596.
19. Ortland, "Godly Wife," 1597.
20. Ortland, "Godly Wife," 1597.
21. Ortland, "Godly Wife," 1597.

Sure, women can contribute to the female version, as they help women have a version they can relate to. But men don't need the female voice as they ponder how God's Word speaks to the male heart, because they see it as a patriarchal structure already.

Producing devotional Bibles specifically geared toward men and women separately shapes the way we do our devotions and the very way we read, interpret, and apply Scripture. It puts a lens of interpretation on God's Word—the lens of biblical manhood and womanhood. The underlying message is that there is a men's version and a woman's version to read. There is a male and a female way to meditate on the Bible's teaching. And this separates the sexes by our cultural gender paradigms. While the intentions of reaching men and women may be good, it conditions men and women to constant reflection on how God's Word is relevant to their own sex. The emphasis is on the differences between men and women. I affirm that there are differences between men and women. God made male and female. But we need to be careful not to reduce us by our distinctions. Men are more like women than any other creature God made. Adam poetically acknowledged this when God made Eve. Men and women are not opposing beings; we are all human beings bearing the image of God. Offering two versions of Scripture separates and isolates our devotion time, ignores our likenesses, and misses all the important nuances in our distinctions.

"DESTROYING [OURSELVES] IN UNHEARD OF CONTRADICTIONS"[22]

Let's return to the question as to whether men and women benefit equally from God's Word. Everyone would answer, "Of course we do!" But the church receives a different answer when we are offered separate Bibles and devotions. Particularly as we see in the *ESV Men's Devotional Bible*, men benefit from receiving only male contributions,

---

22. Charlotte Perkins Gilman, "Why I Wrote *The Yellow Wallpaper*," The Forerunner, www.nlm.nih.gov/exhibition/theliteratureofprescription/education/materials/WhyIWrote YellowWallPaper.pdf.

whereas women benefit from having a version where women can help teach us to relate to God's Word.

Is the Bible a patriarchal construction put together by powerful men? "No!" we insist. And yet the resources flooding the Christian women's genre for Bible reading and devotions send the message that God's Word is so male-centered and authored that women need to create our own resources to help us relate to it.

Are men and women equally called to share in God's mission and joy? "Of course!" we say, "Yes!" But while much of the writing in these devotional Bibles would support that, it is contradicted by other teachings that men are specifically given a task from God and that women serve God through supporting a man's mission, rather than men and women jointly serving in God's mission to humankind.

Church leaders need to address this kind of thinking, because such contradictions don't only hurt women; the whole church is affected by them. While the church today does foster more reciprocity and coactivity in service among brothers and sisters, the vestiges of yellow wallpaper still lingering continue to promote the kind of separate ministries and applications for women that stunt their growth and keep them at arm's length from the rest of the church. How would a better understanding of the function of the female voice in Scripture help to integrate women more into robust theology and life in the church? If men and women benefit equally from God's Word, then it will reflect in the life of the church. If we peel this yellow wallpaper of contradictions away, we are not going to take down the walls with it. Proactive investment following biblical convictions will help the whole church flourish. It will help church leaders, not sabotage their authority. It will also be a witness for the world to see how we are called to communion with the triune God and with one another. So what do we see in God's Word?

PEEL AND REVEAL

When we examine Scripture, we find that it isn't a patriarchal construction. And we find that it is not an androcentric text that lacks female contribution. In fact, we find that the female voice is important and necessary. We can find plenty of female voices in Scripture—we don't need to be a target-marketed add-on for endless customized devotions for reading Scripture. There isn't a male version and a female version of Scripture. Men and women are to read the same Scriptures, and we learn from both men and women in Scripture. And it is in our shared Bibles and covenant communities that we are trained well according to God's design for women as necessary allies with men in God's mission to the church and to the world.

I am building on a fascinating book, *Gospel Women: Studies of the Named Women in the Gospels*, by Richard Bauckham, with this point. Bauckham makes the case that radical feminists are wrong in regarding the canon of Scripture "as a hopelessly patriarchal construction." The women from whom we hear in the Scriptures as a whole are not merely tokens thrown in as props, accidental vestiges that somehow slipped through the canonical process without getting suppressed. Nor are the accounts of these women a patronizing general recognition of the contribution of women. Bauckham's book respects "the fact that these women and their stories are remarkable for their particularity, rather than for their typicality or representativeness."[23]

Throughout Scripture, we get snapshots from a woman's perspective and experience, which is especially remarkable considering its male writers and the patriarchal culture of the time of writing. Bauckham brilliantly introduces the idea of female-centered (gynocentric) interruptions of the dominant male-focused (androcentric) writings of Scripture in his first chapter, "The Book of Ruth as Key to Gynocentric Reading of Scripture."

For illustration, he refers to the novel *The Wall of the Plague* by André Brink. It is written in the first-person perspective of a mixed-race woman, but at the close of the novel it is revealed that the author is actually a white male South Afrikaner. So this man is taking on the perspective of a mixed-race female as he writes "vivid accounts even of distinctively female physical experience."[24] As the voice changes at the

---

23. Bauckham, *Gospel Women*, xix.
24. Bauckham, *Gospel Women*, 1.

end of the novel, he reveals himself as the true author. Is he revealing himself a fraud? Bauckham points out the genius of this method, quoting the male's fears of failure as he attempts to imagine what his lover's world is like.

> "How can I, how dare I presume to form you from my rib? . . . To do justice to you an essential injustice is required. That is the heart of my dilemma. I can never be you: yet in order to be myself I must imagine what it is like to be you." By this ingenious device of two levels of fictional authorship, the real author distances himself from the attempt he has made to imagine what it is like to be this woman. It is, after all, only a white male's attempt to imagine what it is like to be a mixed-race woman. But readers have known this all along. How does the final revelation function for them? . . . What it does is to acknowledge, within the imaginative world the novel has created, the readers' consciousness that behind the female voice lurks the male author.[25]

All along the reader knew the real author. So this technique is a way of the author explaining what he is up to. And he pulls it off! It is not fraud; it is a true investment in learning about this person whom he loves.

Likewise, Bauckham shows us that in the book of Ruth we have the female voice, a Moabite woman's and an Israelite woman's perspective on ancient Israelite society, right up until the last few verses. "Thus the book of Ruth, its conclusion tells us, is the kind of story that official, masculine history leaves out."[26] Bauckham goes on to highlight other gynocentric interruptions in Scripture, where the female voice dominates, not to compete with the man's, but to complement it, exposing "the narrative as pitifully inadequate in its androcentric selectivity."[27] The female voice in the Song of Songs highlights the mutuality of the lovers. The book of Esther has a predominately female voice.

---

25. Bauckham, *Gospel Women*, 1–2.
26. Bauckham, *Gospel Women*, 11.
27. Bauckham, *Gospel Women*, 11.

Peppered throughout Genesis we see the matriarchal voices interrupting the more dominant perspectives of the patriarchs, giving us glimpses of the female voice functioning within the patriarchal context of the time. Bauckham highlights the variations of these gynocentric interruptions. There are the "historically exceptional" cases, such as Deborah, a rare occurrence of a woman having extrinsic power, as well as the "textually exceptional" cases, such as Hannah, "in the sense that they make visible what is normally invisible in the texts."[28]

REVEALING A WOMAN'S WORK

Early in Scripture we see that the canon of God's Word was not merely assembled by the most powerful male voices. Women too were involved in the process of canonical selection. In chapter 3 we will see some cases of women as active tradents passing down the faith, but in this section I wish to highlight a powerful case from the biblical account of the restoration of an important part of the Pentateuch. Sadly, whenever I begin talking about Huldah, I get blank stares. Christa L. McKirland fittingly subtitles a section introducing her with "Huldah Who?"[29] She reasons, "Huldah's vindication comes through the simple act of making her visible once again."[30] While this is true, Huldah isn't pointing to herself at all. She is helping to make God's Word visible to his people.

We have much to pay attention to in this 2 Kings 22 passage and 2 Chronicles 34 parallel. King Josiah sent out his dignitaries to inquire of the word of the Lord once the Book of the Law was discovered. It's sad to read the explanations some commentators give for why they sought the prophetess Huldah, the most unreasonable explanation being that there were no good men available. God could raise up a male prophet anytime he pleased. And this was the same time that Jeremiah and Zephaniah were prophets. Why weren't they sought? Also, it's interesting that Josiah sent out his dignitaries to Huldah. McKirland

---

28. Bauckham, *Gospel Women*, 13.
29. Christa L. McKirland, "'Huldah' Malfunction with the Wardrobe Keeper's Wife," in *Vindicating the Vixens*, ed. Sandra Glahn (Grand Rapids: Kregel, 2017), 213.
30. McKirland, "'Huldah' Malfunction," 213.

explains how the sending out of the dignitaries to her rather than summoning her directly to the king should clue the reader in to the respect both the king and his dignitaries had for her. This was a matter of high importance, as Josiah lamented, "For great is the LORD's wrath that is kindled against us because our ancestors have not obeyed the words of this book in order to do everything written about us" (2 Kings 22:13). Under great duress, they sought Huldah for a word from the Lord.

Huldah answered with the "Thus says the LORD" authoritative formula of a prophet, spoke in the first-person voice of God, confirmed the judgment Josiah anticipated and the details of the charge and, amazingly, the delay of God's wrath because Josiah's "heart was tender and [he] humbled [him]self before the LORD when [he] heard what [she] spoke" (2 Kings 22:16–20). Here we have a prophetess who is described as "arguably the first person to grant authoritative status to the Torah scroll deposited in the temple treasury," authenticating the Word of God largely accepted as the heart of the book of Deuteronomy.[31] What a bright and shining account of a woman authoritatively confirming an important text in the canon of Scripture to "the most righteous king in the divided kingdom's history."[32] Huldah "played a significant role in the last major reformation in the kingdom of Judah before its final downfall."[33] And Josiah had no problem learning from her. He, the kingdom of Judah, and the whole church benefited from her obedience to the Lord. "In the same way that women were the first to testify to the resurrection of Christ, the living Word, how poetic might it be that the first person to authenticate the written Word might also have been a woman?"[34]

WHAT ONE BIBLE REVEALS

No, women were not left out of active traditioning in testifying to and passing down the faith. As a matter of fact, in Scripture we see

---

31. McKirland, "'Huldah' Malfunction," 222.
32. McKirland, "'Huldah' Malfunction," 231.
33. McKirland, "'Huldah' Malfunction," 213.
34. McKirland, "'Huldah' Malfunction," 222.

a testimony to the opposite. Men and women are coactively contributing to and affirming God's Word. There aren't two versions, only one. If the most righteous king in the divided kingdom's history sought out a woman's contribution for something as vital as authenticating the Word of God, maybe it isn't so harmful for men to read women's contributions in their Bible devotions after all. In fact, like Josiah, they should be seeking women out when they are the right person for the task. Our churches need both men and women who recognize the authority of God's Word and speak it to one another. We need life in the local church to be coactive. We need men and women to join together in recognizing our calling under God's mission. And we all need godly interruptions from our default modes of thinking.

We must take a critical look at what's being added to and perhaps, in effect, taken away from our Bibles when they are customized to our sex. God had a reason for not offering feminine and masculine versions of his Word to the church. Women don't need their own version to learn to relate to God's Word, and the women's contributions do not need to be mansplained for the men. Our installation as male or as female image-bearers situates us to speak distinctly and fruitfully in our joint mission under God.

Let's take a closer look at Ruth and some of these gynocentric interruptions that I am talking about and how they affect the way we read Scripture.

QUESTIONS FOR GROUP DISCUSSION

1. We customize our phones, our houses, our coffee, and our social media profiles. Do you find that your time reading Scripture throughout the week has become customized to your own taste, life circumstances, and needs? What types of resources do you use most to help you in studying Scripture?
2. Do you tend to read Christian books and Bible studies that are authored by someone who is the same sex as you? Why or why not?

3. What is the value of separate Christian resources aimed toward men and women? What is the value of men and women attending exclusive Bible study groups for their own sex?

4. What is the value of men and women learning together? What are we missing out on if we capitalize on the benefits from male-only and women-only studies at the exclusion of coed opportunities to learn together?

5. Although we are beginning with the study of the female voice in Scripture, more than half of the book will be on discipleship in the church, reading Scripture as a covenant community, and serving together as active traditioners of the faith. Why would it be beneficial even for men to study the female voice in Scripture?

CHAPTER 2

WHY NOT THE BOOK OF BOAZ?

When I was a little girl, the placement of the book of Ruth always annoyed me. Back when we were memorizing the books of the Old Testament, "Joshua, Judges, Ruth" was an easy order to remember because of how unfair it sounded. Poor Ruth, always being judged. No wonder her mother-in-law was so bitter.

Kidding aside, it is pretty interesting that one of the earliest books of the Bible is named after a woman, a Moabite woman at that. If the Bible were a patriarchal construction, wouldn't we have the book of Boaz? After all, he is the kinsman redeemer in the story who points to Christ. And we see in the closing genealogy that Boaz is from the line of Judah and an ancestor of David. Why the focus on this Moabite woman, an outsider of the covenant people? And the honor and attention to Ruth doesn't stop there. We see Ruth listed in the genealogy of Jesus in the beginning of Matthew (1:5)—that is fascinating, isn't it?

In chapter 1, I introduced the book of Ruth as a model for how the female voice functions in Scripture. The book of Ruth may thus actually aid our reading of Scripture as a whole. It demolishes the lens of biblical manhood and womanhood that has been imposed on our Bible reading and opens the doors to how we see God working in his people. Ruth isn't the first occurrence of a gynocentric interruption in Scripture, but it is a good model for us before we venture into some of the others. In the opening verse of Ruth, we are introduced to a man, Elimelech, his wife, Naomi, and their two sons. He moves his family from Bethlehem to Moab during the famine, and his two sons marry

Moabite women. By verse 5, ten years have passed and all three of the men have died. We are left with Naomi and her two daughters-in-law, Ruth and Orpah. Now we are entering the story through the women's eyes. Like in *The Wall of the Plague*, in the book of Ruth we hear the feminine voice in the text while the male voice pops back in, almost coarsely, at the end. Have you ever noticed how the reading suddenly switches gears at the end of Ruth? In this succinct book of only four chapters, the narrator offers rich layers and details to the narrative as we wonder with Naomi whether the Lord really has opposed and abandoned her (Ruth 1:20–21) and then wonder in awe at his *hesed* love to which the whole story points. But then the voice abruptly changes when we get to the genealogy in the end. It almost seems like it was cut-and-pasted there by someone else.

The book is written in a third-person perspective, so we do not have Naomi's first-person account of her inner turmoil, even as her complete despair and loss, which turn to gratitude and joy, are impressed on us. Likewise, we don't get Ruth's first-person account of what was going on in her mind. But we can still recognize the gynocentric perspective in which it is written, so well that we do get a sense of Ruth's destitution, anxieties, loyalty, bravery, hopes, and climactic celebration. We can also observe that while we have one of the most beautiful pledges of loyalty in Ruth, it is far from the sentimental drivel[1] we see in many of the Christian books marketed to women today. Additionally, even though we get the happy ending, the book does not overlook the plight of women in ancient culture—it exposes their difficulties, and it shows us a faithful, brave woman who took initiative to rescue her family, as well as an honorable response from Boaz.

So why do we have this shift in perspective at the end? Do we have in Ruth a male author taking on the female voice to let the reader see more of the picture? And what more do we see with this approach? Are women like Ruth and Naomi, with the initiative they took and boldness of faith they exercised, exceptions or examples of the Israelite

---

1. I am borrowing this great expression from Carl Trueman. It's one of his best.

culture at that time? What is the Holy Spirit saying to our churches with this approach to the text?

In his book *Gospel Women*, Richard Bauckham explains that we have gynocentric interruptions in Scripture where the female voice counterbalances the dominantly male-centered perspective and the book of Ruth helps us to see a good model of how that functions. The female voice makes visible the invisible. We get the story behind the story. This is what that abrupt insertion of the genealogy in the male voice also reveals. All of the sudden we shift gears from the narrative to a listed patrilineal succession in a genealogy record. This change exposes something. Bauckham explains, "The male voice of the genealogy is that of the traditional compilers of such patrilineal texts, which served to summarize long periods of history by tracing a line of male descent. This male voice is quoted not . . . in order to undermine the female voice of the narrative, but on the contrary, in order to be exposed by the female voice of the narrative as pitifully inadequate in its androcentric selectivity."[2]

He explains that we get the same history from the gynocentric narrative as we do from the androcentric genealogy, but we see now what is lacking in these patrilineal records. "Thus the book of Ruth, its conclusion tells us, is the kind of story that official, masculine history leaves out."[3] But not the Bible.

The Bible isn't a book of masculine history. There is women's literature in Scripture! But it's not the stereotypical women's literature like we have today. This is to be read by men and women alike, for the benefit of both sexes. We are not to look at the gynocentric interruptions in Scripture, such as Ruth, as a "canon within the canon"[4] for women. We don't need to take these gynocentric stories out and publish them in books for women's ministries. All of Scripture is meant for coed reading and understanding.

---

2. Richard Bauckham *Gospel Women: Studies of the Named Women in the Gospel* (Grand Rapids: Eerdmans, 2002), 11.

3. Bauckham, *Gospel Women*, 11.

4. Bauckham, *Gospel Women*, 15.

THE POINT OF RUTH IS NOT ABOUT RUTH

Before we get more into how the female voice functions in Ruth, I want to make sure I'm not being misread or misunderstood when it comes to the main point in Ruth. The book isn't primarily about Ruth or Boaz or Naomi. It's not primarily about the female voice or manhood and womanhood or patriarchy. It is primarily about God. In the beginning Ruth makes a vow to her mother-in-law to follow her God. And yet Naomi says that the Lord has opposed her (Ruth 1:16–17, 20–21). Some commentators have referred to Naomi as the female Job. Naomi's and Job's afflictions both raise the same nagging question that looms throughout both books: Is God good to his people?[5] And particularly in Ruth we wonder, does God care about a woman as insignificant as Naomi?

The setting takes place during the time of the Judges, when everyone "did what was right in [their] own eyes" (Judg. 17:6 NASB). The very next generation after Joshua's "did not know the LORD or the works he had done for Israel" (Judg. 2:10). How does only one generation down from the one God delivered from enslavement in Egypt and blessed with the promised land of Canaan turn away from God to worship idols? Still, even in his righteous anger toward his people for abandoning him and doing evil, even as he hands the Israelites to their enemies, God continues to send them deliverers. We see this play out in the book of Judges, and then in the book of Ruth we see how God is providentially working to send his people the true Deliverer they so desperately need. Like the Israelites during the time of the judges, we too desperately need Jesus Christ our Redeemer. And like the Israelites, without him our hearts are bent to do what is right in our own eyes.

In the beginning of Ruth, we see Elimelech doing what he thinks is right for his family to survive the famine—he moves away from God's people and the land God gave them. Why would we even expect for God to intervene now, when by his choices, Elimelech's remaining

---

5. We can say about the book of Ruth what Christopher Ash says about Job: "The book of Job is not about suffering in general. . . . Rather it is about how God treats his friends" (Christopher Ash, *Job: The Wisdom of the Cross*, Preaching the Word, ed. Kent Hughes [Wheaton, IL: Crossway, 2014], 42–43).

family is left destitute in a foreign land? In this redemptive historical context of the book of Ruth, transitioning between Israel's rule by the judges to the age of the kings, Naomi's situation parallels Israel's. There was famine in the land, as Israel turned away from God. Likewise, Naomi is "empty" (Ruth 1:21). Israel is in a sense a widow like Naomi.[6] Given God's covenant relationship with Israel, we wonder, does God keep his promises? Naomi doesn't expect God to intervene. She is hopeless as she makes her walk of shame back to Bethlehem.

And yet the theme in Ruth is God's *hesed* love for his people. We see this Hebrew word used three times (Ruth 1:8; 2:20; 3:10) in the short, little book, and we see *hesed* also played out in its main characters, Naomi, Ruth, and Boaz. This Hebrew word gets lost in translation, as Carolyn Custis James says, because we just don't have an English word good enough to describe it. She describes this Hebrew word as the summation of how we were created to live before one another. This kind of love is an "active, selfless, sacrificial caring for one another that goes against the grain of our fallen natures. . . . *Hesed* is driven, not by duty or legal obligation, but by bone-deep commitment—a loyal, selfless love that motivates a person to do voluntarily what no one has the right to expect or ask of them. . . . It's actually the kind of love that we find most fully expressed in Jesus."[7] James elaborates on the main point in the book: "The book of Ruth puts God's *hesed* on display. We will learn along with Naomi that God's *hesed* love is indiscriminate, unearned, and persistent. YHWH's *hesed* will reach Naomi through the selfless and relentless commitment of Ruth to fight for her, and Boaz will join Ruth in this effort. Events in the field of Boaz . . . will give Naomi fresh insight in YHWH's *hesed*. What she learns is indispensable to us—because so often we struggle to put suffering and God's *hesed* together in our own stories."[8]

God's *hesed* love is the main thrust of the book of Ruth. We see the text saturated with Christ. In the richness of God's Word, he is

---

6. See Peter J. Leithart, "The Structures of Ruth," *Biblical Horizons Newsletter* 45 (January 1993), www.biblicalhorizons.com/biblical-horizons/no-45-the-structures-of-ruth/.

7. Carolyn Custis James, *The Gospel of Ruth* (Grand Rapids: Zondervan, 2008), 115.

8. Carolyn Custis James, *Finding God in the Margins* (Bellingham, WA: Lexham, 2018), 51.

also showing us how layered with meaning that love is. So the field of text from which we reap is the context and foundation of God's *hesed* love in Christ. Just as Ruth gleaned from a field behind the harvesters, picking up piles of grain left behind specifically for her, what can we glean from the text as we see that love carried out in God's people? We have all kinds of bundles of grain to feed on, all kinds of rich meaning and application for the church today. What can we observe from the perspective in which this account is told and the interactions between the main characters in light of Naomi's charge that God had opposed her and left her empty? We can ask all these questions now that we get the main point.

GLEANING WITH A DIFFERENT SET OF EYES

If the book of Ruth began with the genealogy, we might be more inclined to think that it should be named the book of Boaz. It's all about who fathered whom. But the narrative of Ruth gives us the story that we can't see in the patrilineal genealogy. The focus is on who mothered Obed, why, and how. We see the providence of God at work. We see his undying *hesed* love for his people who are struggling to put his love and their suffering together. We see the birth of Obed, King David's grandfather and King Jesus's ancestor, through the eyes of a woman. These are the eyes of a widow, the eyes of barrenness, and the eyes of an outsider. This perspective teaches men and women something different.

It teaches us layers of different. We see how the female voice is needed in Scripture. This isn't a criticism of the male voice. God put man and woman on this earth, and he intends to use both sexes in his mission. In Ruth men and women see that sometimes we need a different set of eyes to see the fuller picture. And what a beautiful picture it is.

But it doesn't begin that way. In ancient Near Eastern culture, a woman without a husband or a son was marked. Women didn't have their own identity. Their worth and their value hinged on providing sons to be heirs of the patrilineal family name and take care of the family land. Naomi is past childbearing age, Orpah and Ruth never were able to conceive, and now all their men are dead and they have no sons. Not only were their worth and value depleted, but so was their welfare. This is where the strong voice of Ruth first breaks through. Headed back to Bethlehem empty, even in her bitterness, Naomi shows her daughters-in-law kindness by releasing them from any responsibility toward her, bidding them to return to their parents, and blessing them, saying, "May the LORD show kindness [*hesed*] to you as you have shown to the dead and to me" (Ruth 1:8). She continues to express her hope that the Lord will grant them new husbands. But Ruth isn't having it. And she responds,

> Don't plead with me to abandon you
> or to return and not follow you.
> For wherever you go, I will go,
> and wherever you live, I will live;
> your people will be my people,
> and your God will be my God.
> Where you die, I will die,
> and there will I be buried.
> May the LORD punish me,
> and do so severely,
> if anything but death separates you and me. (Ruth 1:16–17)

Naomi invokes the Lord's kindness (*hesed*) toward her daughters-in-law. Ruth displays this great kindness (*hesed*) toward Naomi. This is persistent, sacrificial love in action. But Naomi is too blind to see it at the time. When greeted by all her old friends on entering Bethlehem, with Ruth by her side, she says, "'Don't call me Naomi. Call me Mara' . . . 'for the Almighty has made me very bitter. I went away full, but the LORD has brought me back empty. Why do you call me Naomi, since the LORD has opposed me, and the Almighty has afflicted me?'" (Ruth 1:20–21). *Oh yeah, and there is Ruth, aka "chopped liver," with me.* That's got to be how Ruth felt after Naomi's declaration. But although she too mourned the loss of their men, Ruth gained new life in their God. So in these two female voices, we see utter despair and grief, as well as strength of faith and sacrificial commitment.

Ruth is worse than a nobody. She is a foreigner. She is poor. She is a woman. And she has no husband and no son. Ruth stood out like a sore thumb when she came to Bethlehem with Naomi. She wasn't from any of Israel's tribes. She didn't have a clan to protect her. And not only was she an outsider, but she never bore a child during the decade she did have a husband. Ruth had no value. She was only a burden to society. As we read this account in the history of God's people, it's hard for us to imagine Ruth's vulnerability as we see her remarkable faith in action. We see a strong woman. But her strength could not be in her own abilities or position. She was completely exposed and at risk in this patriarchal culture. That's the story behind the story. James notes, "The book of Ruth turns a spotlight on the plight of women in the world for the whole church to learn."[9] It is a corrective voice. Ruth and Naomi help us see the yellow wallpaper. The widow and the barren woman are made visible to us. And yet "patriarchy is not the Bible's message. Rather, it is the cultural backdrop against which the gospel message of Jesus stands out in sharpest relief."[10] We also see this in Ruth. The extraordinary faith of a Moabite woman works actively to fulfill the vow she made to her mother-in-law, against all odds.

Often we need a different set of eyes to show us our blind spots. Boaz is introduced to us as "a prominent man of noble character" (Ruth 2:1). He is a good guy, a good leader. He is strong and well-to-do in the community. Life seems pretty good for Boaz. By all that is revealed to us, he is a godly man. He enters the scene greeting his harvesters by invoking the Lord's presence: "The LORD be with you!" (Ruth 2:4). Boaz is kind, and he treats those under him with the knowledge that the Lord is with them. When he spots a new, foreign woman using the "the ancient welfare system"[11] to glean from his field, he asks his men who she belongs to. That is how women were viewed in the patriarchal culture; their identity was tied to either their husband or their father.

Although Ruth stuck out like a sore thumb for her status, her reputation was spreading in a different way as well. Boaz already heard

---

9. James, *Finding God*, 22.
10. James, *Finding God*, 10.
11. James, *Gospel of Ruth*, 98.

about this Moabite daughter-in-law who left everything she knew behind her—her parents, her people, and her land—to care for Naomi in a land foreign to her and against her (Ruth 2:11). She was a strong woman. And so the reader gets this story through the eyes of faith.

GLEANING A PICTURE OF MANHOOD AND WOMANHOOD

Whenever a strong woman is portrayed in Scripture, teaching or leading a man in any salient way, the popular explanation is often that God is making a point that there were no good men at the time. This argument never holds traction, as we all know God can use Balaam's ass (Num. 22:21–41) if he chooses. He can raise up men, women, and donkeys to carry out his Word. He doesn't need the so-called important people. And so he decided to work through a Moabite woman to teach Boaz, Naomi, and us all about what kind of God he is.

Ruth had faith in Israel's God, and it was showing all over the place. And the story is told highlighting the providence of the Lord in it all. This foreigner without a clan or man to identify herself with goes off to glean on her own and happens on Boaz's field. Boaz happens to be of the clan of Elimelech. And he returns to his field and notices Ruth working hard. She has already earned herself a reputation in that one day on the field as a hard worker who takes initiative. She is ripping down the yellow wallpaper, not because she's a feminist who wants to show the world what women can do and fight the patriarchy, but because she will do whatever it takes to fulfill her vow to Naomi. When we hear the question she asks Boaz's men about gleaning behind the harvesters, we might not think much of it. Some commentators say that she is merely asking the workers whether she can be one of the gleaners in their field. But the law requires them to allow her to do this already.[12] Others say that this is a request to be able to glean beyond what the letter of the law requires. The harvesters cut and piled the stalks of grain, and the gatherers came behind them to bundle it and take it to the threshing floor. The poor had to wait until after the work

---

12. See Lev. 19:9–10; 23:22; Deut. 24:19–22.

of the gatherers before they could glean what was left behind. This was grueling and often unsafe work for a little food to put on the table. Ruth is asking pretty boldly for permission to glean behind the harvesters before all the bundled grain is tied up and moved off the field. In this case, Robert Hubbard exclaims, "Ruth showed herself to be anything but a modest, self-effacing foreigner. Rather, she emerges as courageous if not slightly brash . . . present[ing] a model of risk-taking devotion to be emulated."[13] Either way, she is working as hard as she can for as much as she can. Man or woman, this is godliness.

Matthew Henry seemed in awe as he introduced this section of Scripture in his commentary, saying, "There is scarcely any chapter in all of sacred history that stoops so low as this to take cognizance of so mean a person as Ruth, a poor Moabitish widow, so mean an action as her gleaning corn in a neighbor's field, and the minute circumstances thereof."[14] God sees this risk-taking devotion, and so does Boaz. Boaz respects what she is doing, placing herself in the shameful position of a gleaner to help meet the basic needs of both herself and her hurting mother-in-law. He generously responds to her request, even elevating Ruth's status. Hubbard explains, "In modern terms, by giving access to the water cooler (v.[1:] 9) and the lunchroom (v.[1:]14), Boaz resembled a boss showing a new employee around the company."[15] Ruth bows down in gratitude, asking why she has found such favor with him. Boaz doesn't think his actions come close to the reward she deserves for her devotion to Naomi. He answers in prayer, "May the LORD reward you for what you have done, and may you receive a full reward from the LORD God of Israel, under whose wings you have come for refuge" (Ruth 2:12). If you want an amazing example of "biblical manhood," look no further than Boaz, who "in response to Ruth's initiatives, will subvert the very patriarchal mores that most benefit him as a man. Instead, he will sacrificially employ those benefits and privileges to empower Ruth and to

---

13. Robert J. Hubbard Jr., *The Book of Ruth*, New International Commentary on the Old Testament (Grand Rapids: Eerdmans, 1988), 150.

14. Matthew Henry, *Matthew Henry's Commentary on the Whole Bible* (Peabody, MA: Hendrickson, 2001), 375.

15. Hubbard, *Book of Ruth*, 156.

benefit Naomi."[16] James reminds us that this is the Christlike example of manhood the world today so desperately needs to see.[17] Boaz isn't consciously trying to put some brand of manhood on display any more than Ruth is aiming to demonstrate womanhood to all the townspeople who are chattering about her. They are both just living before their God as men and women in their circumstances.

Ruth's initiative and strength spur Boaz to sacrificially give as well, and he too shows *hesed*. At mealtime that day, he does something amazing. He invites Ruth to a seat at his table to break bread with them. Not only that, but he serves her—so much so, that she has leftovers (Ruth 2:14). He treats her as one of the best employees rather than as a gleaner on welfare. The scene reminds me of all the times Jesus shocked those around him by his choice of mealtime companions. It also gives us a glimpse of the great feast we all look forward to in the new heavens and the new earth.

This book of the Bible gives us a picture of manhood and womanhood that is radically different than we see in much of contemporary evangelical teaching. "Ruth herself becomes a powerful catalyst for change." In her we see that "courage, boldness, and godly leadership are important feminine attributes when it comes to living for God."[18] Boaz recognizes this and wants to join in. He is going to rip off any yellow wallpaper that covers up the spirit of the law to help this woman. In this scene, we see *hesed* love at work. He serves her a meal and instructs his workers to leave extra stalks for Ruth to pick up. He commands them not to touch, rebuke, or embarrass Ruth (2:9, 15–16). James points out that Boaz's response is not only to permit, but also to promote.[19] And he makes sure that his workers do the same. This book shows us both feminine and masculine strength. Both are sacrificial strengths that are exercised in faith for the benefit of another. With its gynocentric perspective, the book of Ruth displays "a radical, not-of-this-world brand of masculinity that foreshadows the masculinity

---

16. James, *Finding God*, 10–11.
17. James, *Finding God*, 10–11.
18. James, *Gospel of Ruth*, 105.
19. James, *Gospel of Ruth*, 105.

Jesus embodied."[20] This is something we so desperately need to see displayed today. It is a humble masculinity that recognizes God's work in others and promotes it.

Once Ruth brings home her first shocking load of barley from a day's work (which was worth over two weeks' pay and was the size of a "colossal bag of dog food"[21]) and her bag of leftover food for her mother-in-law, Naomi's faith is reignited. Learning more about where Ruth gleaned, on Boaz's field, she exclaims, "May the LORD bless him because he has not abandoned his kindness [*hesed*] to the living or the dead. . . . The man is a close relative. He is one of our family redeemers" (Ruth 2:20).

THE RESCUE MISSION

In time Naomi cooks up a plan to have Ruth initiate a possible marriage to Boaz. She wants to know her daughter-in-law will be taken care of. There has been no sign or action from Boaz to indicate his interest in marriage to Ruth. And obviously there is no father or male figure in Ruth's household to try and set this up. So Naomi gives Ruth specific instructions:

> "This evening he will be winnowing barley on the threshing floor. Wash, put on perfumed oil, and wear your best clothes. Go down on the threshing floor, but don't let the man know you're there until he has finished eating and drinking. When he lies down, notice the place where he's lying, go in and uncover his feet, and lie down. Then he will explain to you what you should do."
>
> So Ruth said to her, "I will do everything you say." (Ruth 3:2–5)

But she doesn't. Ruth goes off script. At first she does everything Naomi instructs her to do. Now I know Boaz has been abundantly generous and kind to her, but I cannot imagine the level of anxiety

---

20. James, *Finding God in the Margins*, 84.

21. "Somewhere between twenty-nine and fifty pounds of grain" (Ian Duguid, *Reformed Expository Commentary: Esther & Ruth* [Phillipsburg, NJ: P&R, 2005], 161).

and the size of the lump in Ruth's throat as she is hiding out, waiting for the right moment to creep to the foot of Boaz's "bed." And talk about a gynocentric interruption! This man who has worked hard and celebrated the end of the barley harvest lies down to sleep and awakens to Ruth, of all people, right there at his feet.

This is where she breaks script. As bold an act as this is, Naomi set Ruth up to give all the signs for proposal, possible marriage that night, but left the final act of initiation in Boaz's court. So much risk is involved here. Both women are holding on to faith in what God has providentially laid out for them and trusting that Boaz is not going to let any harm come to Ruth. Ruth is supposed to be silent and wait for a response from Boaz, but she has more than marriage in mind. She isn't there to rescue herself so that she will be taken care of. She's there to rescue her family,[22] and she needs a partner, specifically Boaz, to do so. Ruth had the perspective to look beyond the usual way the laws worked and challenged the spirit behind them. "It takes an outsider like Ruth," says James, to "combine two laws and expand their reach." With a "single, innovative sentence"—"Spread the corner of your garment over me for you are a *go'el* of our family"—she "merged the levirate and kinsman-redeemer laws—property and progeny. She was asking Boaz to purchase Elimelech's land and to father a son to become Elimelech's heir and the eventual owner of his land."[23] Hubbard adds, "If successful, [Ruth] set herself up to be the true bringer of salvation in this story."[24] Not only that, she invokes the prayer Boaz said for her earlier: the Hebrew for "'garment-corner' triggered a clever word association" with the Hebrew for "'wings [of refuge]' in Boaz's earlier wish (2:12). In essence, Ruth asked Boaz to answer his own prayer!"[25] She is suggesting that Boaz covering her with the corner of his garment, a sign of protection and marriage, is the means God is using for her refuge under his wings, and even as the reward for her kindness to Naomi.[26]

---

22. See James, *Gospel of Ruth*, 199.

23. James, *Finding God in the Margins*, 75.

24. Hubbard, *Book of Ruth*, 213.

25. Hubbard, *Book of Ruth*, 212.

26. Hubbard, *Book of Ruth*, 212.

How is Boaz going to respond to her gumption? This scene is packed with suspense and sexual tension. Boaz is suddenly awakened to find Ruth, a poor Moabite woman, all doozied up and lying at his feet. Before giving him a chance to take any initiative in the situation, she pops a marriage proposal like no other. It's not a question. It reveals she has a very perceptive grasp of Jewish law. And with that perception she uses some fancy lawyering to stipulate what this marriage will cost him. Boaz is floored by the ingenuity and lengths Ruth will go to rescue her family. He responds:

> May the LORD bless you, my daughter. You have shown more kindness [*hesed*] now than before, because you have not pursued younger men, whether rich or poor. Now don't be afraid, my daughter. I will do for you whatever you say, since all the people in my town know that you are a woman of noble character. Yes, it is true that I am a family redeemer, but there is a redeemer closer than I am. Stay here tonight, and in the morning, if he wants to redeem you, that's good. Let him redeem you. But if he doesn't want to redeem you, as the LORD lives, I will. Now lie down until morning. (Ruth 3:10–13)

And unlike Ruth's response to Naomi, Boaz does do everything she says. He rises early and takes this matter to the place of business, the city gate. In this scene we see that Ruth isn't the only calculating one. He dangles the carrot of purchasing Elimelech's land before the possible kinsman redeemer, who would of course want to purchase it and gain it for his own inheritance. But that's when Boaz adds the Levirate law into the mix: the kinsman (usually a brother, but he is following along with Ruth's liberal application) is to marry the widow to carry on the line of the deceased. So the stipulation to purchasing the land as a kinsman redeemer is that he would also have to marry Ruth, and if they bore sons, they would carry out Elimelech's claim on the land. That is too big a risk for this possible redeemer to take, even if Ruth does seem to be barren. Like Orpah in the beginning of the story, he respectfully bows out.

But Boaz, like Ruth, is honored to offer risk-taking devotion.[27] This is truly an amazing story of God's love carried out through his people. And you know the ending: the barren woman bears a son. The blessing that all the people at the city gate gave to Boaz and Ruth is fulfilled. Like Rachel and Leah, Ruth helps to build the house of Israel. Their house becomes "like the house of Perez, the son of Tamar bore to Judah, because of the offspring the LORD [gives them] by this young woman" (Ruth 4:12). As Ruth gives Obed to Naomi, the women bless her,[28] saying that Ruth is better to her than seven sons. Frank Spina connects the dots even more, saying, "Like Tamar before her, Ruth the outsider has acted to save her own future, Naomi's future, and Israel's future."[29] Our question is answered as Ruth gives Naomi that baby: God is good to his people, even to an "insignificant" woman like Naomi. She has a daughter that is better than seven sons, and yet "'a son has been born to Naomi'" (Ruth 4:17). Naomi is full. Then we get the patrilineal genealogy, starting with Perez, showing Obed in that line as the grandfather to David. Fast-forward to the birth of our true Deliverer, Jesus Christ, and Ruth is named in Matthew's genealogy right beside Boaz. God is good to his people, even to an outsider like Ruth. He has sent the promised Deliverer. Mission accomplished.

REVEALING TRADENTS OF THE FAITH

Tradents, those who hand down the oral traditions and history of the faith, were extremely valuable to God's people in this oral culture. They didn't have multiple Bibles per household. God's Word to his people and his covenant faithfulness were preserved through those who faithfully taught them to others. Tradents were valuable sources over the thousands of years that the canon of Scripture was being formed. They were the scribes, the teachers, the exegetes, the rabbis,

---

27. "Hence, as ch. 1 set the ordinary *hesed* of Orpah beside the extraordinary *hesed* of Ruth, so this scene did with the kinsman and Boaz" (Hubbard, *Book of Ruth*, 246–47).

28. Presumably, the same women who greeted Naomi at the beginning of the story.

29. Frank Anthony Spina, *The Faith of the Outsider: Exclusion and Inclusion in the Biblical Story* (Grand Rapids: Eerdmans, 2005), 136.

and the preachers. But we will see throughout this book that all of God's people are responsible to be active traditioners of the faith, even today. And in Ruth we see the importance of women tradents. We can glean even more from Ruth's gynocentric interruption. While the writings in Scripture are dominantly androcentric, what do stories like Ruth's reveal about women tradents?

We have already seen Huldah granting authoritative status to canonize a large section of what we know as the book of Deuteronomy. But throughout Scripture we see women in less formal roles passing down the oral traditions and history of the faith to God's people. As we glean from the book of Ruth, three women stand out in playing an important role as active traditioners. The first one isn't mentioned in Ruth, but her influence and teaching is all over the pages. In Matthew's genealogy of Jesus, we see Rahab listed as the mother of Boaz.[30] Now this is very interesting. Boaz's mother was a Canaanite prostitute who openly professed her faith in the God of Israel and was then welcomed to become a member of God's household.[31]

Rahab, like Ruth, was an outsider with no status who helped to rescue her family by trusting in the true Deliverer (see Josh. 2). Rahab is such a fascinating person in history. Her part in helping the Israelite spies who were scouting out Jericho revealed a faith full of bravery, initiative, discernment, and resolve.

Here we have another gynocentric interruption to the text, where two male spies depend on the actions of a prostitute. Rahab is sent word from the king of Jericho to bring out these two men who recently entered her house. As a prostitute, she is used to men entering her house, right? Due to their view and treatment of her, she probably didn't regard men as having much integrity. John Calvin reasoned that these two spies most likely picked her place out of convenience.[32] It was close to the city wall and in a remote spot where they would be more

---

30. For an argument making the case that 1 Chron. 2:54–55 is the exegetical basis for Salma and Rahab's marriage, see Bauckham, *Gospel Women*, 34–41.

31. See Josh. 2.

32. John Calvin, *Commentary on Joshua and Psalms 1–35*, vol. 4, trans. William Pringle (Grand Rapids: Baker, 2003), 43–44.

likely to be concealed. What is she going to do when these two men—Israelite spies—enter her home?

Rahab must make a swift decision about whether she is going to help these Israelite men. These aren't her people. And they are two strange men. But they are Israelites, and Rahab has faith in their God. So she acts in bravery, against her own king and her own people, securing their safety. She acts quickly to hide these men, as she knows watchmen are lurking and rumors would spread fast about these Israelite men in her house. Calvin commented that when the king's men come asking for them, "their life hangs upon the tongue of a woman, just as if it were hanging by a thread."[33] Rahab risks her own life to protect these men. She doesn't hide herself but "comes boldly forward"[34] to detract the king's men from the spies.

We can add initiative to Rahab's bravery. She doesn't act like a victim of circumstance here. She knows the authorities are going to come knocking on her door, so she preemptively hides the Israelite spies. Scholars even know the time of year when this happened by her method of concealment. The stalks of flax drying in open air on her roof reveals that it was around the end of March or beginning of April.[35] They couldn't have pulled off that hiding spot had they waited until the knock at the door. Taking the initiative to hide them preemptively puts Rahab in position for her next move.

After the king's men leave, fooled by Rahab, she then takes initiative with the two spies to secure salvation for herself and her family. Before they can fall asleep on the safety of her roof, she charges them, "Swear to me by the LORD that you will also show kindness [*hesed*] to my father's family, because I showed kindness [*hesed*] to you." She then asks, "Give me a sure sign that you will spare the lives of my father, mother, brothers, sisters, and all who belong to them, and save us from death" (Josh. 2:12–13).

Rahab exercises this great bravery and initiative because she has a discerning faith. She doesn't just take a chance on these two men.

---

33. Calvin, *Commentary on Joshua and Psalms 1–35*, 45.
34. Calvin, *Commentary on Joshua and Psalms 1–35*, 45.
35. Calvin, *Commentary on Joshua and Psalms 1–35*, 45.

She doesn't just follow some gut feeling she had from their first impression on her. No, Rahab says,

> "I know that the LORD has given you this land and that the terror
> of you has fallen on us, and everyone who lives in the land is pan-
> icking because of you. For we have heard how the LORD dried up
> the water of the Red Sea before you when you came out of Egypt,
> and what you did to Sihon and Og, the two Amorite kings you
> completely destroyed across the Jordan. When we heard this, we
> lost heart, and everyone's courage failed because of you, for the
> LORD your God is God in heaven above and on earth below."
> (Josh. 2:8–11)

Those first two words, "I know," reveal a certainty of Rahab's faith. She knows what's real. She knows how to separate the truth from the lie—that's what discernment is. That means there is content involved. And Rahab expresses exactly what she knows is going on and who is behind it, concluding, "For the LORD your God is God in heaven above and on earth below." She knows who is Lord!

Knowing the Lord changes everything. It changes a person. This prostitute's actions reveal that she is a new creation. And it changes her status. She will not act as a Canaanite prostitute but as a sister to these two spies. When confronted with the truth, we either align ourselves with it as allies or buck against it as opponents. To have resolve requires sacrifice. And that is what Rahab is now confronted with. Her bravery, discernment, initiative, and resolve are fruits of her faith and a revelation to God's people about his openness to welcome Gentiles into his covenant community.

Now, what do you think Rahab would have taught her son Boaz about their amazing God? Do you think she would withhold any detail of his mighty love and work? The evidence is all over the text in Ruth. Boaz already knows the richness of God's love for the outsider—his mother was one! He knows the history of their faith, God delivering his people from slavery and bringing them to the new land. He is now living in the time of the judges when everyone did what was right in their own eyes. But he still has the story of God's covenant love for his people burning in him. Rahab was a tradent teaching God's *hesed* love to Boaz.

Boaz already knows that God works through women in mighty ways. A strong, godly woman raised him. So he too has the discernment to see God working in Ruth. He sees that same bravery, discernment, initiative, and resolve in Ruth as the fruit of her faith. And he is not threatened by her but rather wants to join her as a blessed ally[36] in God's mission.

So we look backward just one generation, and we see God using Rahab as an influence on her son. I should point out that Salma too, who may have been one of those Israelite spies depending on her,[37] would also influence Boaz. This man, the son of Nahshon, "the leader of the descendants of Judah" (Num. 2:3), joins forces with a Canaanite prostitute to carry out the Lord's work. The alliance of Salma and Rahab had a rich testimony to hand down about the God of their faith. Naomi, Boaz, and Ruth also had an amazing account to tell about the Lord. We see that the narrator of Ruth is telling this account generations later, either during David's or Solomon's reign (the genealogy extends to David), and even needed to explain the custom of a man handing his sandal to make the exchange of property legally binding (Ruth 4:7). So there had to be some serious active traditioning going on for these details to be preserved. And to be able to tell most of the story from the female perspective, we expect that female tradents were responsible for handing down these details—starting with Naomi and Ruth.

Furthermore, the patrilineal genealogy reveals that Obed is King David's grandfather. The narrative scene closes with Obed in Naomi's arms. What did Naomi teach Obed about the fullness of God's love? Naomi experienced God's *hesed* love as he met her in her darkest hour. She didn't have multiple Bibles in her home, she didn't have a husband to teach her from God's Word, and she didn't have any word from

---

36. James, *Gospel of Ruth*, 187–88.

37. See Bauckham, *Gospel Women*, 37; this was possibly a tradition passed down.

the Lord telling her what he was up to. She didn't get the answers to why she was left mourning the death of her husband and two sons, or why God seemed to be absent from that picture. But God showed his presence in his great *hesed* love through his people. Carolyn Custis James notes the quality of faith that was handed down to the man after God's own heart,[38] David, saying that Naomi's influence is all over the Psalms.[39] Oh how Naomi and Ruth must have loved to tell that story— loved to encourage others who were hurting and exhort those who were weak in the faith—of God's *hesed* love. Can we not marvel about these tradents of the faith, passing down God's *hesed* love to Obed, and how that poured into his own grandson? When we read the Psalms, do we wonder at the depth of the poetic and raw expression of David's faith and not think of Ruth and Naomi and Rahab?

PEEL AND REVEAL

If there were no gynocentric texts in Scripture and women played no role in the process of recognizing the canon, then it would be fair to say that maybe Scripture is a patriarchal construction. It would make sense for women to feel the need to have God's Word customized more for us and to want to add in the woman's perspective. But the woman's perspective is not missing from Scripture. And as we see in Ruth and will see from more examples in the next chapter, women played an active role alongside of men in passing down the history and teachings of God's covenant people as tradents of the faith.

We don't want to overemphasize these gynocentric texts over and against the androcentricity of Scripture. That is not what they are meant to do. But as Bauckham points out, they do correct any promotion of androcentrism. The canon itself corrects this kind of promotion.[40] Women aren't left out. They aren't ignored; they are heard. They are more than heard; they contribute. And these gynocentric

---

38. 1 Sam. 13:14.

39. James, *Gospel of Ruth*, 205.

40. See Bauckham, *Gospel Women*, 15.

texts are rich with doctrine-meets-real-life, history-meets-experience, and depth of insight.

Why not the book of *Boaz*? He is the one with the power in this story. He is the man. He is the actual Israelite. Why *not* the book of Boaz? Because God wants us to see this story through the eyes of an outsider who came to his wings for refuge. What does Boaz see when he meets Ruth? He sees the single-minded, risk-taking devotion of Ruth's pledge to Naomi and her God. He sees the godliness of rightly ordered desire. He sees *hesed* kindness in action. What do we see when we meet Ruth? We see the *protoevangelium* of Genesis 3:15 rumbling all over the place. Ruth's single-minded devotion was to provide an heir, who turns out to be the ancestor of David, and then of Jesus, the woman's seed. We see that God keeps his promises. And he does it in unsuspecting ways. Many commentators downplay the significance of the book of Ruth by calling it a love story between Boaz and Ruth. But it is a love story of a different kind. It is the *hesed* love of God to his people. Things are not as they seem. As Israel has turned away from God, broken his covenant, and appears as a widow, God works through a remnant. He brings the outsider to his inner circle, giving her initiative, discernment, and resolve by faith. And he gives Naomi a son.

PEELING AWAY PERMISSION TO SPEAK

Is Boaz threatened by Ruth's initiative, discernment, and resolve? No, he follows Ruth's lead in making it happen. He doesn't only permit, he promotes. It's literally ancient history. And yet the book of Ruth provokes a critical look at the church today. How do we see God's *hesed* love working in his people in the covenant community of our churches? Doesn't he show his kindness to and through both the men and the women in a dynamic way that will fructify his church? Can we recognize it at work in both the men and the women? As we see in Ruth, *hesed* kindness sacrifices to promote the goodness of others.

What do you see when you look at the women in your church? Do you see someone you should learn from? Do you see someone worthy to invest in—to sacrifice for? This is even more of a challenge for churches that hold to male-only ordination, because there is a tendency to keep an eye out for men with theological vigor and leadership gifts as they are potential deacons, elders, bishops, or pastors. They become the ones who are more likely to be invested in. But this is a mistake, as the women in the church have much to teach as well. Church officers need to see the potential in the women, who help with even their own blind spots. As the book of Ruth shows us, there's often a story behind the story.

I sometimes meet with church leaders interested in improving in this area. Their questions often reveal how both the secular and evangelical cultures are shaping the way they are thinking. The church is using the same language as the secular world—whether we're talking about equality and rights or borrowing the same Victorian-age gender tropes and then calling it "biblical." Their questions often revolve around what the women in the church are *permitted* to do. While there is certainly a place to talk about these things, there seems to be little talk about how the woman's contribution is distinctly valued and how they can promote that in their leadership by listening to and investing in their women. The woman's casserole is valued. The woman's nursery duty is valued. The woman's service in VBS is valued. Is her theological contribution valued? Is her testimony valued? Is her advice valued? When she shows initiative, discernment, and resolve, do you see someone who wants to give of herself in service in all these ways, or does that make her less feminine in your eyes?

Gynocentric interruptions shouldn't just be permitted; they should be promoted. The women's voices—not only their casseroles and babysitting skills—are needed just as much as the men's in the life of the church. This means the ones with authority need to show them the water cooler and lunchroom. This means they need to be fed from the depths of the Word and be satisfied.

No, women were not left out of active traditioning in testifying to and passing down the faith. This is a coed endeavor. And the women's literature that we find in Scripture is not accidental.[41] Women have a

---

41. Bauckham, *Gospel Women*, 16.

voice in God's Word, and women were certainly included in the process of recognizing and receiving God's Word to his people throughout the process of the formation of the canon of Scripture. Let's praise God for these things and discuss how they are reflected in our reading, studying, and discipling in God's Word in our churches today.

QUESTIONS FOR GROUP DISCUSSION

1. How do you think the version of this history would be told differently if we were reading the book of Boaz?

2. Gynocentric interruption might help us to consider differently what we would usually attribute as masculine concerns. In Ruth we see how ancient patrilineal genealogy, and all the legal red tape involved when an heir dies, is not only a patriarchal concern. Reread Ruth 4. You see this interplay of the male and female perspective at the end of Ruth when the men are discussing the legal structures at the gate and then when the birth of Ruth and Boaz's son, Obed, is described. What advantage do these legal structures give Ruth, a childless widow and a resident alien? What about for Naomi, a widow who already lost her childless sons? How does this bring light to how the legal conventions benefited the vulnerable ones in Israel?

3. What is a tradent? How might tradents be valuable to God's covenant people in antiquity and to the writers of Scripture? Why is this an important term when we discuss how the Bible was written, the process of recognizing the canon of Scripture, and the contribution of women?

4. I'm talking a lot about a female voice and a male voice, but is there a feminine or masculine way to study doctrine? For example, if your church were to offer a class on the Trinity, the properties of Scripture, sanctification, or eschatology, would there be a need to teach the women on these topics differently than the men? Would you need books written specifically for men and specifically for women on doctrine? Would men and women have different perspectives to share when it comes to

how theology meets life? How would coed studies with active male and female contributions benefit discipling in the church? What is beneficial in also providing exclusive men's and exclusive women's studies?

5. Read the genealogy in Matthew 1. How does it differ from the genealogy in Ruth? Why is this significant to the reader?

CHAPTER 3

GIRLS INTERRUPTED

I hope everyone is having fun with this new term, *gynocentric interruption*. I was talking about Richard Bauckham's work and introduced this term to a male professor friend of mine, and he began chuckling with the revelation that his life as a husband and father of three daughters *is* one big gynocentric interruption. Academic terms sometimes have a way of taking on a humorous life of their own.

Let's look at some more gynocentric interruptions, where Scripture takes us behind the scenes and gives us a story behind the story through the female voice, as well as implementing women as tradents of the faith. This is not an exhaustive look by any means. My hope is that you will begin identifying how this coactivity of the male and female voice functions more and more in your regular reading of Scripture and consider its implications in church life.

DELIVERING BABIES AND THE TRADITION

Genesis has plenty of texts we could look at, but an excerpt from Exodus 1 particularly stands out. The book starts with another patrilineal succession genealogy and tells us of the new king of Egypt who did not know Joseph, and how he oppressed the Israelites with forced labor out of fear that they would take over Egypt. This did not curb the population of the Israelites, as they multiplied exponentially even under severe oppression. Ironically, as the pharaoh aims to eliminate the Israelites' strength, he underestimates where strength can be found. Scripture gives us a look behind the scenes from the perspective of a couple of midwives to show how God is working to deliver his people:

> The king of Egypt said to the Hebrew midwives—the first whose name was Shiphrah and the second whose name was Puah—"When you help the Hebrew women give birth, observe them as they deliver. If the child is a son, kill him, but if it's a daughter, she may live." The midwives, however, feared God and did not do as the king of Egypt had told them; they let the boys live. So the king of Egypt summoned the midwives and asked them, "Why have you done this and let the boys live?"
>
> The midwives said to Pharaoh, "The Hebrew women are not like the Egyptian women, for they are vigorous and give birth before the midwife can get to them."
>
> So God was good to the midwives, and the people multiplied and became very numerous. Since the midwives feared God, he gave them families. (Ex. 1:15–21)

James Montgomery Boice never used the term *gynocentric interruption*, but he camps out on this portion of Scripture for his series on the life of Moses:

> The midwives were sensitive to God. They did the right thing and would not participate in the killing of newborns. We have their names when we are not even told the name of the pharaoh. In those days, who would have paid any attention to these midwives? Yet everybody knew the pharaoh and his father and the pharaoh before him, and their names were written on the monuments. In the book of Exodus, God does not record the pharaohs' names, but he remembers these two women, Shiphrah and Puah, because they did the right thing.[1]

---

1. James Montgomery Boice, *The Life of Moses* (Phillipsburg, NJ: P&R, 2018), 26.

These two women, Shiphrah and Puah, are faced with a question—whom do they fear more, the pharaoh of Egypt, or the Lord God Almighty? These women who deliver babies have faith in the true Deliverer. They will not murder his children. Shiphrah and Puah are not two insignificant women after all. They have the strength to choose life for these male babies; and for that, the Lord blesses them. And Pharaoh is not as mighty as he thinks he is. We see in this account that things are not as they seem. The weak are strong and the strong is weak. The Lord is at work, and therefore "it would be better to be a Hebrew midwife than to be Pharaoh."[2]

Boice told us why Shiphrah and Puah's names were preserved and written in God's Word, but how were their names preserved? How did Moses get this story about the midwives? We have these details because the midwives told their story and it was passed down. The midwives not only feared God and loved God's Word; they were active traditioners, tradents of the faith.

You see, these women aren't merely interrupting the androcentric perspective with their narrative in the text. They served God's people in more than one way. Not only did they deliver babies, and not only did they preserve the male infants' lives against the orders of the pharaoh, but they passed down the heritage and tradition of God's people by sharing how God worked through them.

THE CAMERA ANGLES IN JUDGES

The book of Judges reads like a culmination of different narrative camera angles showcasing the downward spiral of the Israelite people as they absorb the Canaanite lifestyle and do what is right in their own eyes. It is a brutal book to read. One of the ways we see the progressing depravity of the Israelites at this time is by the way the women are viewed and treated. We get snapshots of increasing wickedness toward women as the Israelites continue to abandon God. Most of these camera angles are viewed through the androcentric lens and center around the lives of

---

2. Boice, *Life of Moses*, 27.

men as we see this pattern of God's people turning away from him in sin, the Lord handing them over to their enemies, the Israelites crying out, and God then hearing their prayers and sending another deliverer. Again and again. Each time the Lord sends them another judge, his people are saved from their oppression. But after the death of each judge, the Israelites progressively become more corrupt.[3] Their hearts quickly turn from the Lord, and they become more and more debased.

The first judge or deliverer was Othniel, Caleb's youngest brother. Given the patriarchal culture of the time, Caleb promised to give his daughter in marriage to the man who could overcome Kiriath-sepher. It's difficult to read this with our modern-day sensibilities and not see a woman objectified as a voiceless trophy wife. But while following the custom of fathers arranging their daughters' marriages, Caleb is setting his daughter up to marry the best of the best. He knows Othniel is a good leader. The land had peace for the forty years he was a judge.[4] And we do hear Caleb's daughter's, Achsah's, voice. As Barry Webb notes in his commentary, "From the moment of her entry (v. 14) Achsah ceases to be an object acted upon by two men. She seizes the opportunity to get something which neither her father nor her husband has considered."[5] In addition to the dowry of land her father gave, she takes the initiative to request springs. And he grants this to her, giving Achsah both the upper and lower springs, which are valuable in this dry land.[6] Things start off pretty well.

As the Israelites turn more and more to their own ways and abandon the Lord, women are used for sexual pleasure, manipulation, sacrifice, and baby mamas, with one woman even being offered to savages to be brutally raped in place of a man being raped. After this particular gang-rape victim dies from the night of violence done to her, her master—a Levite who threw her to the rapists to protect himself—cuts up her body and delivers its pieces to the tribes of Israel. This is his way

---

3. Judg. 16–19.
4. Judg. 1:12–13; 3:11.
5. Barry G. Webb, *The Book of Judges*, New International Commentary on the Old Testament (Grand Rapids: Eerdmans, 2012), 104.
6. Judg. 1:14–15.

of calling for justice and vengeance against the tribe of Benjamin for protecting these wicked men. While the tribes unite for battle and civil war breaks out, the book concludes with the Israelites stealing women and giving them over as brides to the six hundred men in the tribe of Benjamin who survived. Clearly the war was not because the Israelites valued the life of the woman who was raped and left for dead. And if Achsah was a trophy wife for the best warrior in the beginning, everyone gets a trophy in the end, no need for a father's oversight, arrangement, or even permission.

Again, I want to keep the main thing the main thing. The main point in Judges is not the treatment of women. Chapter 2 lays out the pattern of the whole book, giving us the big picture. The narrative then unravels, displaying the details from different camera angles. After all God had done to deliver his people from Egypt and bring them to the new land of Canaan, just one generation later they turn from him. But he is still their God. They may break his covenant, but he will not. He reveals their hearts, and they pay the consequences. We see the depravity of life in our own eyes apart from God. Yet in his grace God continues to hear the cries of his people and delivers them from oppression. This all points to our great need for the true Judge, the true Deliverer, Jesus Christ, to come. He gives us new life and new hearts that turn to him. He delivers us from sin's enslavement and brings us into communion with the triune God. But as we have the big picture, we can observe that one of the glaring evidences of the Israelites' increasing depravity is displayed in their degradation of women. This is marked evidence of human depravity even today. And it stands in stark contrast to the gynocentric interruption that we have in the song of Deborah, earlier in the narrative, as well as the active traditioning by the daughters of Israel a little later. They give us two different camera angles in such a dark room of a book.

PRAISE TO THE GOD OF ISRAEL

Deborah enters the scene after the third judge dies. God's people once again do evil, and God hands them over to Jabin, king of Canaan, and his powerful army commander, Sisera. After twenty years of cruel oppression, the Israelites cry out to God. We typically associate a judge as a magistrate, but the judges here in Scripture function as deliverers of God's people. Although, unlike the other judges described, Deborah is a judge who is also a prophetess and one whom people did seek out for judgment.[7] This is important to the narrative, because when she speaks for God to Barak, asserting that he is to gather ten thousand men to battle Sisera, Barak says, "If you will go with me, I will go. But if you will not go with me, I will not go" (Judg. 4:8). Barak has earned a bad reputation in the church for this response. Many of us have been taught that he is cowardly to insist that Deborah come along. But these words are wise and full of faith. We see this in the story told through Deborah's perspective, which is a beautiful song of praise to the Lord.

Barak's meager army of unarmed Israelites was no match against Sisera's nine hundred chariots. Prophets played a very important role in a battle like this:

> Barak couldn't run down to the local Walmart in Bethel and buy a 5.99 bible. Revelation was not complete at this time. They had the books of Moses, but those would not have been accessible to the general public. They would have known the 10 commandments, but other than that, where would one go for the word of God?
>
> They could go only one place: Deborah. She WAS the word of God to Israel.[8]

Rather than go without the direction of the Lord and seek the glory for himself, Barak insists that Deborah come. This wasn't an unusual request. In military battles such as this, prophets were more important than weapons. Having God's Word to encourage warriors and tell them when to strike and what to do is better than nine hundred chariots. "Prophets are such an important presence in battle that Elijah

---

7. Judg. 4:4–5.

8. Sam Powell, "In Defense of Barak," *My Only Comfort*, December 3, 2014, https://myonlycomfort.com/tag/barak/.

and Elisha are called 'Israel's chariot and cavalry.'"[9] Deborah's response that she will gladly go, but that a woman is going to have the honor of taking down Sisera, is not a rebuke. Barak wasn't after his own glory; he sings along with Deborah, glorifying God for the victory.

In Deborah's song she reveals that the Israelites were without weapons.[10] The only weapon they had was the word of the Lord. Deborah gives Barak God's word to rush down Mount Tabor toward Sisera's army with his unarmed men, motivating him with the assurance that the Lord has gone before him. And in faith, Barak does just that. He doesn't ask her to go into the battle with him. He doesn't hesitate. He descends the mountain, charging after the nine hundred iron chariots in obedience to the word of the Lord. Deborah's song reveals the details about the Lord going before Barak. God sent a flash flood that rendered all the nine hundred chariots useless.[11] Here Deborah reveals that Israel's God had ultimate power of storm and rain, exposing the ineptitude of the Canaanite's storm god, Ba'al. Their chariots are powerless in the muddy waters, and Barak is able to descend on them victoriously. "Deborah has announced God's victory, Barak has facilitated it, and God has saved Israel."[12] Sisera flees, only to be tricked and defeated by a woman. God, not Barak, gets the glory.

Interestingly, during a time of crucial battle for Israel's deliverance, we see a contrast of mothers. Deborah calls herself a mother of Israel. Not only has she counseled her people; she also preserves the Israelite heritage and protects them in battle by advising them with the word of the Lord.[13] Here we see a mother figure actively working in the public sphere. She contrasts herself with Sisera's mother, who is described as waiting at home for her son to return victoriously, envisioning him returning with many women trophies as spoils of battle. Sisera's mother is kept in the domestic sphere, promoting the sexual abuse of Israelite

---

9. Tikva Frymer-Kensky, *Reading the Women of the Bible* (New York: Schocken, 2002), 48. See 2 Kings 2:11; 6:13–18; 13:14–16.

10. Judg. 5:8. Her entire song is recorded in Judg. 5.

11. Frymer-Kensky, *Reading the Women of the Bible*, 49.

12. Frymer-Kensky, *Reading the Women of the Bible*, 49.

13. Frymer-Kensky, *Reading the Women of the Bible*, 50. This section on the contrast of mothers borrows from pp. 50–60.

women. Both mothers are protective of their own people, but Deborah is victorious. We see more motherly language as Jael invites Sisera into her home, covering him with a blanket and giving him milk.[14] Sisera believes he is being nurtured and protected by an ally, and Jael drives a tent peg into his head, aligning with Israel's God. Jael proves to be a warrior within the domestic sphere of her home. "Jael is most blessed of women" (Judg. 5:24)! Both Deborah and Jael are contrasted with Sisera's mother, as servants of God.

As Jael drives a peg into the enemy's head, we are reminded of the *protoevangelium* in Genesis 3:15. Deborah sings, "she crushed his head" (Judg. 5:26). The enemy falls at her feet. We remember that the woman's offspring will strike the serpent's head. Our hope in Christ, the true Servant and Deliverer, is renewed. Things are not as they seem. This woman's home was not a haven for Sisera. And we read this knowing that pegs will be driven through Christ's hands and feet in order to crush the serpent's head.

Deborah celebrates her motherly love for Israel in her song, blessing both Jael's actions and Barak's faith to carry out God's work. Much later we see Jesus lamenting over Jerusalem with motherly language, saying, "Jerusalem, Jerusalem, who kills the prophets and stones those who are sent to her. How often I wanted to gather your children together, as a hen gathers her chicks under her wings, but you were not willing!" (Luke 13:34). Deborah celebrates as the mother of Israel; Jesus laments over his people with motherly language. The Israelites respect Deborah as a prophet and judge. They turn on Jesus. And yet through death and resurrection he delivers his people anyway and is the true Prophet to which all others point. Deborah spoke the word. Jesus is the Word.

I particularly appreciate this gynocentric interruption of Deborah's song in such a dark book. In Judges we see our profound need for a deliverer. It's almost too much to bear. Deborah stands in contrast to the pagan goddesses of the time and to the worst of patriarchal abuses that we see play out in the book of Judges. And once again, through the female perspective, Israel's heritage is handed down in detail as

---

14. Judg. 4:18–19; 5:25.

we get the story behind the story of Sisera's defeat. If the Bible were a patriarchal document, we wouldn't have these details of Deborah, Jael, or Barak. And the best part is that God alone gets the glory.

A COMMEMORATION ANGLE

While we celebrate victory with the mother of Israel, we mourn loss with the daughters of Israel. In another camera angle, we see that even a good judge can make a rash vow, and his own daughter pays the price. Jephthah has that great line in Judges where he declares that the Lord is the judge. It's almost like when an actor breaks the fourth wall, an expression that refers to the invisible wall that separates the actors and the audience. When an actor breaks the fourth wall, they speak directly to the audience. In a similar manner, the narrator in Judges uses Jephthah's voice to do this. Here we are reading the narrative of the judges that God sends to deliver his people, and this line, "Let the LORD who is the judge decide today between the Israelites and the Ammonites" (Judg. 11:27), functions as the character giving us direct information of the whole book. God is the true judge, not them. And he will deliver his people.

But then in his zeal, we see Jephthah make a rash vow to the Lord: "If you in fact hand over the Ammonites to me, whoever comes out the doors of my house to greet me when I return safely from the Ammonites will belong to the LORD, and I will offer that person as a burnt offering" (Judg. 11:30–31). After defeating the Ammonites, he is devastated when his only child, a daughter, is the first to come out of the doors of his house, greeting him with tambourine in hand. Most commentators take this at face value, giving the interpretation that his daughter was offered as a burned sacrifice. The consensus is that Jephthah should never have made such a rash vow and that he should not have honored the vow, as this was an abomination to God.[15] A few commentators interpret the sacrifice to be of a different nature, saying that he consecrated his daughter to the Lord as a perpetual virgin living

---

15. See Deut. 12:31; 18:9–12; cf. 2 Kings 3:27; 23:10; Isa. 57:5.

in seclusion. It is a difficult text either way. And this is Jephthah's only child that he is "offering" to the Lord.

But it doesn't end there. We read, "Thus it became a custom in Israel, that the daughters of Israel went yearly to commemorate the daughter of Jephthah the Gileadite four days in the year" (Judg. 11:39–40 NASB). It's interesting to note the contrast between the godly lamentation of Israel's daughters and the role lamentation of goddesses played in the pagan culture of the time. "Goddesses [sang] laments over their dead sons, lovers, and brothers."[16] They also lamented for their cities. But these daughters of Jerusalem are commemorating and lamenting the loss of a daughter. Here, in the book of Judges of all places, we see a young woman honored for the value of her life.

I wrote an article for my blog on the female voices in Scripture, and James Duguid gave an enlightening comment:

> I've often thought that generations of women must have played a significant role in passing down the traditions that served as sources for the book of Judges particularly. There is just so much in the book about women and the abuse of women. In the story of Jephthah's daughter we actually have evidence for such a process: It is the "daughters of Israel" (Judg. 11:40) who keep her memory alive through a yearly ritual. The author of Judges must have used other sources about Jephthah as well, but it seems likely that his most important source was handed down to him from generations of Israelite women.[17]

This is such a fascinating point. Do you see the coactivity of male and female voices in God's Word at work here? Once again we see a male narrator using what would typically be thought of as insignificant voices, the daughters of Israel, as tradents of the faith. Clearly the

---

16. Tikva Frymer-Kensky, *In the Wake of the Goddesses* (New York: Fawcett Columbine, 1992), 36.

17. James Duguid, comment on Aimee Byrd, "The Female Voices in Scripture," *Housewife Theologian* (blog), Mortification of Spin, November 10, 2016, www.alliancenet.org/mos/housewife-theologian/the-female-voices-in-scripture#.WzEEyBJKgyk.

writer of Judges is not advocating the abuses that he records in detail. It is descriptive, not prescriptive. And with all these camera angles, two being gynocentric interruptions, we see more vividly the horror of turning from the LORD and doing what is right in our own eyes. And we also see just how transformative the grace of God is. He did not make a rash vow but covenanted to send his only begotten Son to live the life we could not and bear the curse for our wretched sins. God doesn't only deliver us from his wrath but gives us goodness.

TWO WOMEN CAPTURING THE SAME SHOT

Let's connect some of these gynocentric interruptions found in the Old Testament with a few snapshots through the lens of the female voice in the New Testament. What do Rahab, a dog, and the Canaanite woman have in common?[18] Answer: they all foreshadow the great commission. And this will make some people who really want to know about dogs in heaven happy. But I'll come back to the dog part later. First, let's look at two women, separated by more than fourteen hundred years.

Rahab is one of the Gentile women Matthew named in the genealogy of Jesus. Looking at the women in Matthew's genealogy is an interesting study. While we are used to seeing the women in our own ancestral family trees, as I mentioned earlier most genealogies in that time were patrilineal. And yet along with the fathers, Matthew included Tamar, Rahab, Ruth, and Bathsheba. This is a curious choice of women to include. These women may not sound like what we are used to being taught regarding "biblical womanhood," which often encourages women to be passive. But here they are in the genealogy of our Savior.

Why did Matthew include Rahab, for instance? Bauckham insists that it is because Rahab represents God's openness of his covenant community to the Gentiles. She was a Canaanite, a prostitute even, who openly professed her faith in the God of Israel and was then

18. This section is adapted from a talk I gave at the Quakertown Women's Conference 2018, "Women at the Feet of Jesus," sponsored by the Alliance for Confessing Evangelicals and Grace Bible Fellowship Church, May 18–19, 2018, Grace Bible Fellowship Church, Quakertown, PA. Used with permission.

welcomed to become a member of God's household. But not only was Rahab admitted into the covenant family; she also has a spot in this blessed genealogy. We covered her story in detail in the last chapter, but now I'd like to connect her with another gynocentric interruption.

Interestingly, Matthew gave us a snapshot of another Gentile woman in his gospel. In Matthew 15:22 we have a Canaanite woman who persuades Jesus to change his mind. That's a pretty big deal, right? We read, "a Canaanite woman from that region came and kept crying out, saying, 'Have mercy on me, Lord, Son of David! My daughter is severely tormented by a demon.'" Bauckham picks up on some parallels explaining this encounter between Jesus and the Canaanite woman as "a new Rahab encountering a Messiah who could be a new Joshua":

> Her address to Jesus, "Son of David," is equivalent to Rahab's confession of the true God that is inseparable from her recognition that this God has given the land to his people Israel (Josh. 2:9). Like Rahab she takes initiative and asks boldly for the kindness she so desperately needs (Josh. 2:12–13). Like Rahab she receives the mercy for which she had asked (Josh. 6:22–25). Finally, and very importantly, like Rahab, because of her faith she is a first exception to the rule about Canaanites.[19]

Let's read the rest of the interaction between Jesus and the Canaanite woman:

> Jesus did not say a word to her. His disciples approached him and urged him, "Send her away because she's crying out after us."
>
> He replied, "I was sent only to the lost sheep of the house of Israel."
>
> But she came, knelt before him, and said, "Lord, help me!"
>
> He answered, "It isn't right to take the children's bread and throw it to the dogs."

---

19. Richard Bauckham, *Gospel Women: Studies of the Named Women in the Gospel* (Grand Rapids: Eerdmans, 2002), 44.

"Yes, Lord," she said, "yet even the dogs eat the crumbs that fall from their masters' table."

Then Jesus replied to her, "Woman, your faith is great. Let it be done for you as you want." And from that moment her daughter was healed. (Matt. 15:23–28)

This text has gotten under my skin in the past. Jesus doesn't have very kind words for this desperate woman at first. But a closer look makes this first response from Jesus appear as if he is throwing her a softball rather than being cruel. Matthew was certainly throwing one to us as readers. He had just opened his gospel with some of these supposed "dogs" named in the ancestry of Jesus. In a footnote, Bauckham reminds us "that Jesus cannot ultimately reject this woman for her ethnicity without repudiating two of his ancestors in the genealogy."[20]

Just as with Rahab, we see a Canaanite woman—about as valuable as a dog—exercising bravery, initiative, discernment, and resolve. By describing this woman as a Canaanite, Matthew was gesturing to the tension of this encounter—the Jewish nationalism of the time was "not only directed at the Roman occupying power but also at the presence of pagans in the land of Israel, which they polluted with their idolatry and immoral lifestyle."[21] But this woman doesn't only approach Jesus; Mark described her as falling at Jesus's feet (Mark 7:25), what looks to be both a desperate and humble move. It reminds me of the woman who suffered from twelve years of bleeding who touched Jesus's robe. When Jesus discovered her, Luke said, "she came trembling and fell down before him" (Luke 8:47). Here too we have a desperate, brave woman, begging for mercy at the feet of Jesus.

Obviously, she took initiative by seeking out Jesus. In a parallel text in the gospel of Mark, just before his account of this story, Mark said that Jesus was trying to keep his location on the down-low at this point. Perhaps his desired concealment was working with the Jews, the people

---

20. Bauckham, *Gospel Women*, 44, quoting Craig S. Keener, *A Commentary on the Gospel of Matthew* (Grand Rapids: Eerdmans, 1999), 415.

21. Bauckham, *Gospel Women*, 43.

who actually have the promise and who have seen his miracles. But this pagan woman was able to seek him out. She was looking for Jesus.

And what does Jesus do as she bravely falls at his feet begging for mercy? He ignores her. John Calvin said that this silence was a "sort of refusal."[22] He was answering her by not answering her. That seems pretty cruel right there. Maybe that's what we think sometimes when we are praying and see no answer in sight. But that does not stop our Canaanite woman, does it? She reveals her faith, and "it will not be taken away from her" (Luke 10:42).

This pagan woman gets into a sort of humble theological battle of wits with Jesus. Falling at his feet, she uses a particular title for Jesus, saying "Have mercy on me, Lord, Son of David!" (Matt. 15:22). Richard Bauckham points out an added bravery and cleverness of employing a title to address Jesus that actually "should make Jesus her enemy."[23] It is through David's line that the expected Messiah, who was going to deliver Israel and conquer her oppressors, would come. This Gentile woman is identifying Jesus as the Messiah. How remarkable is this for her to know? What a discerning Gentile! She didn't have the Law or the Prophets, and yet we see in this confession that some crumbs have already fallen from the table: Israel's neighbors have heard about the promised redemption.[24] This woman had a daughter taken over by a demon and was going to risk it all to implore the only One who had power over evil to help her.

Addressing Jesus as the Son of David spices things up in another way. Bauckham draws the reader's attention to how this title evokes the genealogy with which Matthew opens his gospel and presses the question of what this title means.[25] What is the Messiah coming to do? How is Jesus then going to respond to this relentless woman who confirms his title? Is she his enemy after all? Jesus's answer "echoes Ezekiel 34 (cf. 34:16, 30), as Davidic messianic prophecy (see 34:23–24)

---

22. John Calvin, *Commentary on the Harmony of the Evangelists, Matthew, Mark, and Luke*, vol. 2, Calvin's Commentaries 16, trans. William Pringle (Grand Rapids: Baker, 2003), 264.

23. Bauckham, *Gospel Women*, 44.

24. See Calvin, *Commentary on the Harmony of the Evangelists*, 263.

25. Bauckham, *Gospel Women*, 44.

that is not anti-Gentile, but has nothing to say about Gentiles at all. Matthew's narrative thus situates itself in intertextual relationships with Deuteronomy–Judges, with Ezekiel 34, and with Matthew's own genealogy of Jesus."[26] Fascinating!

So, who is this Jesus, this Son of David, and what is he going to do? Does his answer reveal what the Jewish nationalists expect of him?

Is the Davidic Messiah's role to be that of a new Joshua who, this time, will lead an obedient Israel in driving out the Canaanites who survived the original conquest, repossessing and cleansing the land? Or is his role confined to that of the shepherd of God's scattered and injured sheep, healing and gathering them, saved at last from oppressive leaders and threatening nations alike as in Ezekiel 34? Or do the Canaanite women in his ancestry require a more positive relationship with the Gentiles? All this is at stake in Jesus' encounter with the Canaanite woman, who could have stepped out of the genealogy in order to press her claims on her descendant.[27]

This Canaanite woman is discerning. And Jesus knows it. His initial silence provokes her to persist. She humbly acknowledges her own unworthiness when replying to him. She even accepts the designation of a dog. Yet she is so theologically sharp. She knows Jesus is the Redeemer and that even she has a claim to his grace.[28] So she doesn't waver.

And she is resolved. Jesus makes what looks like a terribly racist and demeaning remark. But like I said, he is tossing her a softball. Jesus knew this woman had bravery, initiative, discernment, and resolve. She had not been able to be one of the blessed disciples who sat at his feet learning. She was not raised in the Jewish tradition. And yet she took hold of the crumbs Israel dropped at the table, and her faith is strong from that diet. The Spirit of God can work with crumbs. That's the power of God's Word. And this woman is sharp. "What the Canaanite woman does, with the clever twist she gives to Jesus' own saying (Matt. 15:27),

---

26. Bauckham, *Gospel Women*, 44.

27. Bauckham, *Gospel Women*, 44.

28. See Calvin, *Commentary on the Harmony of the Evangelists*, 269.

is persuade Jesus that he can act compassionately to her without detracting from his mission to Israel. Like Rahab, with her exceptional faith she secures an exception that can set a precedent. . . . By placing Jesus briefly in salvific relationship to many Gentiles, Matthew seems to be indicating that the Canaanite woman's precedent is not to be an isolated exception but the beginning of the messianic blessing to the nations."[29]

Matthew ended his gospel with Jesus the Messiah authoritatively proclaiming this "precedent constituted by the Canaanite woman" at "a universal scale"[30] with his great commission: "All authority has been given to me in heaven and on earth. Go, therefore, and make disciples of all the nations, baptizing them in the name of the Father and of the Son and of the Holy Spirit, teaching them to observe everything I have commanded you. And remember, I am with you always, to the end of the age" (Matt. 28:18–20).

These women's bravery, initiative, discernment, and resolve are models of faith for us all. Rahab's faith led to the birth of our Savior, and both women's actions foreshadow Jesus's blessing on all nations. If we are to follow some of the hyper-masculinity and femininity teaching taught in some conservative circles, these women would look more rebellious than full of faith. Should we regard them as exceptions to the way faith normally operates?

And yet Rahab and this unnamed Canaanite woman do not point to themselves, do they? Their faith wasn't in *their* bravery, *their* discernment, *their* initiative, or *their* own resolve. Their faith was in the Lord. They had faith in his calling, his initiative, and his resolve. They responded to the call. Both Rahab and the Canaanite woman have a lot to teach us. In the account of the Canaanite woman, Matthew actually gave us the woman's perspective. She functions almost as an interruption to the narrative. She's interrupting the disciples, she's interrupting Jesus's concealment, and she's interrupting the dominant male voice that we read in Scripture. What do we learn from this gynocentric interruption? We learn the amazing call of the gospel.

---

29. Bauckham, *Gospel Women*, 44–45.
30. Bauckham, *Gospel Women*, 46.

And we learn that the metaphor the Canaanite woman plays off of to persuade Jesus is powerful! While many of Jesus's contemporaries didn't know what to think of him, used him for his blessings, and even sought to kill him, this woman knew the value in the crumbs that fell from his covenant table.

Now this doesn't fully answer our dog theology question, but it is promising that they will get some eternal crumbs, right?

GYNOCENTRIC BOOKENDS

And as the incarnate Son entered the world, we learn the details through a woman's perspective. The gospel of Luke is practically book-ended with the women's perspective on the birth and the resurrection of our Savior. Richard Bauckham elaborates that in the beginning of Luke "two women meet and converse without the presence of any male character (other than their unborn babies). . . . Elizabeth and Mary are the focus of attention and supply the dominant perspectives that readers are invited to share."[31] Luke gave us details about the angel Gabriel's interaction with Mary and of her visit with Elizabeth. We are invited into their wonder and joy over the Lord's blessing for his people. And like Deborah, Mary also sings a glorious song of praise to God.[32] We see that Mary is quite the informed theologian, echoing the themes from another tradent of the faith who prayed to the Lord eleven hundred years earlier, Hannah.[33] Both Hannah's prayer and Mary's Magnificat teach about the Lord rather than about themselves. Once again we are comforted to learn that things are not as they seem as Mary, building on the same themes as Hannah, praises the holiness of God, his great compassion, power to save, complete sovereignty, and continued faithfulness to his people.

Mary must have been a valuable resource for Luke when writing

---

31. Bauckham, *Gospel Women*, 51, 54.
32. Luke 1:46–45.
33. To see more on the likenesses between Hannah's prayer and Mary's Magnificat, see Aimee Byrd, *No Little Women: Equipping All Women in the Household of God* (Phillipsburg, NJ: P&R, 2016), 142–44.

his gospel. And as he utilizes the woman's perspective in his narratives, we realize that it is impossible to share the gospel without these women's voices. Mary is a tradent of the faith in passing down how Jesus was conceived. And we learn later in Luke's gospel that out of all of Jesus's disciples, it was mainly the women who traveled with Jesus from Galilee who remained with him during the crucifixion. The only male disciple who didn't flee in fear was John.

Once again in Scripture, stereotypes are overturned, as the women exercise bravery, initiative, discernment, and resolve, faithfully remaining by their Lord's side in his darkest hour.

> They remained there while the land was completely dark, from the sixth to the ninth hour—three hours in darkness! They remained there while the Son of God was mocked and given sour wine. Oh the horror of what they saw! The giver of life was struggling for his next breath. The one who had healed them and discipled them cried out to his Father in heaven, "My God, my God, why have you forsaken me?" They remained there while he gave up his spirit. And they were there when "the curtain of the temple was torn in two, from top to bottom. And the earth shook, and the rocks were split." They remained there while the centurion and others who were there exclaimed, "Truly this man was the Son of God!"
>
> How do Matthew, Mark, and Luke know these details? Because, by God's providence, these women remained there, despite the horrors that they saw, and then gave witness to these crucial events in the glorious gospel that we share! John did not flee, but Calvin points out how these women are the ones mentioned, "deserv[ing] preference above the men," which "suggests a severe reproof of the apostles. . . . Accordingly, when they afterwards proclaimed the gospel, they must have borrowed from *women* the chief portion of the history."[34]

---

34. Byrd, *No Little Women*, 107–8, quoting John Calvin, *Commentary on the Harmony of the Evangelists, Matthew, Mark, and Luke*, vol. 3, Calvin's Commentaries 17, trans. William Pringle (Grand Rapids: Baker, 2003), 329 (emphasis in the original). Bible quotations are from Matt. 27:46, 51; Mark 15:39.

Not only do we have the women tradents to announce Jesus's conception and the details of his crucifixion, but the first person Jesus appears to in his resurrected body is also a woman, Mary Magdalene.[35] Luke wrote that the same women who traveled with Jesus and witnessed the crucifixion returned to his tomb to care for his body with spices and perfumes and discovered that the tomb was empty.[36] Two angels proclaim the good news that Jesus has risen, and these women become the "apostles to the apostles," the first to announce the gospel. Only, the apostles did not believe them. Didn't Jesus know that the Jews of his time did not credit women as liable witnesses? The first-century Jewish historian Josephus reflected the common opinion of his Jewish contemporaries when he wrote, "But let not the testimony of women be admitted, on account of the levity and boldness of their sex."[37] If the Bible were a patriarchal construction, the first witnesses of the resurrected Christ to announce the gospel would definitely have been men.

And so the female voice bookends the gospel according to Luke. How do you think he was able to tell these stories in such detail? It's an interesting observation here that women were an active part of the work of *Christ's* ministry, not of mere women's ministry. Sure, we see a need for exclusive ministries for men and women that benefit the whole church. But we need not always separate so that we forget we are all serving under Christ's ministry to us all, brothers and sisters in the faith.

PEEL AND REVEAL

Our relationship with Scripture affects our relationship with our brothers and sisters in God's household. It's time for the church to examine whether we too are sending the same message as the radical feminists who are opposed to God's Word by treating it as an androcentric text that lacks female contribution. It's fascinating to see how God

---

35. John 20:11–18.
36. Luke 23:56.
37. Josephus, *Jewish Antiquities* 4.219 (translation is from William Whiston, *Josephus: The Complete Works* [Nashville: Thomas Nelson, 1998], 138).

incorporates the gynocentric perspective in the context of such radically patriarchal background of both the Old and New Testament times.

We should consider how this knowledge relates to our private time in God's Word. Throughout Scripture we see women treasuring God's Word, meditating on it, and acting on it, not within isolated women's ministries, but connected to the body of faith. Women don't want to be constantly assessed by our femaleness; our contributions and even our presence as females offer a multifaceted, asymmetrical balance when centered on truth. We are adding more than just the perspective of another human being, but not less. We see this missing both when we are stereotyped and when we are absent altogether.

And so later in his book, Bauckham refers to women as active traditioners in the handing down of the faith. He rightly concludes his first chapter, affirming the purposeful inclusion of these gynocentric texts. "Rather than viewing these texts as surprising survivors of the attempt to suppress such literature, we may reasonably suppose that the importance of women in the grassroots process of canonical selection led to their inclusion precisely as women's literature, in order to counterbalance the androcentrism of the rest of Scripture."[38]

We see in Scripture how women are necessary allies to men in God's mission. We see the coactivity of men and women serving together as servants to God, even in such a dark period as the book of Judges. The effects of the fall left us with hearts inclined to turn away from God. But in Christ we have new hearts, restored for our communion with the triune God and with one another. As we read Scripture knowing the big picture, we see the yellow wallpaper all over the place from the effects of sin, but we also see how God has been ripping it off, revealing true complementarity of the sexes.

This awareness of how Scripture incorporates the female voice in an androcentric text should help fortify our congregations in a biblical understanding of brotherhood and sisterhood in God's household with the benefits of both inclusive worship and studies, as well as exclusive initiatives for men and women. Like Achsah, I ask you to consider

---

38. Bauckham, *Gospel Women*, 16.

whether the women in your church have access to the refreshing springs to drink deeply in God's Word. I ask women to consider whether you are exercising bravery, initiative, discernment, and resolve to drink in God's Word and to serve within the opportunities he gives you.

A CONTEMPORARY GYNOCENTRIC INTERRUPTION

We looked a lot at Judges in this chapter, and we saw that as the Israelites capitulated to the Canaanite culture, they turned further and further away from God. Reading all the violence in the book, particularly as it escalates with the degradation of women, is truly disgusting. But are things really different today? As we see our own culture turning further away from God, we are awakened to the objectification of women in pornography and film and the horrors of sex trafficking. The #MeToo movement and #ChurchToo movement have revealed the depths of men abusing their power to harass and sexually assault women. This movement is a gynocentric interruption. Women are using their voices and asking men to listen. How is the church going to respond? We certainly don't want to mimic the culture and adapt the philosophy of the sexual revolution. But in our efforts to combat the reductive worldview of our secular culture, we need to make sure we are not overcorrecting by slapping yellow wallpaper over it. We need to look at our own blind spots and embrace the whole picture given to us in God's Word. Barry Webb offers corrective words:

> The church needs to be reminded of these things again and again if it is to impact the world about it in an authentically Christian way instead of capitulating to it. A church that merely plays catch up to its ambient culture will increasingly have nothing to say to that culture, and in the end, no reason to exist. If we find Judges shocking, that may be no bad thing. It is not the task of the Christian scholar to tame the Bible, but to play his or her part in helping the church to listen to it.[39]

---

39. Webb, *Book of Judges*, 67.

We have the privilege of listening from the perspective of the full revelation of the gospel. What do we have to say to our culture now about the holiness and grace of our Lord God? What do we have to say about the value of men and women made in his image? What do we have to say about his household?

We live in a time where we can cruise over to Walmart and buy a Bible for $5.99. Now that we are armed with a better idea of how the male and female voices operate synergetically in Scripture, let's explore Christ's presence in the Word of God and therefore its relationship to the church.

QUESTIONS FOR GROUP DISCUSSION

1. James Boice asks a good question about the midwives in Exodus: "In those days, who would have paid any attention to these midwives?" And yet their names are recorded in Scripture instead of the pharaoh's. Moses's recording of the names of the midwives is really quite remarkable. Why do you think the Holy Spirit led him to do this? What contribution does their testimony give to the text?

2. Why would the "daughters of Israel" want to keep the memory of abuse to Jephthah's daughter alive, so much so that they had yearly rituals to pass down their stories from generation to generation? Do you think this shows that God cared or did not care about these women? What would a person who is oppressed today learn from these women who kept their stories alive and from the scriptural record?

3. Read Hannah's prayer in 1 Samuel 2:1–10 and Mary's Magnificat in Luke 1:46–55. What similarities can you find between the two? Why do you think they are so similar? What do they teach us about God? What do they teach us about themselves? How is this different from popular stereotypes about women?

4. During a time when a woman's testimony was not trusted, God gives a woman the honor of being the first witness to Christ's resurrection as well as to be the first to tell the news to the

apostles. How did the apostles respond? After the ascension of Christ, did the apostles include the women in anything else significant? What does this say about their attitudes regarding the women's contributions under the ministry?

5. How does the female perspective enhance the accounts of the birth, death, and resurrection of Jesus?

PART 2

RECOVERING OUR MISSION

CHAPTER 4

WHY OUR AIM IS NOT BIBLICAL MANHOOD AND WOMANHOOD

I married fresh out of college—literally, one month after I graduated. The year was 1997, and I was a mere twenty-one years old. Despite my young age, I was eager to be the perfect Christian wife. So I began reading books from trusted evangelical authorities on this matter. Over the years, this led me to go straight to the most exhaustive resource sponsored by the Council on Biblical Manhood and Womanhood (CBMW), *Recovering Biblical Manhood and Womanhood*. As I stated earlier, I remember my young, impressionable mind learning and underlining, and later even quoting from this book. Like the book's many contributors, I too wanted to have a biblical understanding of the sexes. I embraced this word *complementary* and wholeheartedly agreed that we lived in a time when we needed to respond to the new waves of feminism in our culture and affirm the beauty and distinctiveness of male and female.

Some parts of the book were difficult for me to swallow. And yet its teaching was sown throughout the trusted radio programs, books, and corners of the Internet where the "good" conservative Christians gleaned. And that's what I wanted to be: good and conservative. As I gave the benefit to the authors, who were much more educated and experienced than I was, I still didn't feel comfortable with some of the teachings in that book. I thought that maybe I would understand better as I matured in biblical study and marital experience.

But the more experienced in Scripture and life I became, the more troubling teachings I noticed flowing from this book. Even as I tried to participate in the world of complementarianism as a writer, I began to notice that the movement is constructed with a lot of yellow wallpaper that is "dull enough to confuse the eye in following, pronounced enough to irritate and provoke study, and when you follow the lame uncertain curves for a little distance they suddenly commit suicide— plunge off at outrageous angles, destroy themselves in unheard of contradictions."[1] More and more strange teachings on femininity and masculinity have emerged under the rubric of biblical manhood and womanhood, from the bizarre promotion of "sanctified testosterone" and "soap bubble submission," to employing an unorthodox teaching of the Trinity, the eternal subordination of the Son (ESS), in order to promote subordination of women to men.[2] Knowing there are many young, impressionable men and women like me who desire to express their sexuality in a godly way, I wanted to publicly engage with some of the damaging teaching on biblical manhood and womanhood. I do want to note that there are plenty of helpful teachings in *Recovering Biblical Manhood and Womanhood*, written by authors who have benefited the church in numerous ways. This is what makes the troubling teaching all the more disconcerting. I'm not saying that everything the authors have contributed is bad. It's because they have offered so many good contributions to the church that we need to be all the more discerning of their influence on us.

In confronting the peculiar teachings coming from CBMW conferences, books authored by their leaders, and articles from their website, I found a CBMW document from 2001 on their position on the Trinity, connecting ESS directly to the complementarian position.[3]

---

1. Charlotte Perkins Gilman, *The Yellow Wallpaper* (1892; repr., n.p.: Middletown, DE, 2017), 5.

2. For a summary with extra links, see Aimee Byrd, "What Denny Burk Could Do," *Housewife Theologian* (blog), Mortification of Spin, August 11, 2016, www.alliancenet.org/mos/housewife-theologian/what-denny-burk-could-do-0#.W88fcxNKgyk.

3. Bruce Ware, "Tampering with the Trinity," Council on Biblical Manhood and Womanhood, May 1, 2001, cbmw.org/uncategorized/tampering-with-the-trinity/; Wayback Machine, https://web.archive.org/web/20160131073409/cbmw.org/uncategorized/

This doctrine teaches that the Son, the second person of the Trinity, is subordinate to the Father, not only in the economy of salvation but in his essence. The eternal relationship between the Father and the Son is then described as one of authority and submission. After trying to personally interact with the then president of CBMW, Owen Strachan, he assured me that their teaching was biblical and sent me a PDF of his newly released book in response—where he and coauthor Gavin Peacock "ground their understanding of the complementarity of men and women on a relationship of authority and submission in the nature of the Trinity."[4] Rachel Miller was already working to correct these Trinitarian errors, raising awareness on her blog.[5] But few seemed to respond. I expected the same result. So I invited Liam Goligher, a man, and a complementarian pastor-theologian who was concerned about how this errant, influential teaching affects his congregation, to write a series of guest posts on my blog. He indeed ignited the needed flame, which is now known as the Trinity Debate.[6] After a stream of online articles and interactions, patristic scholars weighed in, and books and conferences followed to uphold Nicene Trinitarianism over and against ESS.[7]

The Councils of Nicea, in 325, and Constantinople, in 381, developed and amended the Nicene Creed, which has faithfully served the

---

tampering-with-the-trinity/. Another version found in their journal: Bruce Ware, "Tampering with the Trinity: Does the Son Submit to His Father?," *Journal for Biblical Manhood and Womanhood* 6.1 (2001): 4, https://cbmw.org/wp-content/uploads/2013/05/6-1.pdf.

4. Rachel Green Miller, "The Grand Design: A Review," *A Daughter of the Reformation* (blog), June 23, 2016, https://adaughterofthereformation.wordpress.com/2016/06/23/the-grand-design-a-review/.

5. Rachel Green Miller, "Continuing down This Path, Complementarians Lose," *A Daughter of the Reformation* (blog), May 22, 2015, https://adaughterofthereformation.wordpress.com/2015/05/22/continuing-down-this-path-complementarians-lose/; and Miller, "Does the Son Eternally Submit to the Authority of the Father?," *A Daughter of the Reformation* (blog), May 28, 2015, https://adaughterofthereformation.wordpress.com/2015/05/28/does-the-son-eternally-submit-to-the-authority-of-the-father/.

6. See "Highlights on the Trinity Debate," Alliance of Confessing Evangelicals, accessed October 23, 2018, www.alliancenet.org/trinity-debate.

7. D. Glenn Butner Jr. states that he is "aware of at least fifty scholars who have posted formal online responses." That, of course, doesn't include the conferences and books that have resulted from it, his being one. D. Glenn Butner Jr., *The Son Who Learned Obedience: A Theological Case against the Eternal Submission of the Son* (Eugene, OR: Wipf & Stock, 2018), 1. See also for further discussion of how ESS contradicts what has been historically confessed regarding divine inseparable operations and the singular divine will.

church in preserving an orthodox confession of the faith. We see from these creeds that eternal subordination of the Son contradicts the orthodox understanding of the Trinity.[8] In upholding the wonder of the one divine being, we need to be careful how we talk of the distinction of the persons of the Father, Son, and Holy Spirit. One way we do this is by speaking of order of procession: the Son's eternal generation from the Father and the Spirit's spiration from the Father and the Son. We also distinguish the filial relationship in the Father's love for the Son through the Spirit, and vice versa.[9]

We learn in Scripture that the Son learned obedience (Heb. 5:8). This is because in the incarnation Jesus has two wills—one divine and one human. Finally, in the Son, we have "the first human who does not resist the Holy Spirit"[10] and is submissive to the will of God. When we speak of the Son's submission to the Father in the plan of redemption, we need to understand this distinction in Jesus's obedience to the Father as our mediator.[11]

BACK TO THE BOOK THAT STARTED IT ALL

Many years after first reading it, I decided to skim over this CBMW resource again. Rereading *Recovering Biblical Manhood and Womanhood* as a more mature woman has been shocking to me. While there are good contributions in this book, which builds on the CBMW's foundational Danvers Statement, some parts are actually quite unbelievable. While evangelicals agree that men and women are created with equal value and distinction, organizations such as CBMW have reduced that distinction to an unbiblical principle—one

---

8. See Butner Jr. for a good resource on this, as well as how ESS also interferes with orthodox Christology and soteriology.

9. The doctrine of appropriation is helpful in speaking of how Scripture may appropriate a divine property or action to one of the persons of the Trinity that is still shared by all.

10. Michael Horton, *Rediscovering the Holy Spirit: God's Perfecting Presence in Creation, Redemption, and Everyday Life* (Grand Rapids: Zondervan, 2017), 101.

11. For further reading I suggest Fred Sanders, *The Triune God*, New Studies in Dogmatics, ed. Michael Allen and Scott Swain (Grand Rapids: Zondervan, 2016); Lewis Ayers, *Nicaea and Its Legacy: An Approach to Fourth-Century Trinitarian Theology* (New York: Oxford University Press, 2006).

of ontological authority and submission. This is what led them to err on the nature of the Trinity. One of the patterns in the book is that of male authority and female submission. Several contributors promote the unorthodox doctrine of ESS/EFS/ERAS[12] as they teach ontological subordination of women to men, but coeditor Wayne Grudem lays it out most clearly:

> The orthodox doctrine has always been that there is *equality in essence and subordination in role* and that these two are consistent with each other . . . primary authority and leadership among the persons of the Trinity has always been and will always be the possession of God the Father.
>
> Paul in 1 Corinthians 11:3 simply sets up three distinct relationships: the headship of God the Father in the Trinity, the headship of Christ over every man, and the headship of a man over a woman. . . .
>
> Authority and submission to authority . . . are truly divine concepts, rooted in the eternal nature of the Trinity for all eternity and represented in the eternal submission of the Son to the Father and of the Holy Spirit to the Father and the Son.[13]

Notice how authority and submission is a matter of eternal nature for Grudem, how it is the basis for defining relationships, and how his Trinitarian model is applied to men and women. Perhaps this is not a view shared by all of the contributors, but it is the teaching of one of the editors of the book. And there are no statements made by the editors or endorsers or in the preface of the book nuancing the differing views of manhood and womanhood the contributors may hold or engaging

---

12. Eternal subordination of the Son has also been referred to as eternal functional subordination or eternal relationship of authority and submission.

13. Wayne Grudem in app. 1: "The Meaning of *Kephale* ("Head"): A Response to Recent Studies," in *Recovering Biblical Manhood and Womanhood: A Response to Evangelical Feminism*, ed. John Piper and Wayne Grudem (1991; repr., Wheaton, IL: Crossway, 2006), 457, 462, 463. These quotes, among others in the book, were pointed out to me by Rachel Green Miller, "Eternal Subordination of the Son and CBMW," *A Daughter of the Reformation* (blog), August 12, 2016, https://adaughterofthereformation.wordpress.com/2016/08/12/eternal-subordination-of-the-son-and-cbmw/.

with this particular error of ESS taught within it. In fact, the updated preface is quite bold in claiming the importance of the book's teaching on manhood and womanhood, warning us of the consequences if we fail to follow it.

The 2006 rerelease provides a new preface in which "a practical embrace of biblical womanhood [and manhood] in the local church" is presented as a key aim for "preaching, teaching, and discipleship."[14] We are told that unless we embrace the CBMW teaching of distinctions between the sexes, "Christian discipleship [will become] irretrievably damaged because there can be no talk of cultivating distinctly masculine or feminine virtue. One can only speak of a vague androgynous discipleship. . . . We need masculine males and feminine females in order to generate the kind of discipleship that results in commitment to complementarianism."[15] While I wholeheartedly affirm distinction between the sexes, I am convinced that our choices are not between CBMW complementarianism and vague androgynous discipleship. Statements like these raise many questions. What makes a "masculine male" and a "feminine female"? What are feminine and masculine virtues? Is biblical manhood and womanhood our aim in discipleship? Are there distinct approaches to discipleship that we should be implementing for men and women?

WHAT MAKES A "MASCULINE MALE" AND A "FEMININE FEMALE"?

Some of these questions are answered above in chapter 1, which gives an overview of the meaning of masculinity and femininity. Two definitions are introduced and broken down:

At the heart of mature masculinity is a sense of benevolent responsibility to lead, provide for and protect women in ways appropriate to a man's differing relationships.

---

14. Ligon Duncan, "Preface," in *Recovering Biblical Manhood and Womanhood*, ed. Piper and Grudem, x.

15. Duncan, "Preface," xii.

At the heart of mature femininity is a freeing disposition to affirm, receive and nurture strength and leadership from worthy men in ways appropriate to a woman's differing relationships.[16]

I find these definitions troublesome. They are one-dimensional. The "heart" of masculinity and femininity provided here is all about male leadership. Nowhere does Scripture state that all women submit to all men. My aim in life is not to be constantly looking for male leadership. And it's very difficult for a laywoman like me, who does see some theological teaching for God outfitting qualified men for an office[17] to see this kind of reductive teaching and call it complementarianism. Perpetuating this constant framework of authority and submission between men and women can be very harmful. My femininity is not defined by how I look for and nurture male leadership in my neighbors, coworkers, or mail carriers.[18] I am not denying the order needed in both my personal household and in the household of God, but I do not reduce the rights and obligations in a household to mere authority and submission roles.[19] Paul teaches mutual submission among Christians even as he addresses husbands and wives specifically.[20] I uphold distinction between the sexes without reduction, as Scripture does.

Notice in these CBMW definitions that masculinity is active and potent, and femininity is merely an affirmation of this fact. In contrast to CBMW's definition of femininity, masculinity exudes strength, provision, and protection. We see God's provision and protection for Israel in verses like Psalms 20:1–2; 33:20; and 121:2, describing him as *ezer* in Hebrew. These Old Testament verses describing God as Israel's

---

16. Duncan, "Preface," 35–36 (capitalization in the original).

17. Based on Adam's vocation to "keep/guard" the garden/sanctuary in Gen. 2:15, which is a priestly function.

18. See Piper's further application of masculinity and femininity to the workforce in John Piper, "Should Women Be Police Officers?," *Ask Pastor John*, Desiring God, August 13, 2015, www.desiringgod.org/interviews/should-women-be-police-officers.

19. See Aimee Byrd, *No Little Women: Equipping All Women in the Household of God* (Phillipsburg, NJ: P&R, 2016), 139–40.

20. Eph. 5:21–33.

ezer communicate great strength, for they are saturated in military language.[21] How manly, right?

But wait, this word *ezer*, which first appears in Genesis 2:18, is how the woman is described. Is God using a masculine word to describe woman? Or maybe strength, provision, and protection are not merely masculine qualities. The very first word in Scripture used to distinctly describe the woman teaches us that she is a corresponding strength to the man.

But rather than woman having a unique contribution, the biblical manhood and womanhood definitions above describe the woman's contribution as parasitic. The heart of femininity merely means being masculinity affirmers. This reminds me of the arguments for women's contributions in the nineteenth century, with Sarah Grimké lamenting, "Woman has more or less been made a means to promote the welfare of man" with no regard to how her own *telos* glorifies God.[22] That doesn't sound very distinctive. So more detail is added as the definitions are broken down.

WHAT ARE FEMININE AND MASCULINE VIRTUES?

The further descriptions of manhood in this first chapter of *Recovering Biblical Manhood and Womanhood* are strength, initiative, and decision making. Masculine men are the ones who make the final say if there is a disagreement.[23] They also have a manly way of handling a woman's purse, they seat the woman and order for her at restaurants, and they are the designated driver when their wife is with them.[24] Even as romantic sexuality is discussed, women are warned not to wrongly "attempt to assume a more masculine role by appearing physically muscular and aggressive."[25] If women try to arouse men in a masculine way by building our muscular physique or being too aggressive, we should

21. See Ex. 18:4; Deut. 33:7, 26, 29; Pss. 20:2; 33:20; 70:5; 89:17; 115:9–11; 121:1–2; 124:8; 146:5; Hos. 13:9. Byrd, *No Little Women*, 25.

22. Sarah Grimké, *Letters on the Equality of the Sexes and Other Essays*, ed. Elizabeth Ann Bartlett (New Haven, CT: Yale University Press, 1988), 36.

23. Piper and Grudem, *Recovering Biblical Manhood and Womanhood*, 40.

24. Piper and Grudem, *Recovering Biblical Manhood and Womanhood*, 41.

25. Piper and Grudem, *Recovering Biblical Manhood and Womanhood*, 40.

not expect men to meet our feminine needs.[26] We are the softer, responsive sex that needs guidance, and "to the degree that a woman's influence over a man is personal and directive it will generally offend a man's good, God-given sense of responsibility and leadership, and thus controvert God's created order."[27] This needs to be at the forefront of our minds while we are interacting with men.

In the introduction, I questioned whether God's created order is that delicate—that women need to so manipulate their words to be careful not to damage the male psyche if they have something they could teach men. Has God designed men to be so fragile that a woman ordering for herself threatens their manhood? If a husband holds his wife's purse the wrong way, will his man card be taken away? Is this the biblical picture of manly men and feminine females? Or has God equipped men for something more meaningful than making the final call in a disagreement? Paul's teaching to the Ephesians would counter this flattening "husband gets the final say" argument, as husbands are called to sacrificially give for their wives, to put themselves underneath and elevate their wives, promoting their holiness, as Christ does for his church. As Sarah Coakley explains, the point of headship in a household, whether we are talking about a personal household or the household of God, is not executive dictatorship, but responsibility for the "well-being of the whole." "A whole transcending its parts"[28] understanding presents more of a "bottom-up" than a "top-down" model. And whether we are talking about husbands and wives or men and women in general, disallowing personal or direct influence of a woman over a man silences the crucial, unique contributions that women are to give as *ezers*. In Scripture we see women functioning as necessary allies[29] in ways such as warning men to turn away from

---

26. Piper and Grudem, *Recovering Biblical Manhood and Womanhood*, 41. Also, it is probably important to note that there are many reasons women may want to work on strengthening their muscles other than arousing men.

27. Piper and Grudem, *Recovering Biblical Manhood and Womanhood*, 51.

28. Sarah Coakley, *God, Sexuality, and the Self* (Cambridge: Cambridge University Press, 2013), 320.

29. The term "necessary ally" as well as these functions of a necessary ally and Scripture references are taken from John McKinley, "Necessary Allies: God as *Ezer*, Woman as *Ezer*,"

evil;[30] acting as cobelligerents with men against evil enemies;[31] mediating the Word of the Lord;[32] giving wise instruction and counsel;[33] collaborating in service to others;[34] responding to God as examples of faithfulness;[35] and influencing men from a gift of empathy and relatedness.[36]

And as far as muscles go, not all women have soft, curvy bodies. We are all built differently. We do not want to question our biblical femininity in comparison to our muscle mass.[37] The softness of our bodies shouldn't determine whether our husbands will meet our "feminine needs." Thankfully, in contrast to these teachings, we have ourselves a swarthy woman in the one book in Scripture that shows us playful, intimate interaction between a bride and her groom. Her work in the vineyard affected her appearance to the point that she says, "Do not stare at me" (Song 1:6).[38] She explains that she had to neglect her own "vineyard" because of all her laborious duties. This doesn't

lecture, Hilton Atlanta, November 17, 2015, mp3 download, 38:35, www.wordmp3.com/details.aspx?id=20759.

30. See Abigail in 1 Sam. 25:1–42; unnamed woman in 2 Sam. 20; Deborah in Judg. 4:1–5:31; and Huldah in 2 Chron. 34:22–28.

31. See Abigail in 1 Sam. 25:1–42; Esther; Rahab in Josh. 2.

32. See Miriam in Ex. 15:21; Deborah in Judg. 4:1–5:31; Hannah in 1 Sam. 2:1–10; Huldah in 2 Chron. 34:22–28; Mary in Luke 1:46–55; Anna in Luke 2:36–38; Phillip's four daughters in Acts 21:9; the women announcing the resurrection of Jesus in Luke 24:9; women prophesying in Corinth in 1 Cor. 11:5; and Prisca informing Apollos about the gospel in Acts 18:18–28.

33. See wisdom as a feminine metaphor in Prov. 7:4; Titus 2:3–5; Prisca in Acts 18:18–28.

34. See Prov. 31; women serving at the door of the tent of meeting in Ex. 38:8; Phoebe in Romans 16:1–2; Euodia and Syntyche in Phil. 4:2–3; Prisca, Mary, Persis, Tryphaena, Tryphosa, Junia, and Rufus's mother in Rom. 16:3–4, 6–7, 12–13; and the wealthy women who funded Jesus's ministry, hosted churches in their homes, and also provided hospitality for traveling evangelists.

35. See Naomi and Ruth in Ruth 3, Elizabeth in Luke 1:25, 42; Lydia in Acts 16:11–40; the women instructed in 1 Peter 3:1–2; and others already mentioned: Rahab, Deborah, Esther, Mary, the women at the crucifixion and resurrection; the women at Pentecost (Acts 1:14).

36. See Mary and Martha in Luke 10:38–42; John 11:23–27, 28–37; Matt. 26:6–13, Mark 14:3–9, John 12:1–8.

37. This isn't an argument against the obvious fact that men generally have a larger muscle mass than women biologically. But women who train with weights, are athletically built and inclined, and are muscular are not necessarily trying to look masculine.

38. For a great sermon connecting the woman saying she is dark yet lovely (Song 1:5) to the believer's knowledge of sin as well as union in Christ, see Liam Goligher, "The Bruised Reed," Tenth Presbyterian Church, February 4, 2018, www.tenth.org/resource-library/sermons/the-bruised-reed.

sound very feminine according to our contemporary authors. And yet her groom calls her "most beautiful of women" (1:8). The poetry that follows assures me that her feminine needs were met. Even as a metaphor for Christ's great love for his church, we see the mutuality honored between the husband and wife figures playing out in the story. Christ elevates his bride!

IS BIBLICAL MANHOOD AND WOMANHOOD OUR AIM IN DISCIPLESHIP?

Will Christian discipleship become irretrievably damaged if biblical manhood and womanhood are not the key aim for preaching, teaching, and discipleship? What is the key aim for men and women? Grimké's words return to me again: "It is impossible that we can answer the purpose of our being, unless we understand that purpose. It is impossible that we should fulfill our duties, unless we comprehend them; or live up to our privileges, unless we know what they are."[39] Do men and women have separate aims with a common adjective—biblical manhood and biblical womanhood?

In Scripture we don't find that our ultimate goal is as narrow as biblical manhood or biblical womanhood, but complete, glorified resurrection to live eternally with our Lord and Savior Jesus Christ. We don't find a command anywhere in Scripture for all women to submit to all men. We don't find directions for women to function as masculinity affirmers. We find that men and women are called together in the same mission: eternal communion with the triune God. Both men and women are to pursue the same virtues as we await our ultimate blessedness, the beatific vision—to behold Christ!

Christ lays these virtues out for us in the Sermon on the Mount, which is surprisingly not a gendered pursuit:

> "Blessed are the poor in spirit,
> for the kingdom of heaven is theirs.

---

39. Grimké, *Letters on the Equality of the Sexes*, 31.

> Blessed are those who mourn,
> for they will be comforted.
> Blessed are the humble,
> for they will inherit the earth.
> Blessed are those who hunger and thirst for righteousness,
> for they will be filled.
> Blessed are the merciful,
> for they will be shown mercy.
> Blessed are the pure in heart,
> for they will see God.
> Blessed are the peacemakers,
> for they will be called sons of God.
> Blessed are those who are persecuted because of righteousness,
> for the kingdom of heaven is theirs.

> "You are blessed when they insult you and persecute you and falsely say every kind of evil against you because of me. Be glad and rejoice, because your reward is great in heaven." (Matt. 5:3–12)

Many of these virtues sound quite feminine according to our cultural stereotypes. These are the priorities our Lord gave us for true blessedness. And what we have here is a description of Christ himself. Our Christian hope is presence and communion with the triune God, made manifest to us through Jesus Christ, who in his human nature revealed what it means to be poor in spirit, mournful, humble, hungering and thirsting for righteousness, merciful, pure in heart, a peacemaker, and persecuted for righteousness. He articulated that aim for which our hearts cry out: to attain the kingdom of heaven, true comfort, inheritance of the earth that we feel so estranged in, fulfillment, mercy, "the invisible God mak[ing] himself visible to us,"[40] and to be called sons of God. We can rejoice in Christ because our reward is great.

---

40. Michael Allen, *Grounded in Heaven: Recentering Christian Hope and Life on God* (Grand Rapids: Eerdmans, 2018), 87.

Men and women are called to be Christ's bride. This is something women understand more than men, but nonetheless, it is a joint *telos*. Men and women are called to be sons of God, sons in the Son.[41] This is something men understand more than women, but nonetheless, it is a joint *telos*. However, this is not an androgynous calling. All those who hold to the authority and inerrancy of Scripture will agree that in creation we find equality of value between the sexes, as well as distinction. We wouldn't even be talking about equality if there were no distinction. But the differences come when we begin to talk about what that distinction is and what that might mean for our relationships.

While evangelical egalitarians agree on distinction between the sexes, they often downplay these distinctions and empty them of their meaning. I think this is why so many women in egalitarian churches feel just as undervalued, because even though there is an ostensible consensus that man and woman are equal, the work hasn't been done to acknowledge the enrichment that distinct feminine and masculine contributions bring to the church. On the other hand, complementarians often set up femininity and masculinity as something to strive for in itself. There are no exhortations in Scripture for men to be masculine and women to be feminine. As the Roman Catholic theologian Dietrich Von Hildebrand points out, the calling for both man and woman, our *telos*, is "to be transformed in Christ, to become holy and glorify God, and to reach eternal communion with God. . . . The specific tone of masculinity and femininity must appear by itself" as we strive together toward this same mission.[42]

Rather than encourage us in this way by pointing to the beatific vision as our aim, or even the Ten Commandments or the Beatitudes to guide us, popular complementarian leaders point to the NASB translation of 1 Corinthians 16:13 to teach "biblical manhood": "Be on the alert, stand firm in the faith, act like men, be strong." The current president of CBMW put it this way: "The biblical norms of

---

41. See David B. Garner, *Sons in the Son: The Riches and Reach of Adoption in Christ* (Phillipsburg, NJ: P&R, 2016).

42. Dietrich von Hildebrand, *Man and Woman: Love and the Meaning of Intimacy* (Manchester, NH: Sophia Institute Press, 1992), 60–61.

manhood and womanhood apply wherever human beings appear in the world. That is why the apostle Paul applies those norms to hair-length (1 Corinthians 11:14). The law of Moses forbids cross-dressing (Deut. 22:5). When Paul wants people to behave courageously, he tells them to "act like men" (1 Corinthians 16:13)."[43]

The former president of CBMW also liked to use this verse to teach biblical manhood, as he does in his book he sent me. He calls this verse "the Corinthian challenge"[44] for men:

> Here is the central command: "act like men," not like boys and not like women. Even as he calls all believers to maturity, Paul recognizes that there is a specific way that a man should act with manly bravery.[45]

Other Bible translations exhort the Corinthians to be "courageous," "valiant," or "brave," rather than to "act like men," as this more accurately represents the military metaphors the language is conveying in the text. He is writing his final exhortations of the letter, telling Corinthian brothers and sisters to act like mature Christian adults. This is certainly an obscure verse to build a teaching on masculinity, but I'm sure readers can name numerous women in your own lives off the top of your head, as well as from Scripture, who are alert, courageous and strong, and stand firm in the faith. This admonition is addressed to both men and women, as in the following verse 15, Paul addresses them as brothers and sisters. "Act like men" does not appear to be a helpful translation. Nonetheless, as Dr. Valerie Hobbs pointed out, "A Christian's character is not derived from their sex, but from the object of their faith."[46] This is why Paul continually points both men and women to Christ as our only hope, and the One whom we are to "act like."

---

43. Denny Burk. "Thin Complementarianism?," *Denny Burk* (blog), September 17, 2015, www.dennyburk.com/thin-complementarianism-firstthingsmag/.

44. Owen Strachan and Gavin Peacock, *The Grand Design* (Ross-shire, UK: Christian Focus, 2016), 47.

45. Strachan and Peacock, *Grand Design*, 54 (emphasis in original).

46. Valerie Hobbs, "Act Like Women," The Aquila Report, January 9, 2018, www.the aquilareport.com/act-like-women/.

Men and women bear the image of God. This means that both genders are representatives of the presence of God! In the ancient Near East, idols were not valued simply as carved, inanimate objects. They were worshiped because they were "a manifestation of a divine presence in the world."[47] The idol was considered a living thing once it went through proper cultic ritual whereby divine presence is considered infused into the idol that was crafted by human hands.[48] Marc Cortez explains that this background is important to understand as we grasp being made in the image of God, saying, "We need to view the *imago Dei* as a declaration that God intended to create human persons to be the physical means through which he would manifest his own divine presence in the world."[49] He further explains that in the New Testament we see this image is focused on a "christological reality in which we have been invited in to participate. Indeed, this is precisely what we have been destined for since before the creation of the world (Rom. 8:29)."[50]

"The New Testament authors consistently identify Jesus as the one through whom God manifests his divine presence in the world. Jesus is 'God with us' (Matt. 1:23), the eternal word dwelling with us (John 1:14), and the one in whom 'God was pleased to have all his fullness dwell' (Col. 1:19)."[51] The Spirit's work is fundamental to this as "Paul demonstrates the connection of Jesus, the Spirit, and the *imago Dei* in a single intriguing statement: 'And we all, with unveiled faces reflecting the glory of the Lord, are being transformed into the same image from one degree of glory to another, which is from the Lord, who is the Spirit' (2 Cor. 3:18 NET). . . . The christological reorientation of the *imago Dei* asserts the central importance of the Spirit for understanding what it means to be human," which "involves manifesting God's own presence through the indwelling power of the

---

47. Marc Cortez, *ReSourcing Theological Anthropology: A Constructive Account of Humanity in Light of Christ* (Grand Rapids: Zondervan, 2017), 109.

48. See Cortez, *ReSourcing Theological Anthropology*.

49. Cortez, *ReSourcing Theological Anthropology*, 109.

50. Cortez, *ReSourcing Theological Anthropology*, 114.

51. Cortez, *ReSourcing Theological Anthropology*, 114.

Spirit."[52] Christian men and women don't strive for so-called biblical masculinity or femininity, but Christlikeness. Rather than striving to prove our sexuality, the tone of our sexuality will express itself as we do this.

I do see in Scripture that God made man and woman as true complements in this mission. My contributions, my living and moving, are distinctly feminine because I am a female. I do not need to do something a certain way to be feminine (such as receive my mail in a way that affirms the masculinity of the mailman). I simply am feminine because I am female.

DISTINCT MALE AND FEMALE DISCIPLESHIPS?

When I was in my early twenties, some young women asked me to lead a Bible study. I was not equipped to do this, and I knew it. I wanted to be learning from women who were wise in the Scriptures and more mature than me. But my young church plant did not have anything available like that. I do see a benefit in exclusive studies for men and women, as we have shared experiences and responsibilities within our own sex, and exclusive studies do provide an environment where we feel we can share on a more vulnerable level. After putting these women off for a while, they prevailed on me to be the one to step up and lead the group. But first I asked my pastor for his help. I wanted it to be a church group that was under the shepherding care of our leadership. And I needed that for my own growth and accountability as a teacher.

Thrilled to have a women's study to offer to the church, my pastor lent me a book on systematic theology. I didn't know what systematic theology even was. Receiving this large book full of doctrines on God, man, the Bible, and the work of Christ was life changing for me. I ended up ordering my own copy so that I could have it forever and mark it up as I wished. I began our first study on the doctrine of Scripture. This book was well written to be digested even by a layperson like me and was a helpful introduction into the world of systematic theology.

---

52. Cortez, *ReSourcing Theological Anthropology*, 115.

However, the women in my group, who were growing in number and diversity of ages, were no small talkers. We all were eager to learn and make applications to our lives. They asked excellent questions. And I was full of questions of my own. I wanted to get some feedback from my pastor.

Although I was happy with my new book, there were parts that seemed to me to contradict themselves, and other parts that I was reserved to embrace. I was respectful of my pastor's time. I did not constantly approach him but usually saved my questions and waited for him to check in on me—which he did. At first my pastor was giving some satisfying answers to my questions. But I clearly remember the response he gave me once that sent me a message about women and discipleship. He began chuckling a bit, as if I were a small child asking about quantum physics, and said something to the effect of, "Aimee, I think you are taking this women's Bible study a little too seriously." I felt like Ralphie asking Santa for a Red Ryder BB gun in the movie *A Christmas Story* and getting the answer, "You'll shoot your eye out, kid!" He basically said, *Why are you women worrying your pretty little heads with such difficult theological questions?*

I have since worked through what I found to be so troubling about that book's teaching on my own. And my husband and I eventually found a different church. But I continue to see this same attitude and approach when it comes to discipling women, in contrast to discipling men. Titus 2 is often a popular text taught to promote women's ministries. Rather than upholding the strong connection Paul is making between teaching healthy doctrine and its fruitfulness in our personal lives, the doctrine part gets ignored and women are merely delegated to a domestic sphere that is disconnected from serious theological study. The women's ministry is often a separate faction of the church that is drowning in theologically anemic books marketed specifically to them.[53] To the credit of my pastor back then, at least he gave me a systematic theology and not the latest bestselling book for Christian women!

---

53. For a closer look at this phenomenon see Byrd, *No Little Women*.

Sure, men and women have some distinct relational responsibilities that color our discipleship. Men will never be daughters, sisters, aunts, wives, or mothers. Women will never be sons, brothers, uncles, husbands, or fathers.[54] Because of this, it is beneficial to have opportunities for exclusive fellowship and study for women and for men, as well as a need to worship, study, fellowship, and serve together so that the whole household of God benefits from the reciprocity of male and female contributions. In the following two chapters, I go into more detail about discipleship in the church. At the end of chapter 5, we will see a picture of this reciprocity in Paul's greetings in Romans 16, which contrasts to *Recovering Biblical Manhood and Womanhood*'s one-dimensional teachings that promote a factioned and fractioned discipleship centering on male authority and female submission.

It is this ontological argument, teaching the sole distinction between the sexes from the creation account, consisting in male/authority and female/submission, that leads to an androcentric focus on theological teaching in discipleship. And that's just not in the creation text. Unlike the surrounding pagan cultures and myths, Genesis teaches that God granted man *and* woman authority over the earth and its creatures.[55] Creation of woman, and the first description of her, points to man's need for a strength equal to him in a corresponding way—his need for a colaborer to reign with him. The focus of the text is unity and reciprocity. There are no implications of male/female distinction being authority and submission, which is what much of complementarian teaching insists is *the* creation distinction between man and woman. And we even see that in the fall Eve was equally culpable for her sin, as God directly addressed her.[56]

Interestingly, Adam was called to a special submission in three areas. Before the fall, Adam and Eve served in a holy temple-garden. Adam bore a priestly responsibility of the vocation to guard or protect,

54. On a different level, there is the spiritual reality of men and women as the bride of Christ and sons in the Son.

55. See Phillip B. Payne, *Man and Woman, One in Christ: An Exegetical and Theological Study of Paul's Letters* (Grand Rapids: Zondervan, 2009), 43.

56. See Payne, *Man and Woman*, 49.

which is the meaning of the word *keep* in this text: "Then the LORD God took the man and put him into the garden of Eden to cultivate it and keep it" (Gen. 2:15 NASB). Adam was called to submit, or sacrifice himself, in this way.[57] Second, Adam had to sacrifice a piece of his own body for the creation of Eve (Gen. 2:21–22). And third, even in describing the union of marriage, we see that unlike the surrounding ancient patriarchal culture of the time when Moses wrote Genesis, in which the woman left her family and was then under the authority of her husband's family, the man was to leave his family and cleave to his wife (Gen. 2:24). So if we want to call this leadership, yes, it is the best kind. But it is also submission—sacrifice of the man's own rights and body for the protection of the temple and home and out of love for his wife. These are proleptic representations of Christ, the true keeper of our souls (see Ps. 121), who left his heavenly home, took on flesh, lived the life that we could not, and died the death that we could not so that he can hold fast to his own bride, the church.

But not only does CBMW teach male authority and female submission as the key ontological distinction in creation; they also see this as an eternal matter. When pondering how our sexuality will transcend in the new heavens and the new earth, guess what the first question is regarding our gender distinction?

> Given that gender identity will remain, is there evidence that functional distinctions will likewise remain in the new creation? Will resurrected saints as male and female have gender-specific roles? How will we relate to one another? Will male headship apply? . . . Complementarians, who view male headship and gender-specific roles as part of God's original plan for creation (and for the present age as well) are more likely to answer these questions in the affirmative.[58]

---

57. See Aimee Byrd, *Why Can't We Be Friends? Avoidance Is Not Purity* (Phillipsburg, NJ: P&R, 2018), 133–36.

58. Mark David Walton, "Relationships and Roles in the New Creation," *Journal for Biblical Manhood and Womanhood* 11.1 (2006): 4, http://cbmw.org/wp-content/uploads/2013/05/11-1.pdf.

The argument is that even though there will be no more marriages in heaven, because the whole church will be the bride of Christ, men and women will still relate under the rubric of headship and submission because this is our created nature, our ontological identity. So as we are preparing for the new heavens and the new earth, discipleship will be affected by these two categories: men learn to lead and women to submit. I wonder, if complementarianism stakes their male/female distinction in male authority, how do they disciple men for their *telos* as Christ's bride? And if women's key distinction from man is ontological subordination, how is she then equal to him?

I'm thankful to see a complementarian scholar outside of the CBMW influence describe marriage differently, as well as the eternal social implications we should take from it:

> The perfection of marriage serves as an intellectual prompt for thinking about the social facets of our eschatological hope more broadly. On the one hand, we see the deepest purpose of marriage perfected by human communion being transposed into the ultimate divine-human covenantal fellowship and intimate presence. Thus, our current commitment to marriage has integrity and deserves our concern and commitment, precisely because it prepares for and is perfected in eternity to come. On the other hand, marriage will no longer be marked by sexual activity, by procreation as a related end, and so forth. If marriage's perfection involves such radical changes to its reality, we must be humble in our expectations about what other social realities might be like in that new creational hereafter.[59]

Teaching about gender and relationships using unbiblical notions regarding the new heavens and the new earth is harmful. Our focus should be on divine covenantal fellowship and intimate presence.

Furthermore, applying this unbiblical ontological category of authority to all men downplays the real authority God gives to the

---

59. Allen, *Grounded in Heaven*, 123–24.

ordained office of the ministry. This should be important to those who do hold to male ordination. The authority a pastor has from the pulpit is not a "role" of masculinity, it is an authorization from God to a qualified and ordained person to speak God's Word to his people in the context of the covenant renewal ceremony of corporate worship. The special governing authority given to elders is not due simply because they are men but because they are specifically called, qualified, and ordained to lay down their own lives and guard and shepherd his flock. I take that very seriously and do not think we should diminish the gifts Christ gives his church—the office of the ministry—by flattening that authority as some sort of "role" for all men. Later I will also discuss how we downplay the real authority given to the office of ministry when we mimic it in parachurch organizations.[60]

PEEL AND REVEAL, FIRST LAYER

One of the patterns in the language of biblical manhood and womanhood that *confuses the eye in following*, is *pronounced enough to irritate and provoke study*, and *when you follow the lame uncertain curves for a little distance they suddenly commit suicide—plunge off at outrageous angles, destroy themselves in unheard of contradictions*—is the usage of the word *role*. Kevin Giles has peeled back this pattern in the wallpaper, revealing, as the swordsman Inigo Montoya from the 1987 movie *The Princess Bride* put it, "You keep using that word; I do not think it means what you think it means."

> This word is not found in any of the most common modern English translations of the Bible. It was first used in the theater in the late nineteenth century, and then in sociological texts in the twentieth century. It only came into common usage in the 1960s when people started talking about how male-female roles were changing. In everyday usage the term refers to characteristic behavior that can change. In complementarian speak it is a code word for fixed

---

60. See chap. 6.

power differences allocated on the basis of gender. What defines a man is that he has been given by God the leadership "role," and the woman the subordinate "role." This can never change.

Without ever telling their readers that they are using the word "role" in a way no dictionary defines it, complementarians say that the primary issue in contention is "God-given male-female role distinctions," or "distinct and nonreversible male-female roles." These gender-allocated roles, they argue, give to men and women their "identity.". . . The primary issue in contention is not who does the housework, shopping, childcare, gardening, or household repairs, as the use of the word "role" would suggest to anyone not a complementarian.[61]

We need to stop using the word *role* in reference to permanent fixed identity. Roles can change, especially in different cultures. My sexuality is not a role I play. I don't need to *act* like a woman; I actually *am* a woman. Furthermore, role playing is neither our identity nor our eternal aim.

CBMW bases all their complementarian teaching on one foundational document. They hold this document higher than our ancient creeds when it comes to what unifies them. When CBMW caused commotion on their ESS/EFS teaching on the Trinity, and many called for them to make retractions and align themselves to confessional Nicene Trinitarian teaching, the president of CBMW affirmed:

I am a Danvers complementarian. That view of gender is not and never has been reliant upon an analogy to the Trinity. Biblical complementarianism neither stands nor falls on speculative parallels with Trinity. . . .

CBMW exists to promote the Danvers vision, which is silent on this current controversy. For that reason, my view is that CBMW does not need to be adjudicating the Trinity debate.[62]

---

61. Kevin Giles, *What the Bible Really Says about Women* (Eugene, OR: Cascade Books, 2018), 13–14. Quoting from Andreas and Margaret Köstenberger, *God's Design for Man and Woman: A Biblical-Theological Survey* (Wheaton, IL: Crossway, 2014), 196, 182, 19, 160. See also, 14, 15, 18, 74, 161, 163, 269, et al.

62. Denny Burk, "My Take-Away's [*sic*] from the Trinity Debate," *Denny Burk* (blog), August 10, 2016, www.dennyburk.com/my-take-aways-from-the-trinity-debate/.

Notice CBMW's lack of apology or retractions for their biblically errant teaching. And you can't make a claim that ESS and CBMW complementarianism aren't connected when there was an official statement regarding the Trinity on the CBMW website connecting the two and when much of the teaching in books, articles, and conferences from the organization not only promotes ESS but also bases its teaching on gender on it. At a CBMW conference, the former president pushed the matter, saying, "The gospel has a complementarian structure."[63] The implication is that anyone who does not subscribe to his teaching on complementarity, the teaching that directly connects ESS to "biblical" manhood and womanhood, is denying the gospel. I firmly disagree. This is exactly why I cannot call myself a complementarian. And although I do hold to ordination of qualified males, I join hands with evangelical egalitarians (many who fought for the Nicene teaching on the Trinity) in the gospel, as male ordination is a secondary—not a primary—doctrine.

However, notice how The Danvers Statement is *the* unifying authoritative teaching for CBMW. The current president calls it their "true north."[64] It matters more how one views the "roles" of men and women than holding to orthodox teaching on a first-order doctrine.[65] CBMW introduces the statement this way: "The Danvers Statement summarizes the need for the Council on Biblical Manhood and Womanhood (CBMW) and serves as an overview of our core beliefs. This statement was prepared by several evangelical leaders at a CBMW meeting in Danvers, Massachusetts, in December of 1987. It was first published in final form by the CBMW in Wheaton, Illinois, in November of 1988."[66]

Given all the teaching coming from CBMW linking an ontological role of authority and subordination within the Trinity to womanhood

---

63. Owen Strachan, "The Goodness and Truthfulness of Complementarity," presented at CBMW preconference to T4G 2016, "The Beauty of Complementarity," April 12, 2016, See www.youtube.com/watch?v=AUBeqe5donQ&feature=youtu.be.

64. Burk, "My Take-Away's [*sic*] from the Trinity Debate."

65. A first-order doctrine is a teaching that one must believe in order to be a Christian. What we confess about the Trinity is a first-order doctrine.

66. "The Danvers Statement," CBMW, https://cbmw.org/about/danvers-statement/.

and manhood, I am concerned by what they mean with some of the language in their statement. For example, this first affirmation on which the others build:

> 1. Distinctions in masculine and feminine roles are ordained by God as part of the created order, and should find an echo in every human heart (Gen. 2:18, 21–24; 1 Cor. 11:7–9; 1 Tim. 2:12–14).[67]

Here we see that word *role* being used as a fixed, ontological identity—so much so that we are to find an echo of it in every human heart. How can this be, when the Bible never even mentions these so-called ontological roles being the very thing that distinguishes men and women? We don't see it in the creation account, the Ten Commandments, the Sermon on the Mount, or anywhere Christ teaches about our mission. Nor do we see it in the verses provided on the Danvers document.

I do not need to try and conjure up some echo in my heart that matches cultural role stereotypes for my gender. This kind of thinking will only add damaging fuel to those who suffer with gender dysphoria. Our genders are not limitations to exercising virtue. Jesus himself transcends this stereotype. In both the incarnation and Jesus's resurrection, we see that embodiment and sexuality are essential to human existence.[68] Jesus is not a woman; he is a man. So what do we do with the manliness of Jesus? Is that a problem for women equally made in the image of God? Do we need to look to someone else, like Mary, to know what virtues to emulate? And how do we see Jesus function as a man? Since Jesus has a "particular body with individual characteristics,"[69] we see that we too need particular bodies with individual characteristics. "But none of this entails that any particular characteristic would also need to be viewed as similarly paradigmatic."[70] Like Jesus, I have a sexuality of a man or a woman. (I also want to recognize the dignity of

---

67. "Danvers Statement."
68. See Cortez, *ReSourcing Theological Anthropology*, 197–98.
69. Cortez, *ReSourcing Theological Anthropology*, 197.
70. Cortez, *ReSourcing Theological Anthropology*, 197.

those who suffer with intersex biology, which is a physical reality for some as a result of the fall.[71]) And like Jesus, I have a particular height, hair color, and ethnicity. This diversity within the way God has created us all plays into our being image bearers. We read nothing in Scripture about needing a certain echo in our hearts to affirm this.

While Jesus is most certainly a male, when we learn that he is the wisdom of God, the One whom Proverbs describes using feminine language, it doesn't diminish his masculinity one bit.[72] We don't see him filling mere roles of what the Jewish or Greco-Roman culture expected for manhood. We see him exposing many of those roles as inadequate, subverting them beyond expectations, and then revealing a better picture of God's design. Just think of the way Jesus showcases leadership in the washing of feet and how differently he exercises his own authority as the Son of God, in contrast to the one-dimensional ways taught in biblical manhood. He doesn't play the man card, or even the Son of God card! He serves. He listens. He teaches. He fulfills. He gives his whole self. He equips and empowers men and women. And he calls them to do his work. He does not call them to different roles or different virtues.

REVEALING TRUE MEANING, LAYER TWO

While I am challenging what many say are essential differences and expressions of femininity and masculinity, I am not saying that we should not affirm biological and even gendered differences between the sexes. I agree with Mark Cortez that we can still affirm some cultural norms associated with gender without holding that these must be essential to our sexuality.[73] However, while cultural norms may not be essential to our sexuality, men and women are both equal in dignity and distinctly differentiated by our sex. We need to talk metaphysics, or the nature of reality, a bit when we discuss sexuality. Roman Catholic

---

71. To learn more visit Intersex and Faith, www.intersexandfaith.org/.

72. See Cortez, *ReSourcing Theological Anthropology*, 207–8, for further description of Jesus being identified with wisdom/Sophia/logos tradition.

73. Cortez, *ReSourcing Theological Anthropology*, 208.

philosopher Sister Prudence Allen has done extensive work in this area that is much more robust than the teaching on so-called biblical manhood and womanhood. Based on the essential hylomorphic understanding of the body and soul, a metaphysical[74] understanding that has been developed throughout history (since Aristotle) that recognizes "the human being as a soul/body composite identity,"[75] we understand that as the image of God there are "two distinct ways of being a human being as a male and as a female."[76] This is not something we have to force under an artificial ontological framework of authority and submission or under cultural stereotypes. The word *complementarian* has been hijacked by an outspoken and overpublished group of evangelicals who flatten its meaning and rob it of true beauty and complementarity. Complementarity presupposes difference but also communion through giving of the self in and through these differences.[77] Whether we are talking about mutual self-giving in union of marriage or self-giving reciprocity in communion of friendship, vocation, church service, or neighborly activity, men and women give "of the specific richness of their respective humanity."[78]

Although every human is equal in dignity, we are not "equal" in what we give. Every human is "a unique, unrepeatable person."[79] How glorious that God has created so many human beings to bear his image in such creative ways!

As we think about two ways of being human, as males and as females, do our physical differences mean anything other than the fact that women are men's sexual counterparts? What is the meaningfulness in being male and female? What is beautiful about it? It is certainly

---

74. Meaning a philosophical study of the nature of reality, how things are and how they relate.

75. Prudence Allen, *The Concept of Woman, Volume 3, The Search for Communion of Persons, 1500–2015* (Grand Rapids: Eerdmans, 2016), 492. This contrasts with Plato's dualistic view of the body and soul.

76. Allen, *Concept of Woman*, 464. Allen recognizes that most of us are male or female, but because of the fall, a small percentage of people, who should receive equal dignity, suffer with intersex biology.

77. See Allen, *Concept of Woman*, 460.

78. Allen, *Concept of Woman*, 460.

79. Allen, *Concept of Woman*, 469.

important to note that men and women are sexual counterparts—woman is not made as a sexual counterpart for woman, and vice versa. It is the union of man and woman that is considered one flesh. And this union is fruitful. Some have written about how a woman's body is continuously preparing itself to receive and create life within herself, in contrast to how man creates life outside of himself, leading to different dispositions or "complementary roots of femininity and masculinity." In this teaching, a woman "has the disposition to receive and foster the growth of particular persons in her sphere of activity; a man has the disposition, after accepting responsibility for particular persons in his sphere of activity, to protect and provide for them."[80]

I agree with the teaching in so far as men and women have something distinct to give. And yet both genders are called to all these virtues in our spheres of activity. So I would not want to overgeneralize every man's or woman's disposition. Even in Scripture, we see women, such as Moses's mom and sister, and Pharaoh's daughter, receiving *and* letting go to foster growth *and* protect.[81] I wonder about being too rigid by assigning these dispositions as masculine and feminine when, for example, as a mom I intimately know how fierce my disposition to protect is.[82] I see in Scripture how God successfully employed "feminine" protection (i.e., the Jewish midwives, Rahab, and Jael, to name a few). Nevertheless, men are built with an even greater physical capacity to do so and are called to be the first to lay down their own lives—to leave their mothers and fathers, to sacrifice their own lives for their wives', to care for their wives' bodies, minds, and souls as if they were their own. And for much of their lives, women have a monthly

---

80. Allen, *Concept of Woman*, 478, where Allen is summarizing Pope John Paul II's teaching on the genius of women and men (see 475–78).

81. Also, "Abigail protects her husband and the men in her household from a violent death (1 Sam. 25). Rahab protects the male spies (Josh. 2). An unnamed woman protects the people of Thebez from being burned to death (Judg. 9:50–55). The unnamed 'wise woman' of Abel Beth Maakah protects the men and women of her city from an invading army (2 Sam. 20). Esther protects her people, the Jews, from being massacred (Esth. 2:19–9:19)" (Andrew Bartlett, *Men and Women in Christ: Fresh Light from the Biblical Texts* [London: Inter-Varsity Press, 2019], 89).

82. And while my husband looks the part of a "manly man," I have learned much from his inclination to receive others and foster growth in them.

menstrual cycle that reminds them of their own potential to receive and nurture new life, as well as the bloody sacrifice involved in creation of life. This makes us both strong and vulnerable. And even if a woman or man does not marry, these differences still exude into our wills, personalities, and intellect. And yet there are many expressions of how this affects unique persons as male and female.

Pope John Paul II contrasted fractional complementarity teaching with integral complementarity. Prudence Allen sums up this teaching, saying, "In *fractional complementarity* a woman and a man are described as contributing fractional portions to a relation that together add up to one single person. In *integral complementarity* a woman and a man are each considered as a whole person, and together they synergetically generate something or someone more."[83] Man and woman are not $1/2 + 1/2 = 1$, or more commonly taught in fractional complementarity, $3/4 + 1/4 = 1$, but rather one whole + one whole = 3.[84] The holy communion of whole persons is one that produces fruit. We see this clearly in the fruit of offspring between men and women. But this is true in a spiritual and relational manner as well when we talk about friendship, vocation, and church life. The challenge for the church is to see the relationship between men and women not as fractional, but integral, in that men and women are whole persons and "together they synergetically generate something or someone more."[85] Therefore it is inadequate merely to describe the nature of man and woman without also describing the dynamic of communion between the sexes and where we are headed.

The work of Paul A. Zancanaro and Julián Marías parallels the teaching of Prudence Allen and Pope John Paul II, and its necessary metaphysical component.[86] "Each sex, as embodied persons,

---

83. Allen, *Concept of Woman*, 8.

84. See Prudence Allen, "The Concept of Woman," YouTube, www.youtube.com/watch?v=dZAyxea_Qg0.

85. Allen, *Concept of Woman*, 8.

86. Thanks to Anna Anderson for directing me to Paul. A Zancanaro, "Julián Marías on the Empirical Structure of Human Life and Its Sexuate Condition," *International Philosophical Quarterly* 23.4 (December 1983): 425–40, www.pdcnet.org/ipq/content/ipq_1983_0023_0004_0425_0440?file_type=pdf; and Julián Marías, *Metaphysical*

co-implicates the other, which is reflected in the biological fact that each 'complicates' the other."[87] In co-implicating one another, men and women must be ordered toward one another to be able to actualize their own humanity "such that to live for each sex is to direct his or her life toward the other."[88] Our sociohistorical context does factor into how we view one another as men and women, as "we each live always with our face turned toward the other sex. Man realizes himself in woman and woman realizes herself in man."[89] This too is an integral understanding of personhood, as both man and woman are whole persons with personality, future-oriented dynamism, and agency to act within our multiple realities of the context of our choices.[90] This is what moves us to communion of persons, as our integral humanity is more fully actualized "through exercising reciprocal activities that flow from [our] reciprocal structures."[91]

Marías, like Allen, answers the question of woman by looking both to the beginning of creation and to our eschatological future. God does not create Adam and Eve at the same time. Why does he create Adam first, and why does he create animal life in between? Adam, and the reader, discovers that he is "not suited to be alone."[92] What does Adam see when Eve is created from him? Talk about a gynocentric interruption! He sees that "what it is to be man consists in being related to women."[93] He sees his *telos*, as we see it played out in the rest of the pages of Scripture. He sees his bride, but this bride symbolizes to all of humanity what we are called to become—the church as Christ's collective bride. Prudence Allen builds on this, as she discusses the works of Saint Teresa of Àvila, Saint John of the Cross, and Pope John Paul II.

Anthropology: The Empirical Structure of Human Life (University Park, PA: Penn State University Press, 1971).

87. Marías, *Metaphysical Anthropology*, 137.

88. Zancanaro, "Julián Marías," 433.

89. Zancanaro, "Julián Marías," 433.

90. See Zancanaro, "Julián Marías," 430.

91. Zancanaro, "Julián Marías," 434.

92. Zancanaro, "Julián Marías," 434.

93. Zancanaro, "Julián Marías," 434 ("and vice-versa for women" [434]).

Saint John of the Cross often referred to himself as the "bride of Christ." Saint Teresa of Àvila's analysis of her religious experience also incorporated her self-understanding as a spiritual bride of Christ. How does a man in his ^{spirit}soul$_{psyche}$/body identity become self-described as both different from and similar to a woman's act of existence? More specifically, the question arises how a man, who is a religious called into a spousal relation with Jesus Christ, can understand this spiritual reality analogously to a woman. Generally speaking, a woman can consider herself a spiritual bride of God by drawing upon a *horizontal analogy* with other women who are brides in the world and then, *qua* woman, making a *transcendental analogy* with spiritual marriage. A man, however, has to make a second step: he has to die to himself a little (to his strict identification with his male body as his primary identity) to be able to make the horizontal analogy with women who are brides in the world.[94]

Man cannot make that feminine transcendental analogy until he is able to account for this greater horizontal difference.[95] And so we see in the beginning, Adam had to die to himself a little, we even see him put down, as God takes from the side of man's body to create woman.[96] Perhaps this is sounding similar to the André Brink novel, *The Wall of the Plague*, that we looked at in chapter 1, where the white male African narrator takes on the first-person voice of his mixed-race lover, saying, "'How can I, how dare I presume to form you from my rib? . . . I can never be you: yet in order to be myself I must imagine what it is like to be you.'"[97] Pope John Paul II explained it this way:

> For the analogy implies a likeness, while at the same time leaving ample room for non-likeness. This is easily seen in regard to the person of the "bride." According to the Letter to the Ephesians,

---

94. Allen, *Concept of Woman*, 102.
95. Allen, *Concept of Woman*, 104.
96. Gen. 2:21–22.
97. Richard Bauckham, *Gospel Women: Studies of the Named Women in the Gospel* (Grand Rapids: Eerdmans, 2002), 1, quoting A. Brink, *The Wall of the Plague* (New York: Summit, 1984; London: Fontana, 1985), 445.

the bride is the Church, just as for the Prophets the bride was Israel. She is therefore a collective subject and not an individual person. This collective subject is the People of God, a community made up of many persons, both men and women.

Christ has entered this history and remains in it as the Bridegroom who "has given himself.". . . In this way, "being the bride," and thus, the "feminine" element, becomes a symbol of all that is "human.". . .

From a linguistic viewpoint we can say that the analogy of spousal love found in the Letter to the Ephesians links what is "masculine" to what is "feminine," since, as members of the Church, men too are included in the concept of "Bride."[98]

But it's not only men who need to project toward women for a teleological understanding of their humanness. "Something similar must happen in the thinking of a woman who can die spiritually to her female identity in order to understand herself as a son in the Son . . . inheriting eternal life."[99] As Allen says, these teachings "demonstrate . . . a wonderful flexibility of thought combined with an acute self-understanding *qua* man or *qua* woman. Their alacrity in writing about transcendental and existential analogies anticipates important developments in the search for communion in twentieth-century existential personalism"[100] and beyond.

Like the narrator in *The Wall of the Plague*, like the writer of Ruth, like Luke, and like the many other instances we saw in Scripture in part 1 of this book, men and women need to invest in fostering mutual knowledge of one another. When we look at each other, when we listen to each other, when we cooperate, promoting holiness, men and women are affirming and participating in our ultimate purpose. Oriented in Christ, this kind of communion is truly meaningful. And we don't merely have the exclusive sexual relationship of marriage to

---

98. Allen, *Concept of Woman*, 106, quoting John Paul II, *Mulieris Dignitatem* (Boston: St. Paul Books and Media, 1988), #25.

99. Allen, *Concept of Woman*, 109.

100. Allen, *Concept of Woman*, 109.

express this. We are brothers and sisters in Christ, placed in a dynamic, synergetic, fruit-bearing communion. Zancanaro sums it up: "Men and women, installed in their respected sexes, live mutually—each project-ing toward the other. Consequently, neither man nor woman can be defined—insofar as humans can be defined at all—without entailing the other. . . . This mutual projection of man for woman and woman for man is more fundamental than any sexual need, for it involves their very biographies."[101]

Putting this all together, I need to quote from my good friend Anna: "Men and women aren't merely a static balancing act, but more like a Ripstick, where the very act/art of balancing propels us forward toward our eschatological goal, the end for which God made His male and female image-bearers. Our dependence is dynamic, a fruit-bearing synergism."[102] This is where we find a true actualization—in meaning-ful communion of persons. "'Being a person means striving towards self-realization . . . which can only be achieved *through a sincere gift of self.*'"[103] Have you ever tried to ride a Ripstick? It takes work to learn the balance. But once you invest in that, the ride begins to flow much easier, joyfully so. And the great joy and success of this analogy is the direction in which it is headed, to behold our Bridegroom.

WHO PICKS UP THE TAB WHEN WE FAIL TO RETRIEVE, REFORM, AND RENEW?

The above concept of man and woman is far more robust than I have seen in either complementarian or egalitarian teaching. And if we com-pare it to the definitions of femininity and masculinity provided for us to pursue "biblical manhood and womanhood," we find that teaching to be fractional, reducing our personhood and hindering the dynamic fruition of our *telos*. Frankly speaking, my reasons for writing this book are not academic. And they are not to target certain organizations

---

101. Zancanaro, "Julián Marías," 435, 436.
102. Anna Anderson, personal email.
103. Allen, *Concept of Woman*, 480, quoting John Paul II, *Mulieris Dignitatem*, #7, referring back to *Gaudium et Spes* (emphasis original).

or people. I have the opportunity to speak in many churches. I get to speak at women's retreats and coed conferences, as well as at universities and seminaries. I do this as a laywoman. And I see the toll that the yellow wallpaper is taking on my friends from countless churches, my loved ones, and all those I meet through these engagements and who seek me out online.

You see, it doesn't hurt many of the top names in certain evangelical circles to endorse these books teaching ESS or ERAS, to affirm the orthodoxy of errant teaching on the Trinity, complementarianism, and gender roles, and to continue to headline together at conferences. But I see who picks up the tab for this irresponsibility—the regular churchgoing people who are trying to honor God in their singleness or as wives and husbands.

I have seen the cost in my own experiences, and I am seeing it in all the emails I am getting from women who can't use a word like *career*, lest it sound too ambitious; women who have no voice in their churches because the men are the leaders who have all the valuable input; women who are stuck in ministries that teach "true womanhood" and are considered divisive if they point out heretical teaching on the Trinity in their book study[104]; women who are frustrated because they do not fit into the "biblical womanhood" box of nursery duty and potlucks and feel marginalized in their own church; women who have expressed their conflict of desiring to be "good complementarians" while wanting to cry when they read some of the material marketed to them by so-called trusted Christian resources; and women who are encouraged to go to seminary for a master of arts degree but then discover doors closed for most paying jobs for which they are qualified. Worse, I hear from women who are in and who have come out of abusive situations under this kind of irresponsible teaching. When this so-called complementarian teaching, advocating such poor theology and environment for women, is presented as our design from creation and part of the gospel structure, I'm not surprised that some end up questioning their faith.

---

104. See Rachel Green Miller, review of *True Woman 101: Divine Design* by Mary A. Kassian and Nancy Leigh DeMoss, *A Daughter of the Reformation* (blog), May 8, 2015, https://adaughterofthereformation.wordpress.com/2015/05/08/true-woman-101-divine-design/.

I am writing because we need to recover a better way. We need to peel off this yellow wallpaper and reveal our true biblical aim. We are not directed to biblical manhood nor biblical womanhood; we are directed to Christ. Our aim is to behold Christ, as his bride, as fellow sons in the Son. In the next chapter we'll continue to look at how we can better be prepared to attain this goal.

QUESTIONS FOR GROUP DISCUSSION

1. A false dichotomy has been offered to us: either we embrace the modern-day teaching on biblical manhood and womanhood (which looks a lot like a rebranded PG version of the ancient Greco-Roman model), or we irretrievably damage the church with vague, androgynous discipleship. We've seen descriptions of this biblical manhood and womanhood teaching in this chapter. What would vague, androgynous discipleship look like? Explain why this is a false dichotomy.

2. How would you describe mature masculinity and mature femininity? If Christ ultimately shows us what it means to be human, how does this affect our ideas of masculinity and femininity?

3. How can your church better uphold distinction between the sexes without reduction? What areas might be blind spots for you? How do our distinct relational responsibilities color our discipleship? How would cultural or class differences color our discipleship?

4. Name some examples of how women in your church are serving as necessary allies to the men in warning them to turn away from evil, acting as cobelligerents with men against evil enemies, mediating the Word of the Lord, giving wise instruction and counsel, collaborating in service to others, responding to God as examples of faithfulness, and influencing men from a gift of empathy and relatedness. How can you facilitate this culture of coed labor better in your church?

5. What gender norms within our culture do you think are worth affirming? How might they help us to relate as men and women? Are they essential to being biblically faithful to our sexuality?

CHAPTER 5

WHAT CHURCH IS FOR

Back in 2014 I had a moment of clarity that I now refer to as the pizza revelation. My oldest daughter, Solanna, was fourteen. She and her friend had about an hour before volleyball practice. I put a pizza in the oven for them and walked to the bus stop to pick up my son. The bus was running late, so I called Sol and told her she needed to take the pizza out of the oven. Simple enough. But it wasn't. She began giving me all the reasons why she couldn't do it: she might burn herself, the Pampered Chef pizza stone was awkward to grab, she might break it . . . I couldn't even believe I was having this argument. As I was trying to reason with her that a fourteen-year-old should be able to take a pizza out of the oven, she cut me off, saying, "Never mind, Cory did it."[1] Cory's parents are divorced. She lived with her dad and was a much more independent young woman.

I stood there at the bus stop with a terrifying thought. My oldest child might be out of the house and away at college in three-and-a-half years, and she still couldn't take a pizza out of the oven. I realized that I do way too much for my children still, and I have a different kind of work to do. While it was often my joy to do things for them, my job is to prepare them for adulthood. I needed to raise a contributing member of society. Thankfully, we've come a long way since the pizza revelation, and my daughter is thriving at the university.

I see this as a metaphor for the church. A lot of Christians today

---

1. I changed the friend's name for privacy.

don't know how to take the metaphorical pizza out of the oven. That is, they don't even have a good understanding of the basics of the faith: the doctrine of God, his Word, or his church. They don't have a mature understanding of what kind of book the Bible is and how to do the work of reading for understanding. Our churches are packed with people who never grew out of an adolescent stage in their faith, are insecure about their ability to read and interpret Scripture, and barely have the attention span to make it through a whole sermon.

At fourteen Solanna always imagined I would take the pizza out of the oven—Mom would handle the hot stove for her. But I needed to expand her view of her growing function in our household and equip her to be able to contribute in more mature ways. The pizza revelation helped me to step back and recalibrate my parenting according to the big picture. Applying this as a metaphor for the household of God provokes some questions. How do we view Christ's church, and what is God's eternal purpose for us? How do we prepare for that?

PARTICIPATING IN THE LOVE OF GOD

The triune God pursues his people for eternal fellowship with him according to his good pleasure. God calls us into communion with himself. That sounds like such a simple proposition, but reflecting on it should absolutely fill us with wonder! And it provokes some basic questions in our preparation for eternity. What is that communion like? How has God designed us for this communion? How does he prepare us for it? Does he tell us?

These questions direct us to consider the fellowship between the persons of the Trinity. God has always communicated. Scott Swain explains:

> The eternal life of the Father, Son, and Holy Spirit is a life of perfect communication and communion. In the Holy Trinity, there is perfect communication (i.e., "making common") *of* one divine life and perfect communion (i.e., "sharing, holding in common") *in* one divine life. The Father eternally communicates his life to

the Son (Jn. 5:26), who is his perfect Word, radiance and image (Jn. 1:1; Heb. 1:3; Col. 1:15). And the Father with the Son eternally communicates this self-same life to the Spirit, breathing him out in their perfect, mutual love and fellowship. We come to know this perfect triune life of communication and communion because God graciously unveils it to us in the gospel.[2]

God's triune life has perfect, eternal communication and communion *ad intra*, or we might say internally. He lacks nothing. And although God has no need whatsoever for further communication and communion, we learn from Scripture that "he desires to communicate his own glorious and blessed life to us—in a manner appropriate to our creaturely status—in order that we too might have communion and fellowship with him, that we might become friends with God" (John 15:15; 2 Cor. 13:14).[3] I like how Swain describes communication as "making common" and communion as "sharing, holding in common." This is a movement toward another to truly be known and an invitation to participate in holy goodness. How is it that we, mere creatures, get to participate in this intratrinitarian communion as God's friends?

The answer is in Christ. In the incarnation we have God's affirmation of both creation and humanity. God isn't stingy with his love for the Son but is outgoing, generously calling us to share and participate in that love with him. Kelly Kapic says, "In Jesus, God actualizes his call to us to enter communion with him through the Son and by the Spirit."[4] By the act of the incarnation, we see that the Father's love for humanity is preeminent in Christ, the One into whose likeness we are being transformed in our sanctification. God created us to share in the Father's love for the Son by his Holy Spirit.[5] John Owen affirms, "*We are never more like God than when we love his Son through his*

---

2. Scott R. Swain, *Trinity, Reading, and Revelation* (New York: T&T Clark, 2011), 5.

3. Swain, *Trinity*, 5–6.

4. Michael Allen and Scott R. Swain, eds., *Christian Dogmatics: Reformed Theology for the Church Catholic* (Grand Rapids: Baker Academic, 2016), 166.

5. See Kelly M. Kapic, "Anthropology," chap. 8 in *Christian Dogmatics*, ed. Allen and Swain, 167.

Spirit."[6] This isn't just some esoteric expectation for our future. This is what new creations in Christ are equipped by his Spirit to do now, growing in sanctification, as we are more and more oriented in the love of Christ.

There is another element to this communion. The triune God calls us not only into communion with himself but also with one another. His love overflows to a love for all his people. It's a package deal! We see this in the greatest commandment. "Love the Lord your God with all your heart, with all your soul, and with all your mind. This is the greatest and most important command. The second is like it: Love your neighbor as yourself" (Matt. 22:37–39). And we see these two commands perfectly come together in the incarnate Christ. Michael Horton explains:

> With Jesus, we are dealing with God assuming the nature and commission of humanity in creation so that he can shower his compatriots with the riches that he achieved in our nature, as our human representative and in the power of the Holy Spirit. Jesus is God. But he is also the first human being who finally does not resist the Holy Spirit. Instead he obeys the word of the Father in full acquiescence to the Spirit's power—and he does all this for us, in our name, as our new Adamic head. He gives the Spirit without measure because he first possesses the Spirit without measure, and through union with him we too are anointed as prophets, priests, and kings.[7]

God is outgoing with his love. And so Jesus fulfilled all of his holy law perfectly on behalf of his people, even as he incurred the full wrath of God to pay the debt of our sins. He has brought us into union with him, giving us his Spirit without measure so that we too can love God and neighbor. And as we love the Son through the Spirit, we will love the whole Christ, that is, Christ and his church.

---

6. Quoted in Kapic, "Anthropology," 166 (emphasis original).
7. Michael Horton, *Rediscovering the Holy Spirit: God's Perfecting Presence in Creation, Redemption, and Everyday Life* (Grand Rapids: Zondervan, 2017), 101.

THE WHOLE CHRIST

How long has Jesus thought about the church? We know that we are always on his mind now, since Jesus Christ has ascended to the right hand of the Father where he is continuously making intercession for the saints. And that is quite a wondrous thought to think about. So it really blows our minds to consider that the church has been on Christ's mind from all eternity. We learn in Scripture that before time began, the persons of the godhead made an intratrinitarian covenant of redemption, whereby God the Father promised to give the Son a bride, the Son promised to secure the redemption of his bride, and the Holy Spirit promised to apply his work to his people. Jesus alluded to this in the High Priestly Prayer when he said, "Father, I want those you have given me to be with me where I am, so that they will see my glory, which you have given me because you loved me before the world's foundation" (John 17:24). This claim that Jesus was making about a people that the Father had given him presupposed some kind of prior agreement. Jesus was referring to this oath, this covenant of redemption that was made in eternity.[8]

But as Jesus is now at the right hand of the Father, we can understand that our union goes beyond just being in his thoughts. Even as we are told about the great mystery of husband and wife becoming one flesh, picturing Christ and his church, have we fully grasped what this union with Christ means? Because of our own sinful natures and the pure holiness of God, perhaps we dare not think about the reality of the church being part of the whole Christ. Herman Bavinck wrote:

He went to heaven to prepare a place for his own and to fill them here on earth with the fullness that he acquired by his perfect obedience. What he received as a reward for his labor for himself and what he received for his own cannot be separated. He is all and in all (Col. 3:11). The pleroma (fullness) that dwells in Christ must also dwell in the church. It is being filled with all the fullness of God (Eph. 3:19; Col. 2:2, 10). It is God whose fullness fills Christ

---

8. See also Ps. 110; Rom. 8:34; Heb. 7:25; 9:24; 1 John 2:1.

(Col. 1:9), and it is Christ whose fullness in turn fills the church (Eph. 1:23). The church can therefore be described as his *pleroma*, that which he perfects and gradually, from within himself, fills with himself (Eph. 4:10), and is therefore itself being filled by degrees. As the church does not exist apart from Christ, so Christ does not exist without the church. . . . Together with him, it can be called the one Christ (1 Cor. 12:12).[9]

Paul told us that Christ is the "head over everything for the church, which is his body, the fullness of the one who fills all things in every way" (Eph. 1:22–23). This is why Christ could say to Paul, "Saul, Saul, why are you persecuting me?" in reference to Paul's persecution of the church (Acts 9:4). To persecute the church, the body, is to persecute Jesus, the head.

This blessed truth is the foundation from which Augustine interpreted the Psalms. "Throughout understanding the Psalms as a prophecy of the mystery of Christ in his totality—of Christ, head and body (the *totus Christus*)—Augustine had found a hermeneutical key of expounding them, which enabled him to plumb the utmost depths of the Old Testament words and make them immediately available to Christian understanding."[10] Although the Old Testament writings were veiled by figurative language before the incarnation, Augustine followed the lead of the apostles' interpretation of those writings, understanding that "the Church together with Christ is the central content of holy scripture: 'Christ and his Church, that total mystery with which all of the Scriptures are concerned.'"[11]

Doesn't that blow your mind? What kind of God is this who would share his Word and Spirit, the revelation of who he is, along with the life that flows from it, with mere creatures, so much so that we are considered part of the *totus Christus*? Doesn't this lead you to wonder

---

9. Herman Bavinck, *Reformed Dogmatics*, vol. 3, *Sin and Salvation in Christ*, ed. John Bolt, trans. John Vriend (Grand Rapids: Baker Academic, 2006), 474.

10. Michael Fiedrowicz, "Introduction," in Augustine, *Expositions of the Psalms*, 1–32, ed. John Rotelle, trans. Maria Boulding (Hyde Park, NY: New City, 2000), 43.

11. Fiedrowicz, 44, quoting from Augustine, *Expositions of the Psalms* 79.1.

and awe? Does it not make you delight in him? I love how Michael Reeves expresses this in *Delighting in the Trinity*: "God's innermost being (hypostasis) is an outgoing, loving, life-giving being. The triune God is an ecstatic God: he is not a God who hoards his life, but one who gives it away, as he would show in that supreme moment of his self-revelation on the cross. The Father finds his very identity in giving his life and being to the Son; and the Son images his Father in sharing his life with us through the Spirit."[12]

As those of us in Christ together make up the whole Christ, it's important to note the love that we should then have for one another. We *must* love those whom he loves. Paul described the husband leading the way in modeling this kind of love that Christ has for us in the way he loves his wife, saying "In the same way, husbands are to love their wives as their own bodies. He who loves his wife loves himself. For no one ever hates his own flesh but provides and cares for it, just as Christ does for the church" (Eph. 5:28–29). Mothers experience this in a rich way, as our children are fashioned and come forth from our own bodies. And as husbands and wives can express this in the most intimate ways, Paul used this same description of the body to describe how Christ's whole church is diversely gifted as parts of one body to serve in unity in Christ (1 Cor. 12:12–29). And he said, "If one member suffers, all the members suffer with it; if one member is honored, all the members rejoice with it" (v. 26). If we are part of the whole Christ, then we are to join with him as the source of love to our brothers and sisters, and then together mediate his presence to the watching world. Does the world know us for the love we have for one another (John 13:35)? We often stumble badly in this most important area. We will get into more detail about our relationships with our brothers and sisters in Christ in chapter 8, but as we participate together in the love of God, preparing for eternity with him, we must look to Christ, our head, as the source of this love. The unity and harmony in God's household should model a picture for us of the cosmos of the new heavens and new earth.

---

12. Michael Reeves, *Delighting in the Trinity: An Introduction to the Christian Faith* (Downers Grove, IL: IVP Academic, 2012), 45.

CHRIST WHO GIVES

God has not left us alone while we wait for the consummation of his love, which promises eternal communion with the triune God in glorious new bodies joined with holy minds fit for the new heavens and the new earth. Paul explained that Jesus Christ is restoring God's household to order, even after the chaos of the fall. Notice the household language in Ephesians 1:9–10: "He made known to us the mystery of His will, according to His kind intention which He purposed in Him with a view to an administration suitable to the fullness of the times, that is, the summing up of all things in Christ, things in the heavens and things on the earth" (NASB). Jesus is the household manager, administratively summing up all things in heaven and on earth toward his mission to prepare us to dwell with him for eternity. The fall brought chaos and division, but Christ brings order and unity in himself.

Filling us with himself, Christ blesses us as we grow in sanctification. And he gives his household a commission to prepare us for eternal fellowship with him. That is what church is for. Jesus gives his great commission to the church to spread the good news of salvation in Jesus Christ, who is the only way to fulfill our calling to love God and one another, through the preached Word, discipleship, and administration of the sacraments (Matt. 28:18–20). We are to communicate, *make common*, the gospel of Jesus Christ, so that all whom the Father gave to the Son will commune, *share, hold in common*, with him.

When Christ ascended victoriously to the right hand of the Father, he gave his people the prizes of his victory: "When he ascended on high, he took the captives captive; he gave gifts to people" (Eph. 4:8). These gifts are people, officers of the church, to lead the way in carrying out his great commission. They do this through serving us his Word and sacraments, "until we all reach unity in the faith and in the knowledge of God's Son, growing into maturity with a stature measured by Christ's fullness" (4:13). Christ is filling us with himself through the work of his Spirit and the ministers of his means of grace. Paul said that Christ "gave some to be apostles, some prophets, some evangelists, some pastors and teachers" (4:11). "The officers he mentions are associated with the proclamation of the Word, since it's through this gift that the Spirit makes us all cosharers in *the* gift."[13] Christ's gift to his people of the service of the Word is the primary, foundational way he prepares us for eternal life with him. We see this service is "for the perfecting of the saints, for the work of the ministry," and "for the edifying of the body of Christ" (4:12 KJV).[14] Christ appoints ministers to serve us in preparation for eternity.

The priority of these gifts for the ministry of the Word serves God's household so that we first get to receive before we gratefully serve in response. The ministry unifies and matures us in good doctrine so that we can then "[speak] the truth in love," "grow in every way into him who is the head—Christ," and "[promote] the growth of the body for building up itself in love by the proper working of each individual part" (Eph. 4:15–16). We come to church first to receive these gifts of the ministry, the means of grace whereby Christ gives us himself, *the* gift. Michael Horton has written helpfully on the dynamic effect of our receiving. While Christ qualifies and authorizes some to serve in the office of ministry, "all believers are exhorted to teach, exhort, rebuke, encourage, and keep an eye out for each other's spiritual warfare."[15] Through his Spirit, Christ has gifted all of the members of his household to work in harmony toward his mission.

So we laypeople don't make the effort to roll out of our comfortable beds on Sunday mornings just to sing Jesus some loves songs and let the pastor take the pizza out of the oven for us by motivating us with a powerful message to get us through another week. And we don't go to church for self-improvement. Sanctification is not an individual process. We serve a God who is extroverted with his love, and his "Spirit drives us outside of ourselves by a public word and ministry that makes us extroverted—looking up to Christ in faith, looking forward

---

13. Horton, *Rediscovering the Holy Spirit*, 231.

14. For an argument for the KJV rendering of Eph. 4:12, and for how this verse is not about every-member ministry, see Horton, *Rediscovering the Holy Spirit*, 231–34.

15. Horton, *Rediscovering the Holy Spirit*, 234.

in hope, and looking out to our neighbors in love."[16] Our holy God is summoning us to corporately gather with our brothers and sisters, to receive Christ through Word and sacrament, to offer him praise for who he is and what he has done, to cry out in confession and lament, to hear his words of affirmation, and to be commissioned and sent back out to the world with a benediction. "Both the Spirit and the bride say, 'Come!' Let anyone who hears, say, 'Come!' Let the one who is thirsty come. Let the one who desires take the water of life freely" (Rev. 22:17).

PEEL AND REVEAL

Maybe you are thinking that my pizza metaphor has fallen apart. I opened the chapter by saying that many laypeople can't take the metaphorical pizza out of the oven, that many are missing the basic doctrines of the faith. Then I went on to say that a foundational part of discipleship is to be served the means of grace by the ministers God has gifted to the church. Yes, this departs a little bit from the simple act of pizza retrieval. We are to first be served. But that does not mean that we are not active participants in the service. We don't just passively wait to be fed our slice of pizza. Perhaps, at the risk of adding extra cheese to my metaphor, we could say that the ministers prepare the pizza and put it in the oven to bake. Then they hand over some oven mitts to the brothers and sisters in God's household. Part of the liturgy, or the way our worship service is conducted, is our active response in retrieval. And when we taste the pizza and see that it is good, we begin to be nurtured, equipped members of God's household who serve one another in important ways. In the next chapter, we are going to discuss what happens when we do not prioritize the foundational means God has given us for discipleship, which is a big peeling and revealing of how this affects men and women in the church. But as we look at this great responsibility of church officers in preparing men and women for eternity, there are two spots behind the wallpaper that I would like to address.

---

16. Horton, *Rediscovering the Holy Spirit*, 318.

PEEL AND REVEAL: PROCLAIMING THE WORD

Ephesians 4 shows us that Christ has ordained the proclamation of his Word as a foundational means to communicate and commune with us. By this means, he gives us himself through his Spirit. Earlier in his epistle, Paul said that God's household was "built on the foundation of the apostles and prophets, with Christ Jesus himself as the cornerstone" (Eph. 2:20). We no longer need new revelation, but we still need the proclamation of the Word. Both men and women need to be addressed by the Word of God. But findings show that in more conservative churches, male pastors tend to be preaching more to the men. Dr. Valerie Hobbs, senior lecturer in applied linguistics at the University of Sheffield, is conducting a study on this and has presented some of her findings in an academic paper.[17] She summarizes her findings[18]:

Are women invisible to male Christian pastors? Some evidence:

One of my first projects on divorce sermons revealed that male Christian pastors may be mostly preaching to men.

I decided to investigate this in a larger corpus of over 100 sermons on various topics from conservative pastors.

I wanted to know, to what extent are male pastors talking **about** men and **to** men? The results were pretty telling.

1. References to named men (excluding Jesus) far outnumbered references to named women: 5,164 to 635.
2. Unnamed women are also rarely mentioned compared to men (see pic).
3. There is also evidence that even supposedly gender-neutral pronouns (you, anyone, everyone, whoever, etc.) refer to men. The evidence for this is more complicated, but here's

---

17. Valerie Hobbs, "Men Talking to Men? Gendering the Congregation in Conservative Christian Sermons" (paper presented at the Big Data, Big Theory Conference, University of Sheffield, UK, 27 April 2018). See also idem, *An Introduction to Religious Language in Contemporary Contexts* (London: Bloomsbury, forthcoming).
18. Summarized findings shared in personal communication, with permission.

an example. The pronoun "you" behaves grammatically more like "man" in sermons than "woman." So the audience is primed to consider even the pronoun "you" as male.

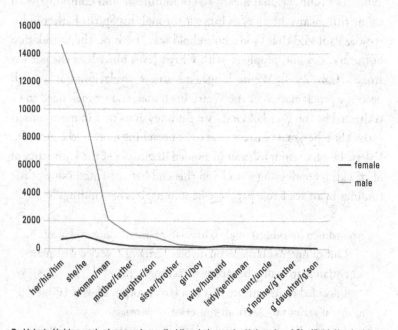

Dr. Valerie Hobbs, senior lecturer in applied linguistics at the University of Sheffield. Used with permission.

This tendency of preachers to address men more than women is a blind spot that needs to be dealt with. I am happy to say that some are doing just that. I've twice been invited to speak to a Communications and Preaching class at Reformed Theological Seminary, DC, on this very topic of preaching to women. While introducing me, the professor who invited me explained to the class that he had invested five years in his own preaching before he realized that he wasn't really preaching to the women. Now he is also a professor who is being proactive about this blind spot.[19] Interestingly, these young pastors in training were

---

19. For the talk I gave, see Aimee Byrd, *No Little Women: Equipping All Women in the Household of God* (Phillipsburg, NJ: P&R, 2016), chap. 10.

taking notes on small, practical tips as I spoke, such as making eye contact with women, not using gender-stereotypical illustrations, using more feminine pronouns in illustrations that describe an intelligent or perceptive person, stimulating women to think during the sermon, and asking them good questions during the week to gain insight while preparing sermons.

This isn't the only time I have worked on this blind spot with pastors and elders. I am being invited more and more to speak with church leaders on the topic of equipping women well in the church as competent allies to the men. The responses to these talks often validate my passion to talk to church leaders about this gap in communication to men and women. One more experience that stands out was when I was invited to talk to a Presbyterian Church in America presbytery of about eighty pastors and elders, a room full of men. I did not know how my talk was going to be received, as I was pretty blunt about the poor condition of women's ministries and how women are often kept at arm's length from the church. This made me nervous about the Q&A that followed the talk. Hand after hand was raised, with pastors connecting the dots between what I taught regarding their responsibility to both equip and listen to the women in their church and the level of damage control they had been dealing with in different women's ministry situations. One pastor raised his hand and said, "I am in my midfifties. In all my years of seminary, pastoring, and presbytery training, I have never heard this before. Thank you for being so brave and passionate to come talk to us." His comment was extremely validating and yet so utterly revealing. Why isn't there more proactive training for pastors about how to minister to and better equip the women in their churches? How much interaction are they having with women academics or even popular female writers? Why are many pastors so terribly unaware of the market of poor theology being sold to women in the form of "Bible studies" and topical studies for women's ministry? We will get into this market in more detail in the following chapter. But in peeling back the yellow wallpaper, pastors need to be asking themselves how they are preparing both the men and women for eternity through the proclamation of the Word and the fruit of that ministry in their church.

PEEL AND REVEAL: COED COLABORERS

If Paul gave us a picture of Christ's gifts laying the foundation for preparing us for eternity in Ephesians 4, he gave us a picture of the fruit of that in our church life in Romans 16. The personal greetings with which he signed off his letter reveal a glimpse of men and women reciprocating the gifts that have overflowed to them under the ministry.

Paul kicked off this idea of reciprocity when he began his closing greetings with, "I commend to you our sister Phoebe, a deacon of the church in Cenchreae. I ask you to receive her in the Lord in a way worthy of his people and to give her any help she may need from you, for she has been the benefactor of many people, including me" (Rom. 16:1–2 NIV). Paul began his commendation of Phoebe by describing her as "our" sister. As siblings in Christ, we share a status of value with one another that will carry over into the new heavens and new earth. This special family relationship carries rights and obligations. "As a sister in the household of God, Phoebe would be expected to use her resources to better the lives of her brothers and sisters."[20] Next, Paul described Phoebe in two leadership positions in which we see her doing just that.

Paul said Phoebe was a deacon of the church of Cenchreae. A lot of debate has centered on whether Phoebe held an actual office or Paul was merely describing Phoebe as a "servant" in the church. Lynn Cohick, among others, rightfully reminds us not to read our own modern ideas of the diaconate into the first-century text. "Instead, a careful examination of the *diakonia* word group suggests a sense of representation or agency. That is, in calling Phoebe a deacon, Paul was identifying her as his agent or intermediary carrying his gospel message, or most specifically, his letter to the Romans."[21] In highlighting examples of the *diakonia* word group used this way throughout Scripture—such as in the previous chapter when Paul spoke of his "ministry" to Judea (15:31), in 1 Corinthians when he wrote of his and Apollo's "service" in bearing the message of God (3:5), and in Colossians when he referred

---

20. Lynn H. Cohick, *Women in the World of the Earliest Christians* (Grand Rapids: Baker Academic, 2009), 304.
21. Cohick, *Women*, 304.

to Tychicus as "a dear brother, a faithful minister," who acted as Paul's emissary in delivering his letter to the Colossian church (Col. 4:7), to name a few—Cohick explains that "in the case of Phoebe, then, Paul is likely stressing her role as a go-between for the Corinthian churches and the Roman congregation, as well as her specific duty to carry Paul's letter, with his authority."[22] Furthermore, the fact that Paul told the Romans to receive Phoebe, our sister and a deacon of the church of Cenchreae, "in contrast to all the other people whom he convey[ed] 'greetings,' indicates that Phoebe was the bearer of the letter to the Romans."[23]

Paul must have certain confidence in Phoebe to entrust her with this responsibility. She was essentially taking the pizza out of the oven and delivering it hot and fresh to the Roman church. Michael Bird asks an important question: *"If the Romans had any questions about the letter, such as: like 'What is the righteousness of God?' or 'Who is this wretched man that Paul refers to about halfway through?' then who do you think would be the first person that they would ask?"*[24] Let me ask the most educated reader, have you ever had any questions when reading Romans? Wouldn't you love the opportunity to ask, if not Paul himself, then the one whom he sent to deliver it with his authority? Consider the weight of his decision:

> This is Romans—Paul's attempt to prevent a potentially fractious cluster of house churches in Rome from dividing over debates about Jewish law. This is Paul's effort to return to Jerusalem with all of the Gentile churches behind him. This is Paul's one chance to garner support from the Roman churches for a mission to Spain. This is Romans, his greatest letter-essay, the most influential letter in the history of Western thought, and the singularly greatest piece of Christian theology. Now if Paul was opposed to women teaching men anytime and anywhere, why would he send a woman

---

22. Cohick, *Women*, 305.

23. Philip B. Payne, *Man and Woman, One in Christ* (Grand Rapids: Zondervan, 2009), 62.

24. Michael F. Bird, *Bourgeois Babes, Bossy Wives, and Bobby Haircuts* (Grand Rapids: Zondervan, 2012), 20 (emphasis original).

like Phoebe to deliver this vitally important letter and to be his personal representative in Rome? Why not Timothy, Titus, or some other dude? Why Phoebe?[25]

Phoebe was a competent woman of influence, an ally to Paul, who he was confident could represent his teaching. He wanted her to take the pizza out of the oven.

Phoebe is also described as a *prostatis*, or benefactor of many, including Paul. This is a leadership term, which "almost always refers to a position of authority."[26] Biblical scholar Philip Payne asserts, "Every meaning of every word in the NT related to the word Paul has chosen to describe Phoebe as a 'leader' (προστάτις) that could apply in Rom. 16:2 refers to leadership."[27] He points out Paul's usage of it earlier in the letter when Paul exhorted Christians to exercise their gifts in good stewardship, "If it is to *lead*, do it diligently" (Rom. 12:8 NIV, italics added). So it is surprising to see Paul placing himself under the patronage of a woman in such a patriarchal culture. Cohick explains how even in ancient culture there were areas of status where women had much influence. "For all its faults . . . the institution of patronage was in many respects gender-blind. As such, it allowed freedom of movement at most social levels for women to participate in the social, economic, and political environment without any cultural condemnation. Thus, while a woman might otherwise be stigmatized for speaking or acting publicly on economic, religious, or political matters, a patroness had liberty to exercise her ideas and interests with society's blessings."[28]

Cohick's emphasis on Paul's embracing of reciprocity as the key aspect of patronage is both God-glorifying and enlightening. In Paul's fashion, he turned the cultural model right-side-up so that we see God as the "ultimate Patron, and all Christians as his clients. Thus to place himself in the socially inferior role of a client to the Romans is not threatening, for he is also on a mission for God, which counterbalances

---

25. Bird, *Bourgeois Babes*, 21.
26. Payne, *Man and Woman*, 63.
27. Payne, *Man and Woman*, 62.
28. Cohick, *Women in the World*, 320.

the social equation. So too with Phoebe—her benefaction does imply her socially superior status. But her role as emissary (deacon) for Paul and the church at Cenchreae mitigates the harshness of the asymmetrical relationship."[29]

As Paul further demonstrated the fruit of reciprocity in his following greetings, we continue to see women laboring with him under the ministry. He first greeted Prisca (Priscilla in some versions) and Aquila, whom he called his "coworkers in Christ Jesus," noting how all the Gentile churches are grateful for this wife-and-husband team. Paul said they risked their own necks for his life. Then he greeted the whole church whom they hosted in their home. Again, we are seeing a woman as a patron, hosting the church. Throughout Scripture, we see Prisca and Aquila using their resources—material and theological—to better the lives of their brothers and sisters. We will examine this active couple in more detail in chapter 7. But I want to note the significance of Paul calling them coworkers or fellow workers. He called Urbanus a coworker in these greetings as well (v. 9), and later passed along Timothy's greeting to them, calling him his coworker (v. 21). Paul referred to himself and Apollos as God's coworkers (1 Cor. 3:9). It's a special term he used to describe specific people who were working synergetically with him to advance the gospel.[30]

Paul continued to show the fruit of Christ's gifts in the early church's life by showing coed labor, even giving special status to women. He used a special commendation for Mary, Tryphaena, Tryphosa, and Persis as women who worked very hard in the Lord (Rom. 16:6, 12). Paul often used the words "work hard" to describe his own ministry, as well as to characterize the labor of other preachers and teachers of the Word.[31] These were people putting their hands in the hot oven. They were equipped with the gospel and knew how to handle its truths in serving others. Payne points out that Paul even associated these hard

---

29. Cohick, *Women in the World*, 307.

30. See also 2 Cor. 1:24, 8:23; Phil. 4:2–3; Col. 4:10–11; 1 Thess. 3:2; Philem. 1:1, 24; 3 John 1:8.

31. See 1 Cor. 4:12; 15:10; 16:16; Gal. 4:11; Phil. 2:16; Col. 1:29; 1 Thess. 5:12–13; 1 Tim. 4:10; 5:10. This was first brought to my attention in Payne, *Man and Woman*, 67, and Kevin Giles, *What the Bible Actually Teaches on Women* (Eugene, OR: Cascade, 2018), 100.

workers with authority, "Now we ask you, brothers and sisters, to give recognition to those who labor [κοπιῶντας] among you and lead you in the Lord and admonish you, and to regard them very highly in love because of their work" (1 Thess. 5:12–13).[32]

And I haven't even gotten to the hotly debated doozy of a line where Paul said, "Greet Andronicus and Junia, my fellow Jews who have been in prison with me. They are outstanding among the apostles, and they were in Christ before I was" (Rom. 16:7 NIV). We will save that for another chapter. But suffice it to say, Paul's greetings at the end of his epistle to the Romans reveal the beautiful fruit of the work of the ministry. It is a portrait of coed laboring for the gospel as Christ is preparing his bride for eternity. And why wouldn't it be? The church isn't to be pointing to itself or even its leaders, because the church isn't an end to itself. We are preparing as we await our great consummation to behold the face of God and to enter holy communion with him in the new heavens and the new earth for eternity. Both man and woman praise Christ our Redeemer together! Therefore, we are to communicate, *make common*, the gospel of Jesus Christ together, so that all whom the Father gave to the Son will commune, *share, hold in common* with him. Again, I need to quote from my dear friend, Anna, who said it best:

> [Woman] stands not as an extension of Adam, but with Adam as bone of Christ's bone and flesh of Christ's flesh, having faithfully mirrored in this life in type and shadow what He has prepared for those who love Him. Stated otherwise, as God's diverse *ekklesia*, we stream together, shoulder to shoulder, side by side, to the city God has prepared for us because we belong to Him (body and soul, in life and in death). [We] belong to the Triune God Himself. Women and men were made for Him. To the extent that we overshadow that with our theology of women, we defraud God of the worship due Him and foster idolatry.[33]

---

32. See also 1 Cor. 16:16; Payne, *Man and Woman*, 67.
33. Anna Anderson, personal email.

This is why we are faithful to the ministers of the Word who serve us in our churches, "because they are God's means of directing our eyes to Himself and acclimating us to what awaits us."[34] And this is why ministers of the gospel will labor beside laymen and laywomen, equipping us to serve one another in preparation for that Great Day, so that we can reciprocate God's, our Great Patron's, generosity toward us.

QUESTIONS FOR GROUP DISCUSSION

1. How does the communication and communion in your church model a picture of the cosmos of the new heavens and the new earth?

2. Here is a text message I received on a Saturday evening last year: "We're gonna go do something instead of church tomorrow. Got a bunch of preaching today at the memorial service." How does this view of the church contrast with God's summons to corporate worship? And how does this mind-set contrast with the way God has ordained to prepare us for eternity?

3. Do you think there is any correlation between the lack of women academics and teachers in conservative seminaries and Dr. Hobbs's findings regarding the lack of women being addressed in preaching? Why or why not?

4. What are some practical ways in which your church leadership is already, or may need to begin, providing oven mitts to help laymen and laywomen take the pizza out of the oven?

5. In these things, are the women in your church utilized more as an extension of the male leadership, or as coworkers laboring side by side?

---

34. Anderson.

CHAPTER 6

THE GREAT DIVORCE THAT YOU DIDN'T SEE COMING

Where did you first hear the gospel? Many believers are brought to Christ through parachurch ministries. This is a wonderful thing. These organizations can often show the fruit of the ministry of the church by "coming alongside" in specific ways, such as in evangelizing; in serving college students who just left home and are asking deeper questions about life; in preparing pastors and Christian educators, missionaries, writers, and teachers through Christian colleges and seminaries; in publishing materials about the faith; and in serving the secular community through many means as salt and light. We have much to be thankful for with all the parachurch ministries available to us.

But a funny thing is happening. I was having a conversation with one woman who would consider herself a strong, committed Christian. I can testify that she does strive to live a godly life, raise her children in the faith, and grow in Christ. She proceeded to tell me that she loves to listen to the sermons of a popular Christian pastor, author, and speaker. That is fine, even as some of us are embarrassed to admit that we favor some so-called celebrity pastors. Except my friend made the odd comment that she considers *him* her pastor. Now, she doesn't go to this man's church. She doesn't live anywhere near it. She's never met the guy. And the pastor of the church she does go to can preach. But even though she regularly attends the local church, she doesn't really think she needs it because she has this celebrity pastor's sermons available to her. In her mind the church may need her, but she can do pretty well without it.

Additionally, I've heard many people say they are "discipling" another person. This is often not even a person who goes to their church. I wonder what they mean when they use that word detached from the ordinary means of grace that God has given us in his church? How do they view discipleship?

How do the members in your church view discipleship? Where do they look to for discipleship? What do they think their own contributions are? Parachurch organizations can surely benefit the church when used well. And through them we have access to all kinds of Christian books and materials that we think would be good to use to "disciple" people with. But we must not confuse parachurch organizations with the church. This is easy to do in our day with so much customized material at our fingertips.

If the church is to be preparing us for eternal communion with the triune God and one another, then it makes a lot of sense that Jesus commissions the church to make disciples. The church is the school of Christ, as Scott Swain and Michael Allen put it. They point to the words to the church from 1 John 2:27, "As for you, the anointing you received from [the Holy One] remains in you, and you don't need anyone to teach you. Instead, his anointing teaches you about all things and is true and is not a lie; just as it has taught you, remain in Him." "Because the anointing of Christ dwells within the church, the church is the school of Christ."[1] This is the context where *God* makes disciples, in his household, which faithfully retrieves the confessions of our faith and passes them down to the generations. Jesus gave his great commission to the church, under his authority, to "make disciples of all nations, baptizing them in the name of the Father and of the Son and of the Holy Spirit, teaching them to observe everything I have commanded you." And in this he promises, "And remember, I am with you always, to the end of the age" (Matt. 28:19–20).

---

1. Michael Allen and Scott R. Swain, *Reformed Catholicity: The Promise of Retrieval for Theology and Biblical Interpretation* (Grand Rapids: Baker, 2015), 18.

FRIEND TURNED LOVER?

Evangelical parachurch organizations have successfully joined forces across denominational lines to evangelize, to uphold some of the basic tenets of the faith that go under attack, such as the authority of Scripture, and to combat the promiscuous and biblically unfaithful message of the sexual revolution. This is praiseworthy. But in this a separation has been occurring right under the church's nose: that of the church and discipleship. There is another lover—the parachurch. It shouldn't be this way. We should be friends with the parachurch, but we should not confuse our relationship with the church and substitute it with the parachurch. Often it doesn't start out that way; the switcheroo may happen more subtly over time. Other times people are evangelized through a parachurch organization and do not realize their need for membership in a local church. Sadly, I've come across many *leaders* in parachurch organizations who do not even belong to a church!

John Webster reminds us that "the gospel is ecclesial"[2]; that is, the gospel is related to and connected to the church. But the popular mind-set is that while church is still recognized as important, the *real* ministry is taking place outside the church. In working with a parachurch organization, many believe they are going somewhere more real than the place they may or may not have participated in and left on Sunday morning. Parachurch is where the gospel *work* is happening. Parachurch is where the real action is. And yet, Webster explains, "the concrete forms of the church's attestation of the gospel are the proclamation of the Word and the celebration of the sacraments. In Word and sacraments, the church sets forth the presence and activity of the living Jesus Christ. . . . Word and sacrament are the church's visible acts which let God act."[3] Something very real is happening when God's people assemble for corporate worship. Here we are summoned by God to assemble together in his holy household and receive Christ

---

2. John Webster, *Confessing God: Essays in Christian Dogmatics II* (New York: Bloomsbury T&T Clark, 2016), 192.

3. Webster, *Confessing God*, 186, 187.

and all his blessings as we participate in his ordained liturgy. This is what his church does! Even within denominations that do not consider themselves liturgical, there is still some format of the basic elements of worship to which congregants are called to participate. No matter the denomination, "the church is the form of common human life and action which is generated by the gospel to bear witness to the perfect word and work of the triune God."[4] Let's not mistake the parachurch—something auxiliary—for the real thing. The church is commissioned to spread the good news of salvation in Jesus Christ, who is the only way to fulfill our eternal purpose to love God and one another, making disciples of Christ.

WHY DISCIPLESHIP IS LEAVING THE CHURCH

How did discipleship become so associated with the parachurch? Sometimes we are shocked to hear of a married couple splitting. They seemed like such a good couple. Everything looked so right about them. But we may learn that although they are active in the circles we may encounter them in, their common life behind the closed doors of their household has become lifeless. As the loneliness of not being known creeps in, one of the spouses may feel like their contributions are not needed or are unappreciated. This can happen in a church as well. As we uphold the primary means of ministry that God gave his church, what should the common life and action look like in God's household? What does it look like in your church—like Romans 16? Church is our home base. We are affected by our time together in corporate worship. This should generate an outgoing household of believers who continuously serve one another.

Maybe there is more behind my friend's considering a celebrity pastor as her own and her involvement in parachurch ministries. She is someone with a desire to help lead women, as well as a strong reciprocal voice in learning with men, but has not found where she fits in. While the gospel is faithfully preached in her church, there isn't much life

---

4. Webster, *Confessing God*, 175.

flowing from the church. The leaders have their meetings and serve the needs that arise, but the members don't really function as brothers and sisters with household obligations. They greet one another on Sunday morning, chat a little after the service, and are on their way back to *real* life. The church is getting by but not growing to maturity. My friend has a hunger to learn and contribute but has not been invested in. If those who have been called and authorized to shepherd her soul have not recognized this hunger and potential in her, then it must not feel any different to her to call someone her pastor who does not have the responsibility to know her and shepherd her. Consequently, she has gone rogue and developed her own ministry to others that isn't connected to her church. And while she uses parachurch resources (often products from her favorite pastor's ministry), she views her spiritual vocation as one who individually disciples others.

While not as many are ambitious enough to go rogue, many women have given up trying to grow and serve in their local churches, as they have more opportunities to learn, teach, write, and speak in parachurch organizations. As I've looked under the hood of many of these organizations, I would say my friend is perhaps taking their claims about discipleship to their natural conclusions. If we can look to another community besides our local church for discipleship, why can't we just look to individual people?

One popular parachurch ministry boasts that it has reached one million women, and we can help them reach the next million. The IF:Gathering attracts thousands of women to their conferences and has equipped more than seven thousand local leaders with their programs and resources. They state their mission on their website: "We exist to equip women with gospel-centered resources, events, and community so they may learn more about who God is and disciple other women right where they are." The first thing you see on their About page is a picture of women singing together with "Discipleship is what we're about" in large letters across the screen.[5] Now, I would not say that these leaders are directly telling women to use their parachurch

---

5. IF:Gathering website, founder Jennie Allen, www.ifgathering.com/about.

ministry in place of church. But this mission, and their success, reveals that no one is noticing that discipleship belongs to the church.

But this isn't only a trend for women. Men too have their favorite Christian preachers and ministries that they look to for their primary teaching. So do pastors-in-training. A seminary professor once told me that he asked his class who their favorite preacher was, and not one of them mentioned their own pastor. Not only that, but none of them may have even met the pastors they named, as they were all celebrity pastors. Church leaders, laypeople, and parachurch ministries need to stop and ask what our responsibilities are and how God's people are discipled.

When churches do not reintroduce Christ's teaching in light of the challenges of the secular culture, the challenges within the church itself, and the many questions of application that its men, women, and children have, then congregants look elsewhere for answers. This is all part of equipping the saints in discipleship. Parachurch often excels in addressing these issues. I am not trying to paint parachurch resources as the bad guy here. I work for some parachurch groups and am thankful for all the benefits I receive through parachurch organizations. I am saying that it's time to have a "define the relationship" talk. I'm also aiming to provide a wakeup call for church officers. Where do the people entrusted to your care look for discipleship? IF:Gathering? The Gospel Coalition? Christians for Biblical Equality? The Council for Biblical Manhood and Womanhood? Ligonier Ministries? LifeWay? The Ethics and Religious Liberty Commission? Tim Challies? Livestream services from another church? A Facebook group they belong to? Community Bible study? Their favorite podcast? You? Paul? Apollos? We need to be lovingly confronted with the truth of God's Word if we are looking for discipleship in all the wrong places.

We are disciples of Christ. God is the one who causes the growth, and he promises to give us Christ in the ordinary means of grace. He has given his church officers to plant and to water with his Word, nourishing the body, "for the perfecting of the saints, for the work of the ministry, for the edifying of the body of Christ" (Eph. 4:12 KJV). What happens in the church when it is no longer viewed by its members as the place and context in which they are discipled?

WHAT HAPPENS WHEN PARACHURCH MAKES DISCIPLES

The parachurch's discipleship methods are different from the church's. Rather than the passing down of the apostolic traditions and ministering Christ to us through ordinary means of grace and church accountability, the parachurch has often embraced a Biblicist method of teaching Scripture. Biblicists rightly uphold the authority of Scripture but often read the Bible with a narrow, flat lens of interpretation, zooming in on the words in the texts themselves while missing the history, context, and confessing tradition of the faith. Biblicists emphasize proof texting over a comprehensive biblical theology. What often happens unintentionally is that the Biblicist readers become their own authority, since they often don't notice they are also looking through their own lens of preconceived theological assumptions. Indeed, this is something we all need to be aware of in our Bible interpretation. The troubling teaching of biblical manhood and womanhood has thrived under this rubric of popular Biblicist interpretive methods.

I demonstrated this in chapter 4. The unorthodox teaching of the eternal subordination of the Son was conceived by Biblicist interpretive methods. Rather than a more systematic approach of stepping back from the words of the text "to consider the One who is present in the entirety of the text"[6] and what we can know about him from all of Scripture, and without retrieving what has been faithfully handed down to us from centuries of the Holy Spirit's work through tradents of the faith, Biblicists employ a fundamentalist approach to God's Word that doesn't take into account how the church and the Scriptures go hand in hand. Biblicists believe that since the Bible is the authoritative Word of God, then all they need to look to is their Bible to understand what God wants to say to them. But that begs the question of how we read our Bibles.

Our Bibles aren't like other books. When we read a regular book, we are the higher being, in a sense. We are opening up this bound paper and rationally engaging with it. But Scripture is the living Word of God

---

6. D. Glenn Butner Jr., *The Son Who Learned Obedience* (Eugene, OR: Pickwick, 2018), 8.

to his people: "We are instead rational subjects addressed by the divine Subject and called to loving attention and fellowship."[7] It is indeed amazing and glorious that God makes himself known truly, though not exhaustively, to us, his creatures. He does this through his Word, preached to us, made visible to us in the sacraments of baptism and the Lord's Supper that ratify his promises, and in our own reading of it.

Our Reformation cry, "Scripture alone," does not mean that Scripture is alone.[8] It also does not mean that we read it alone, isolated from the community of faith and our historical confessions. Even when we *are* alone studying Scripture or having our devotional time, we read Scripture in the context of our "interpretive communities,"[9] that is, communities that influence us in how we read Scripture. Kevin Vanhoozer additionally uses Michael Polanyi's term "fiduciary framework," which is "an interpretive framework that one takes initially on faith until it proves itself by yielding a harvest of understanding."[10] And even when we affirm the Reformation cry, "Faith alone," we know it is not a faith that is alone. "'Faith alone' means that individual interpreters had best attend to the authoritative apostolic testimony (the primary fiduciary framework) as read in the context of the church (a second fiduciary framework)."[11] Therefore, even though it may sound good, Biblicist does not mean biblical.

If parachurch organizations are making disciples, they are taking the position of a primary interpretive community. Parachurch ministries are often minimally confessional, as they operate as a coalition of denominational affiliations that unite for a common conviction. While they often have "What We Believe" statements so that we can see some of the core doctrines their leaders align with, and some develop their own confessional documents, the whole approach to discipleship and

---

7. Scott Swain, *Trinity, Revelation, and Reading* (New York: T&T Clark, 2011), 7.

8. See Kevin Vanhoozer, *Biblical Authority after Babel: Retrieving the Solas in the Spirit of Mere Protestant Christianity* (Grand Rapids: Brazos, 2016), 111.

9. See Vanhoozer, *Biblical Authority*, 100–103.

10. Vanhoozer, *Biblical Authority*, 100. See also Michael Polanyi, *Personal Knowledge: Towards a Post-Critical Philosophy*, corrected ed. (Chicago: University of Chicago Press, 1962), 266.

11. Vanhoozer, *Biblical Authority*, 102.

Scripture reading can easily become untethered from the means God has given his people.

Tension arises when parachurch organizations mimic the church's discipleship practices. Parachurch organizations are not ecclesial. They do not have the same responsibilities and promises attached to them as churches do. They do not govern with elders or bishops, but usually follow a business model with some sort of board. And yet complementarian parachurch organizations mimic their churches with an all-male board. We must ask, what are their convictions in doing this? Why are women prohibited from being on a parachurch board with no ecclesial authority? Additionally, many parachurch conferences mimic church worship services. For this reason, in complementarian parachurch organizations, women are often not invited or permitted as keynote speakers. And yet, although there may be powerful singing, prayer, and messages from the Word, there is usually no call to worship, no confession of sin, no assurance of pardon, no baptism, no Lord's Supper, and no benediction, and the assembly is not under any ecclesial oversight by shared elders. This is all very confusing. Are only male disciples able to share and communicate God's Word to other disciples? Complementarian parachurch organizations promote a male culture that prohibits reciprocity. This is why there are so many lucrative women's parachurch ministries—they are how Christian women finally get to contribute.

The church needs to reform and renew how we look at discipleship, as well as the contribution of women in discipleship. Discipleship is the church's commission. Parachurch organizations do not make disciples. Individual people do not make disciples. God makes disciples through the ministry and, as a fruit of that, through the men and women tradents in his church. This is an important distinction because it affects the way we view discipleship, read our Bibles, and relate to one another. Distinguishing the parachurch from the church is important so that we do not end up with functional ministers and teachers who do not have any means of accountability in shepherding our souls. When we put the parachurch organizations in proper perspective, we can then enjoy the benefits they offer with discernment and responsibility.

THE COVENANTAL CONTEXT OF DISCIPLESHIP

If the gospel is ecclesial, then there is a covenantal context to discipleship. In chapter 5 I discussed the church's mission to communicate, *make common*, the gospel of Jesus Christ, so that all whom the Father gave to the Son will commune, *share, hold in common*, with him. This is what discipleship is all about. So when Jesus gives the commission to make disciples, he tells them how to do that by "*baptizing* them in the name of the Father and of the Son and of the Holy Spirit," and "*teaching* them to observe everything I have commanded of you" (Matt. 28:19–20, italics added). He then promises to be with them. In Christian baptism we are recognized as having the sign and seal of God's covenant people. Disciples of Christ are initiated into a covenant family. We are baptized within the covenant community of our church, and this marks the church's responsibility to teach us—not some—but all Christ commanded. It also marks our responsibility to learn as disciples.

Disciples learn under someone. Christians are disciples of Christ. In rabbinic culture it was a big commitment and big deal to be a disciple of a prominent rabbi. It didn't merely mean that you were a student of the rabbi; it meant you were to commit to observing everything about the rabbi. You would be with him all the time. And the aim was that you would then become a teacher with your own disciples. Hans Kvalbein elaborates on how this practice changed for followers of Christ. "Jesus had a unique position that couldn't be transferred to his disciples."[12] "But you are not to be called 'Rabbi,' because you have one Teacher, and you are all brothers and sisters" (Matt. 23:8). No matter how great a pastor or theological academic you are, you are not to have disciples. We are all Christ's disciples, brothers and sisters who learn under Christ. But he does expect us to make his teaching common, and to share, hold in common, with him and each other. "The name 'disciples' reminds us that the church from the beginning

---

12. Hans Kvalbein, "Go Therefore and Make Disciples . . . The Concept of Discipleship in the New Testament," *Themelios* 12.1 (January/February 1988): 49, https://s3.amazonaws.com/tgc-documents/journal-issues/13.2_Kvalbein.pdf.

was the 'school' of Jesus. Therefore the teaching function must be very important in the church. But the only real teacher is Jesus himself. The church is basically a fellowship of his students."[13]

So Christians are initiated into a covenant community, and God communicates with us through covenant. We can think of Scripture as a sort of covenant treaty. Our mighty King, who has delivered us from the curse of sin, reveals himself to us and defines our relationship in his living Word. But it's more than that. He has established a covenantal relationship with his people. Scott Swain highlights the importance of the Trinitarian and covenantal context in understanding and interpreting Scripture. He says, "The Bible is one of the preeminent means whereby the triune God communicates himself to us and holds communion with us. And biblical interpretation is one of the preeminent means whereby we draw upon the riches that God has covenanted to us in Christ and whereby we hold communion with him."[14] Thus it is vital for laypeople, not only for academics and church officers, to take Bible interpretation seriously if we want to hold communion with the triune God.

Of course, God's communication with us is more than on paper. "Communication in its deepest sense is a matter of self-giving, a 'making common' of one's life."[15] So, as Swain explains, this communication, this "making common" is more than words, but it certainly isn't less! Building on this, Fred Sanders writes, "There is no surer way to strip the doctrine of the Trinity of all its significance and desiccate most of its interest than to treat it as a transferral of a set of facts about God that were revealed for their own sake as mere information."[16] We don't merely read God's Word to scratch an intellectual itch or even to learn virtue, but to know the One who knows all and who is Goodness. "The triune God communicates not only information but life and energy as well, through Word and Spirit."[17] God powerfully communicates with

---

13. Kvalbein, "Go Therefore," 49.

14. Swain, *Trinity*, 7.

15. Swain, *Trinity*, 8.

16. Fred Sanders, *The Triune God* (Grand Rapids: Zondervan, 2016), 70–71.

17. Kevin J. Vanhoozer, *Remythologizing Theology: Divine Action, Passion, and Authorship* (New York: Cambridge University Press, 2010), 177.

his life-giving Word by the Spirit to commune with us, to be friends with us, to "include us in the blessed life of communication and communion that he is."[18] Swain directs us to 1 John 1:3, "What we have seen and heard we also declare to you, so that you may also have fellowship with us; and indeed our fellowship is with the Father and with his Son Jesus Christ" as a mission statement of sorts for Scripture.[19]

The triune God communicates his life to us and holds communion with us through the means of his covenant. We are not disciples who try to move into the position of our Teacher, but we are disciples who become friends with him and strive for others to savingly know him too. Even though we do not become the Teacher, we are changed by knowing him. We are new creations in whom God himself dwells by his Holy Spirit. And as disciples are formed and grow in his church, we are then sent back into the world with a benediction as we mediate God's presence to the watching world. But even when we leave the holy people and holy place[20] of our covenant community in worship, we are so shaped by this interpretive community that we are not to consider our private reading of Scripture and opportunities to communicate Christ's Word to others as detached from the discipling work God is doing in us through his church.[21]

READING IS A COMMUNAL ENTERPRISE

Even in our private devotions, we don't read God's Word alone. Sure, in one sense we are physically alone when we spend time in the Word privately. This can be intimidating for a lot of laypeople. Combine the sacred nature of the Bible, the vast amount of history it covers,

---

18. Swain, *Trinity, Revelation, and Reading*, 16.

19. Swain, *Trinity*, 16.

20. See Michael Horton, *Holy People and Holy Place: A Covenant Ecclesiology* (Louisville, KY: Westminster John Knox, 2008).

21. See also Scot McKnight's "contention . . . that evangelicalism has a 'salus extra ecclesiam.' That is, if RCatholicism has taught 'nulla salus extra ecclesiam' (no salvation outside the church), evangelicalism's individualism has created a salvation without the church. . . . What we need more of is a gospel that summons folks into the Church as the worshipping, fellowship, missioning Body of Christ" (Scot McKnight, "Gospel and Church," *Jesus Creed* [blog], Patheos, September 26, 2006, www.patheos.com/blogs/jesuscreed/2006/09/26/gospel-and-church/).

the different literary genres, Bible translations, covenants, and difficult passages, and studying Scripture can feel like an overwhelming task. Maybe that is why so many don't even bother. They feel like they need a Bible college or seminary degree to properly understand it.

Or maybe that's why many evangelical teachings have reduced Bible reading into more of a mystical counseling session, as if all we have to do is carve out some "quiet time" with God, summon his Holy Spirit to speak to us in a special way, maybe while reading a short excerpt from Scripture, leaving us with a good feeling and a message that will make our day more meaningful. Otherwise intelligent people succumb to the mind-set that we are just an empty page waiting to be filled each day, and the work of the Holy Spirit becomes trivial.

Of course, many people do dive in, taking Scripture reading to a deeper level of study. Thankfully, many resources are available to assist us. And yet it is easy to fall into a Biblicist approach in private study. Sometimes the doctrine of the priesthood of all believers can mislead well-intended Christians into thinking they are little ministers of a sort, making disciples from the insights they glean from personal Bible study.

What laypeople need to understand is that our time alone in Scripture is connected to our time with our brothers and sisters sitting under the preached Word. Church leadership should be helping us to understand that we aren't disconnected individuals, detached from the whole history of the communion of the saints. Our individual understanding is shaped by the continual ordinary preaching of the Word and faithful discipleship in our churches. This is why dogmatics, the teaching of our churches, is important for laypersons. We care about the preservation of orthodox Christian teaching throughout the history of our faith.

The doctrine of the priesthood of all believers has been sabotaged. Kevin Vanhoozer reminds us that "far from being a pathology that accords authority to autonomous individuals, the royal priesthood of all believers—briefly, the notion that all church members are ministers of God's Word—is actually part of the pattern of authority, indeed, part of a triune economy of authority. *'Royal' signals authority,* '*priesthood*' *signals interpretive community;* '*all believers*' *signals that individuals are not autonomous agents but citizens of the gospel.*" With all the buzz about authority in evangelical circles these days, it seems we are misplacing the "principle of authority (the Triune God speaking in the Scriptures)" and the "pattern of authority, which is to say the pattern of interpretive authority, an economy that identifies Jesus Christ alone as king but accords pride of interpretive place to his royal priesthood." And so Vanhoozer emphasizes, "*The church alone is the place where Christ rules over his kingdom and gives certain gifts for the building of his living temple.*"[22]

So what interpretive communities are we placing ourselves in? What influences from others' teachings impact our own so-called private judgment? Ironically, while we Protestants talk about how thankful we are to escape the trappings of Rome, many of us are looking outside of the church, to the parachurch, to form our theological interpretations, therefore creating our own quasi-magisterial authority—one that has no accountability or proper mode of retrieving the faith of our fathers and continually reforming our confessions to Scripture. We have what's been dubbed "evangelical popes"—favorite celebrity pastors who often become infallible in our eyes.

Who is in your room with you during your quiet time? This is a vital question that is often left out when we talk about Bible interpretation. Yes, the Holy Spirit is with us, and his role is fundamental in our Bible interpretation. But if we want to follow the Spirit, then we must not ignore the way he works and the gifts he has given to the church. God did not leave us to an isolated reading of his Word while we desperately grasp for spiritual illumination of the text. The encounter Philip had with the Ethiopian eunuch in Acts 8:26–40 is a good illustration of this. Philip ran up and heard him reading Isaiah the prophet, and said, "'Do you understand what you are reading?' 'How can I,' he said, 'unless someone guides me?' So he invited Philip to come up and sit with him" (Acts 8:30–31).

---

22. Kevin J. Vanhoozer, *Biblical Authority after Babel: Retrieving the Solas in the Spirit of Mere Protestant Christianity* (Grand Rapids: Brazos, 2016), 29 (italics original).

For Christians, reading is an inherently communal enterprise . . .
for the same reasons that Christianity is a communal enterprise.
God's purpose in the covenant of grace is not simply to reconcile
individual persons to himself. When God reconciles individual
persons to himself in the covenant of grace, he also binds those
persons to other persons, creating a new humanity and interde-
pendent body (Eph. 2:11–20; 1 Cor. 12:12). . . . The knowledge
of the gospel's God is a knowledge obtained and sustained "with
all the saints" (Eph. 3:18; cf. 2 Tim. 3:14–15). For this reason,
the Christian reader of Holy Scripture finds her place as a reader
among the company of those who have been brought from death
to life by the Word of God, gathered together in a common fellowship under the Lord's guidance and teaching, and equipped by the
Lord to instruct and edify one another in the shared faith.[23]

Affirming that the church is a "creature of the Word"[24] and that
Scripture is the supreme authority over the church, Michael Allen and
Scott Swain also remind us that the church is the subordinate servant,
divinely authorized to serve Holy Scripture. This is God's gift to us.
"The church is that community created and authorized by the Word
of God in order that it might obediently guard, discern, proclaim, and
interpret the Word of God."[25] While we have the gift of authorized
ministers, the whole church is made up of active traditioners, parents
instructing children, congregants singing together in public worship,
Christians edifying our neighbors and encouraging and exhorting our
brothers and sisters in the faith.

When I sit down to read my Bible, I remember that I am not alone.
The Scripture is not alone either. I'm not only depending on the Spirit
to work in me for that moment; I know that he has been working in the
church universal through the centuries, preserving orthodox profession

---

23. Allen and Swain, *Reformed Catholicity*, 99–100.

24. Allen and Swain, *Reformed Catholicity*, 100, quoting from Christoph Schwöbel, "The
Creature of the Word: Recovering the Ecclesiology of the Reformers," in *On Being the Church:
Essays on the Christian Community*, ed. Colin Guntin and Daniel Hardy (Edinburgh: T&T
Clark, 1989), 110–55.

25. Allen and Swain, *Reformed Catholicity*, 102.

and testifying to the truth of God's Word. I know he is working in my local church, participating in this retrieval and reformation, looking back to the church universal and "translat[ing] it into our new cultural contexts, thus enlarging our understanding of its achievement."[26] I am thankful for the public reading and interpretation of Scripture in my church and for our orthodox confessions being faithfully handed down, serving as guardrails for me as I read.

We reap the fruit of our interpretive community. The public teaching of the Word shapes our private reading. Scripture is a covenantal text, so Swain concludes, "Reading is therefore a living *conversation* between an eloquent Lord and his attentive servants, a conversation in which the reader is summoned to hear what the Spirit of Christ *says* to the churches (Rev. 2.7)."[27]

While we may not get that mystical feeling during our devotion time or when we leave church after worship, we still hold an expectation that something is supposed to happen. Does one sermon or devotion change us? Sometimes, but it's the continual meeting together under the Word and sacraments, the continual receiving of God's means of grace, the continual benedictions of blessing and call to bear fruit, and continual personal time spent in the Word that truly shapes us.

PEEL AND REVEAL

There is a reason why we confess certain creeds and confessions together in our churches. While parachurch organizations are formulating new statements, there's a reason why these are usually not part of a church liturgy. The church is the context where God makes disciples—in his household—which faithfully retrieves the confessions of our faith, reforms them to Scripture, and passes them down through the generations. We need to be mindful to keep that priority for both men and women.

I explained how easy it is to look outside of the church when we

---

26. Vanhoozer, *Biblical Authority*, 25.
27. Swain, *Trinity*, 139.

don't feel invested in as disciples, when we aren't being trained well to mature in the faith, and when we are stifled in contributing as active traditioners and reciprocal voices. However, both men and women are frequently placed in rooms with yellow wallpaper in the parachurch as well. Parachurch often reinforces bad gender tropes, outfitting and amplifying many of the divisions between men and women in the church. Men's and women's ministries have become a marketable enterprise for publishers, conferences, and websites.[28] And it's interesting to note the contradiction between the individualistic culture in which the biblical manhood and womanhood movement is thriving with its Biblicist interpretive methods, and the traditional values of family and community that CBMW is trying to uphold.

When parachurch organizations such as CBMW develop their own confessional statements, we need to ask if they are replacing the church as an interpretive community in this way. We need to be mindful that parachurch confessional statements can easily function as platforms to be used to push their own propaganda. "As a form of withheld truth, propaganda can be 90 percent true. It's the deceptive 10 percent that gets you."[29] For example, in chapter 4 we looked at the usage of the word *role* in the Danvers Statement. At first glance it appears as if CBMW is helping the church provide a biblical case in response to the rampant sexual revolution of our contemporary culture. Differentiation between the sexes is affirmed. Faithfulness between a man and woman in marriage is affirmed. It's easy to miss that a word derived from the theater that is supposed to mean "playing a part" has been transformed to refer to an ontological creational norm that women are subordinate to men. From this, CBMW has produced many books, conferences, Bible study materials, and resources, for men's and women's ministries have adapted this language. The tropes signify that biblical men are the leaders and

---

28. Consider the endless pink devotionals marketed to women for their "quiet time." Women are a major target market for publishers because we are reading almost twice as much as men. For more information on women's ministry as a commodity, see Aimee Byrd, *No Little Women: Equipping All Women in the Household of God* (Phillipsburg, NJ: P&R, 2016), 113–33.

29. Sue Ellen Browder, *Subverted: How I Helped the Sexual Revolution Hijack the Woman's Movement* (San Francisco: Ignatius, 2015), 14.

initiators, the sex with virility, and the decision makers. Biblical women are submissive, quiet, tenders of the home, and, overall, affirmers for these masculine leaders. As Virginia Woolf put it, "Women have served all these centuries as looking-glasses possessing the magic and delicious power of reflecting the figure of man twice its natural size."[30]

When some of these developments began to be questioned as the Trinity Debate exposed how some leaders were using this ontological subordinate language to describe the Father, Son, and Holy Spirit, CBMW slipped into the background for a while. They shuffled their leadership but still promoted the same teachers. They said that those with different views of the Trinity were welcome in their parachurch umbrella.[31] They did not recant their previous teaching of ESS. And they continued to use this word *role* as an ontological category distinguishing men and women. After briefly taking a back seat, they saw an additional opportunity to speak to the culture with another confession. The Nashville Statement[32] calls the church to faithful witness to God's purposes for human sexuality. It currently has more than twenty-two thousand signatures. Institutions as large as the Southern Baptist Theological Seminary have now adapted it, as well as adapting the Danvers Statement, as an official confessional statement to which their employees must subscribe.[33] "At its Stated Meeting on October 25, 2018, Calvary Presbytery approved an overture asking the 47th General Assembly of the Presbyterian Church in America to declare the Council on Biblical Manhood & Womanhood's 'Nashville Statement' on Biblical Sexuality as a Biblically Faithful Declaration."[34]

---

30. Virginia Woolf, *A Room of One's Own* (New York: Harvest, 1989), 35.

31. See Denny Burk, "My Take-Away's [*sic*] from the Trinity Debate," *Denny Burk* (blog), August 10, 2016, www.dennyburk.com/my-take-aways-from-the-trinity-debate/.

32. "The Nashville Statement," CBMW, https://cbmw.org/nashville-statement/.

33. Andrew J. W. Smith, "Southern Seminary Adopts Nashville Statement as Official Confessional Document," Southern News, Southern Baptist Theological Seminary, October 10, 2017, http://news.sbts.edu/2017/10/10/southern-seminary-trustees-vote-adopt-nashville -statement-official-confessional-document/.

34. Written by staff, "Calvary Presbytery Overtures the 47th PCA GA to 'Declare the "Nashville Statement" on Biblical Sexuality as a Biblically Faithful Declaration,'" The Aquila Report, November 28, 2018, www.theaquilareport.com/calvary-presbytery-overtures-the-47th-pca-ga-to -declare-the-nashville-statement-on-biblical-sexuality-as-a-biblically-faithful-declaration/.

It was passed during the 2019 Presbyterian Church in America General Assembly, with the resolve to "refer the 'Nashville Statement' to the Committee on Discipleship Ministries for inclusion and promotion among its denominational teaching materials."[35] There is more and more pressure to sign this statement, with consequences of losing one's job for those who have objections.

Is this statement something to which our churches should subscribe? I share CBMW's concerns for speaking out against the damage and pain caused by the sexual revolution. I share their zeal for promoting holiness and making known the good news of redemption in Christ available to all. But as I read the fourteen articles, I find that some serious questions are still unanswered. The impact from the Trinity Debate, in which CBMW was of central concern, and the teachings on masculinity and femininity that have been taught from their website, at their conferences, and by their most well-known leaders, still haven't been dealt with.

Seeing CBMW lead the way in retracting the unorthodox, harmful teaching that came from their own movement and leaders would have been relieving. It would have been a great display of leadership at this opportune time to clearly promote teaching that doesn't reduce men and women to stereotypes. But this was not the case. And now we have this new statement, which only provokes more questions.

What does CBMW mean by "divinely ordained differences between male and female" in article 4? The words themselves seem agreeable enough. But CBMW hasn't retracted their teaching on eternal subordination of women by God's design. Just a year before releasing the Nashville Statement, sessions from their conference "The Beauty of Complementarity"[36] connected ESS/EFS to complementarianism in an ontological context of authority and submission. And also just a year before, they promoted the release of then president Owen Strachan and Gavin Peacock's book, *The Grand Design*, which taught this very connection (and is endorsed by others also initially signing the Nashville Statement).

---

35. The Administrative Committee of the PCA, www.pcaac.org/wp-content/uploads/2018/11/Overture-4-Calvary-Nashville-Statement.pdf.

36. See https://cbmw.org/uncategorized/2016-cbmw-conference-media/.

And if this is not the case, then I have to wonder why include CBMW proponents of ESS who used this teaching in conjunction with masculinity and femininity, such as Wayne Grudem, Bruce Ware, and Owen Strachan, as initial signatories? It appears that this is still the accepted teaching. How else should we read it?

CBMW also hasn't retracted any of the hyperauthoritarian, hyper-machismo teaching about manhood and their hypersubmissive and stereotypical teaching about womanhood. Instead, I have seen much more of the same by some of their popular leaders. So once again, I wonder if this is what applies to their "divinely ordained differences"?

Are these divinely ordained differences ultimately expressed in sex and marriage and authority and submission? The statement says nothing about friendship. God didn't design the two sexes only for marriage. What about how we were designed for the new heavens and the new earth? Where's the brother/sister language? How do men and women relate to one another in general? This is an important part of our sexuality that carries over into our eternal bodies when we will not marry. The church needs to speak more into how we were created for communion with the triune God and with one another in platonic—intimate but nonerotic—relationships. This too is a faithful witness against the sexual revolution and for promoting one another's holiness. And a great hope for those who suffer with same-sex attraction.

Others have noted the necessity for the parachurch to take care of its own house before making itself a guidepost for sexual ethics, especially one that is lacking in pastoral sensitivity needed to minister to those who are same-sex attracted and strive for holiness.[37] There are people for whom I have much respect who have signed the Nashville Statement. I am not trying to blacklist anyone or insinuate that everyone who signed or was involved in writing this has some sort of ESS agenda. But I am concerned that so much has been overlooked. CBMW wants to be our leading voice in what they call biblical manhood and womanhood. It's difficult not to see the Nashville Statement

---

37. See Mathew Lee Anderson, "Why I Won't Sign the Nashville Statement," *Mere Orthodoxy* (blog), August 30, 2017, https://mereorthodoxy.com/nashville-statement/.

as a rebranding of their same ontological authority/subordination teaching. No matter how many signatures they get, there's still the issue of whether an organization that continues to teach harmful stereotypes and promote unorthodox teachers that are not in line with Nicene Trinitarian doctrine should be a trusted source. I belong to a church that already subscribes to historically faithful orthodox confessions. I am thankful that I do not need to worry over signing additional statements with questionable theology.

REVEALING WHO IS EXHORTED TO TEACH

And so, with ongoing parachurch statements popping up, asking for signatories and subscription, we are left with some basic questions: Do men and women benefit equally from God's Word? Are they equally responsible for sharpening one another in the faith and passing down that faith to the next generation? Are there limits imposed on laywomen disciples in the church that are not so for laymen?

When we look to Scripture, we see both men and women addressed when it comes to teaching responsibilities of disciples in the church. And we do not need to look to just one isolated verse, for the New Testament features a theme of brothers and sisters in Christ called to serve as they are gifted, including teaching:

> Let the word of Christ dwell richly among you, in all wisdom teaching and admonishing one another through psalms, hymns, and spiritual songs, singing to God with gratitude in your hearts. (Col. 3:16)

> Although by this time you ought to be teachers, you need someone to teach you the basic principles of God's revelation again. You need milk, not solid food. (Heb. 5:12)

> According to the grace given to us, we have different gifts: If prophecy, use it according to the proportion of one's faith; if service, use it in service; if teaching, in teaching; if exhorting, in exhortation;

giving, with generosity; leading, with diligence; showing mercy, with cheerfulness. (Rom. 12:6–8)

But desire the greater gifts. And I will show you an even better way. (1 Cor. 12:31)

Pursue love and desire spiritual gifts, and especially that you may prophesy. (1 Cor. 14:1)

What then, brothers and sisters? When you come together, each one has a hymn, a teaching, a revelation, another tongue, or an interpretation. Everything is to be done for building up. (1 Cor. 14:26)

If the Bible and the church go hand in hand, then our confessions need to have a systematic congruency with the Scriptures. Laywomen in the Scriptures are not addressed as subordinate to laymen. Like their brothers in the faith, they too are encouraged to seek the greater gifts and to mature in their knowledge of the faith so they can teach others. There's no qualifier in these verses, saying that men are not to learn from women or that women are only to teach their own sex and children. Any divinely ordained differences that men and women have do not prohibit women from teaching. It would be disobedient to Scripture to withhold women from teaching.

FRIENDS DON'T LET FRIENDS MASQUERADE

Returning to the function and administration of parachurches, applying a blanket of male authority to parachurch organizations, such as seminaries or conferences, that are missing essential elements of the worship liturgy diminishes the authority of the office of the ministry. These parachurch institutions do not have the office of elder to shepherd God's people, a call to worship, a pastor who is faithfully preaching expositional sermons over long periods of time, a congregational prayer, confession and assurance of pardon, sacraments administered, or a benediction giving God's blessing to his people and calling them to service in the world. We should not confuse the authority given to church officers with the authority of board members. We should not confuse the worship service, where God promises to bless us in Christ, with the classroom or the conference stage.

By defining the terms of our relationship, the church and the parachurch can be friends again. But these are all issues that we need to work through. The distinctives of a local church and denomination are not barriers to separate us, but platforms on which we can stand and from which we can communicate to be up front about our biblical convictions as a body as well as to be sharpened by Christians from other churches. This is why it's also helpful to distinguish between primary doctrinal issues, secondary issues, and even third-order issues of differences.[38] Primary doctrines are what Christians confess to remain orthodox, such as the doctrine of God and what he has done for our salvation, the doctrine of man, and the doctrine of Scripture. Secondary issues, such as what we believe about baptism or ordination of women, may separate us in worship, but we still embrace one another as siblings in the faith. Third-order doctrines are differences such as our views on eschatology and the end times, that we may feel strongly about but should not be a barrier to worshiping together in the same church. The orthodox confessions of the faith are ones we do not budge on. But we sharpen one another with humility even as we may feel strongly about second- or third-order doctrines.

Churches can't do it all. Parachurch organizations can really be a friend in coming alongside the ministry of the church. Church officers can benefit from their many resources and even implement some of them in their teaching. But even as we utilize and incorporate helpful resources from parachurch organizations, the church needs to be careful that she is not outsourcing her discipling privileges and responsibilities. Let's be careful to keep the right perspective as we appreciate the ways the parachurch can help to serve the church and the outside

---

38. For a helpful article on this, see Albert Mohler, "A Call for Theological Triage and Christian Maturity," AlbertMohler.com, July 12, 2005, https://albertmohler.com/2004/05/20/a-call-for-theological-triage-and-christian-maturity-2/.

communities, remembering with discernment that they do it without the ecclesial oversight of elders.

What so easily can happen is that while parachurch organizations particularly market to men and women's ministries, people following them can consequentially develop their own functional ministers. The office of the ministry in the local church can easily be diminished and undermined, as men and women look to their favorite conference speakers, so called "disciple makers," authors, podcasters, online preachers, or Bible study teachers.

Churches can confess the Apostles' Creed and the Nicene Creed confidently, knowing that they have served the church faithfully for many generations over more than fifteen hundred years. One can contest a doctrine from these creeds, but they would be contesting what the church has affirmed as orthodox Christian teaching over the centuries. We should be extra careful with contemporary confessions put together quickly. Even a newer confession, such as the Westminster Confession, written more than three hundred fifty years ago to address additional doctrinal teaching of the church, took the assembly of divines five years to write. From that the Baptists adopted the Second London Baptist Confession (1689). The church uses other time-tested confessions to help in teaching, such as the Heidelberg Catechism or the Thirty-Nine Articles of Religion. These are all viewed as subordinate standards, that is, subordinate to the Bible, which is the supreme standard authority of the faith. But they are very helpful for churches to confess what they believe as it's connected to a historical body of confessing Christians.

In the present unreconciled state of the churches, evangelicals need to offer what they have received for their own traditions to the wider fellowship of the saints. They must do so without stridency or anxiety, with humble confidence and generosity, with attentiveness and a teachable bearing towards those from whom they find themselves separated by reason of confession. But these things can only happen if evangelicals take the time to reacquaint themselves with the deep exegetical and dogmatic foundations of the traditions to which they belong; and, more important still, they can only happen if evangelicals demonstrate the supreme ecumenical virtue of acknowledging that we also need to change. This, at least, the church in the Reformation tradition ought to know: *ecclesia reformanda, quia reformata.*[39]

Having been reformed, the church still needs to be reformed. And she will continue to need reforming to the Word until Christ returns for her.

Webster's words are a beautiful description of what parachurch could look like for us. But it's incumbent on Christians being discipled well in their churches and knowing the teaching of their church. Notice the ecclesial context in all the verses exhorting lay teaching above. We need to be learners who are then able to communicate God's Word well to others. We then mingle with our brothers and sisters from other churches and denominations with humble confidence and generosity.

QUESTIONS FOR GROUP DISCUSSION

1. What parachurch organizations and resources are popular among the members of your church? How can the leaders of the church help to implement these within the context of the church's responsibility to make disciples?

2. Is there a tendency in your church for laypeople to look to the parachurch for discipleship? Are there rogue disciple makers in your congregation? How can the leadership in the church be more intentional in their teaching to understand the church as the school of Christ? What are some ways to help your church to "define the relationship" between the church and the parachurch?

3. What does the common life and action look like in your church? What formal and informal teaching, learning, and serving opportunities are available as a fruit of the ministry of Word

---

39. Webster, *Confessing God*, 192.

and sacrament? Would the church members describe your church as an active, outgoing household of believers? What valid reasons might they have to look elsewhere for discipleship?

4. What challenges, coming from both the secular culture and the theological questions or disputes within the church, need to be addressed by your church? How can Christ's teaching be reintroduced and applied in these areas? Who are some thoughtful and mature men and women in your church who can be invested in and equipped well to help teach in these areas?

5. Do the laypeople in your church have a good understanding of the Trinitarian and covenantal context in interpreting Scripture? How can the leaders help the laypeople to recognize how they fit into a proper pattern of authority as a priesthood of believers and how this helps them to interpret and communicate Scripture? How can church leaders connect this recognition with helping congregants discern their primary interpretive community, creeds and confessions of the church, and be discerning within the parachurch organizations and resources they use? How can church members sharpen one another with this understanding of reading as a communal enterprise?

PART 3

RECOVERING THE RESPONSIBILITY OF EVERY BELIEVER

CHAPTER 7

IS THIS THE WAY IT WAS SUPPOSED TO BE?

Imagine you were having Jesus over for dinner tonight.[1] What in the world would you possibly prepare for him? One thing is for sure, you wouldn't use the store brand jar of spaghetti sauce. No, you might for the first time be thinking about the locally sourced meat and garden-fresh tomatoes to make some Italian dish that you've never heard of before, but thanks to Emeril Lagassé, you can pretend that it's old hat. Bottom line, you want everything to be perfect. And you want your family on best behavior so that your important company thinks that you all adore one another, practice the best manners, and talk about things in a mature way.

Well, let's rewind to the culture Mary and Martha lived in before Martha invited Jesus Christ to their house. And let's just stop and think about the invitation itself. At the very least, Martha views Jesus as an interesting rabbi at this point. It is difficult to get a clear picture of the life of women in ancient Jewish and Greco-Roman history, as the "published" literary works that we have are written by elite men, such as Ben Sira, Philo, and Josephus, portraying women according to their own ideology and convictions. If their prescriptive words were our only

---

1. Much of this section on Mary and Martha is taken from my talk at the Quakertown Women's Conference 2018, "Women at the Feet of Jesus," sponsored by the Alliance for Confessing Evangelicals and Grace Bible Fellowship Church, May 18–19, 2018, Grace Bible Fellowship Church, Quakertown, PA. Used with permission.

resource, the agency of women would have been very bleak. Indeed, Jewish women were not to socialize with men. Rabbis were not even to greet women on the streets. The word of the sages from the rabbinic oral tradition proclaims, "The wise men say: 'Who speaks much with a woman draws down misfortune on himself, neglects the words of the law, and finally earns hell.'"[2]

And we thought the Billy Graham Rule was strict! Here's a popular prayer by a rabbi, Eliezer, who lived at the turn of the first and second centuries, so not very long after the time of Jesus (keep in mind the contrast Paul gives in Galatians 3:28: "There is no Jew or Greek, slave or free, male and female; since you are all one in Christ Jesus"): "Praised be God that he has not created me a gentile; praised be God that he has not created me a woman; praised be God that he has not created me an ignorant man."[3]

In the portrayals that we see in "published" material, women were not to be conversation partners. They were left out of the intellectually and theologically stimulating social circles. And yet Martha invites Jesus into her home. And he accepts the invitation! This is scandalous on more than one level. Martha must have already known something about Jesus having a different teaching than his contemporary rabbis. Perhaps the "published," proscriptive texts do not give us a real-life, on-the-ground description of Jewish women. We can observe contrast between prescribed orthodoxy of gender relations and functional orthopraxy even in our own contemporary debates about men and women. For example, one complementarian leader laments that while many check off the box professing complementarian convictions, they actually live out functionally egalitarian marriages in their own homes.[4] So too the rebuttals and the harsh teachings regarding women's nature and activity might even be defensive measures against the

---

2. Mishnah, Aboth 1:5.

3. Tosefta, Ber. 7:18; Talmud, p. Ber. 13; b. Men. 43.

4. Russell D. Moore, "After Patriarchy, What? Why Egalitarians Are Winning the Gender Debate," *JETS* 49.3 (September 2006): 569–76, www.etsjets.org/files/JETS-PDFs/49/49-3/JETS_49-3_569-576_Moore.pdf. Also see Denny Burk, "Complementarianism or Patriarchy? What's in a Name?," *Denny Burk* (blog), June 7, 2012, www.dennyburk.com/complementarianism-or-patriarchy-whats-in-a-name/.

agency that they do see some women have in society and in religion. Historians looking at evidence from everyday living, such as receipts, personal letters, invitations, legal documents, or even architectural or burial inscriptions,[5] reveal a more complete and complex picture of women's contributions and interactions. Despite the "published" writings, we have evidence of women interacting and contributing in the home, society, and even in the synagogue. Other factors like status, location, and needs of the community factor into a woman's opportunities for education, commerce, and religious service.[6] Although, even in this more well-rounded picture, a woman's agency was typically circumscribed by men, be it her father, husband, guardian, or tutor.[7] Scripture doesn't tell us exactly what status Mary and Martha held in society, but it appears that they were single women who were well off enough to have the means to host people at their home.

And Martha is quite the liberal woman here. We are not yet introduced to Lazarus, their brother, and we don't see Jesus's disciples in this account. Maybe they were all there, but all we have in the picture are just two single women—and Jesus. What a guest to host!

Perhaps Martha brings Jesus home with her thinking about how shocking this is. Was Mary next to her when she invited him in? How excited was she that he said yes? "Mary, guess who *I* brought for dinner?!" We don't know. We often want to give Martha a bad rap for stressing out over her "woman's role" in the kitchen. But Martha shows us with this invitation that she is counterculturally capable.

Now it's time to whip up that Moroccan fish and crispy rice cake with saffron crust that she saved on her Pinterest board. It's not just going to be lentil stew and stuffed grape leaves for Jesus. (Okay, okay, maybe I'm being a little facetious about the menu.) While Martha surely wanted to be a good hostess, she notices that not only is Mary not dutifully helping her, modeling to Jesus what good women they

---

5. Many extant inscriptions are honorary "plaques" on buildings or statues acknowledging a woman's contribution.

6. See Lynn H. Cohick, *Women in the World of the Earliest Christians* (Grand Rapids: Baker, 2009).

7. See Cohick, *Women*, 322–23.

are, but that Mary really breaks with tradition by sitting at Jesus's feet—the position of a disciple who has made it to the inner circle! This is troubling. Jesus is teaching her, and Mary is absorbing every word. Not even bothering to say something to Mary; Martha says to Jesus, "Lord, don't you care that my sister has left me to serve alone? So tell her to give me a hand" (Luke 10:40).

What is Martha upset about here? Is it only that she is the one doing all the work? Jesus answers, "Martha, Martha, you are worried and upset about many things, but one thing is necessary. Mary has made the right choice, and it will not be taken away from her" (Luke 10:41–42). What are the many things? That the saffron crust will brown just right? Well, we do see that she is doing all the serving. That is one thing. But what else might she be worried about?

Let's look into a little more detail regarding this good part that Mary has chosen. Here is a rather long but enlightening excerpt from senior lecturer of Midreshet Ein ha-Natziv and the director of educational development at the Midrasha, Rachel Keren, regarding the attitudes toward Jewish women shortly after Jesus's death and resurrection:

> Throughout the generations, from the destruction of the Temple, Jewish creative and spiritual life revolved around Torah study. All forms of literary expression and spiritual creativity came from Torah study and their purpose was to enrich and deepen it. Jewish history throughout all those generations found expression in spiritual creativity, not in any other form (such as politics). From this we can deduce that women's exclusion from Torah study removed them from the heart of existence, and they were not considered important in passing on the heritage and tradition to future generations. Women had no part in the *bet midrash*, the center of spiritual creativity, or in the religious courts, the seat of the Jewish community's autonomy, because a rabbinic judge must have comprehensive Torah knowledge. Women did not serve in community positions because these roles were identified with knowledge of Torah. This exclusion affected their public image and we may assume that their self-image suffered similarly.

The Mishnah (*Sotah* 3:4) mentions a prohibition that reflects the various paradigms. The Tanna [Tanna: lit. (from Aramaic *teni*) "to hand down orally," "study," "teach." A scholar quoted in the Mishnah or of the Mishnaic era, i.e., during the first two centuries of the Common Era. In the chain of tradition, they were followed by the *amora'im*.] Eliezer ben Hyrcanus (end of the first to the beginning of the second century CE) expressed an extremely harsh opposition to women's Torah study: "Anyone who teaches his daughter Torah teaches her *tiflut*" (BT *Sotah* 21b) [bet midrash (bet ha-midrash): Houses of study (of Torah)]. The word *tiflut* is defined in two ways: 1) sexual license or lewdness. It is feared that the woman will learn how to outwit her husband and sin in secret; 2) The learning itself is considered blemished, an unnecessary thing (Rambam on the Mishnah: Vanity and nonsense) (Mishnah *Sotah* 3:4).

The Jerusalem Talmud (JT) notes the opinion of Eliezer ben Hyrcanus, the Tanna mentioned above: "Women's wisdom is solely in the spindle." He added, "The words of the Torah should be burned rather than entrusted to women" (JT *Sotah* 3:4, 19a).[8]

Rabbi Eliezer's was the accepted opinion until the modern age, with nuances and explanations added. As Ullah put it in the Babylonian Talmud, "Women are a nation unto themselves."[9]

Some rabbis encouraged teaching parts of the Torah to women so that they are morally accountable and know their place, but not for knowledge or love for the Torah itself. "However, the accepted paradigm is that most women, apart from exceptional ones, are incapable of study. Yet even the exceptional ones will not learn the full range of the world of Torah but only appropriate, relevant parts."[10]

So Martha sees what's going on here. She was pretty liberal in inviting Jesus over, but Mary is really stepping over the line. Martha is trying to be a good hostess, but Mary, well, she is getting downright embarrassing.

---

8. Rachel Keren, "Torah Study," Jewish Women's Archive, https://jwa.org/encyclopedia/article/torah-study.

9. b. Shabbat 62.

10. Keren, "Torah Study."

But Jesus's answer turns the tables. In essence he's saying, *You're not the host, Martha, I am. I didn't come for your Moroccan fish; I came for you. . . . "I have food to eat that you don't know about. . . . My food is to do the will of him who sent me and to finish his work"* (John 4:32, 34). *The privilege isn't in being able to serve me; I have come to serve you.*

Notice the significance of what Jesus says in these verses in Matthew. It's not that he's saying, "No, Mary gets to do this now," or in application, "Women are now able to learn and study theology too, if they're interested." No, he says this is *necessary*. It is necessary for Mary to learn his Word—to sit at his feet in the inner circle as his disciple. One thing is necessary. Expectations are turned upside down.

DOES THE CHURCH NOW THINK THE SAME WAY AS JESUS?

Do we think this urgently about women as disciples? This is the one necessary thing for us. Women too need to know Jesus. We need to sit at his feet, that is, do the things disciples do. This means that we must also *participate in creative and spiritual life in the church. We contribute literary expression and spiritual creativity. We must be in the heart of existence. We pass on the heritage of the tradition to future generations,* a most vital task. We are to *serve in roles that identify with knowledge of God's Word.* And *this inclusion will affect our public image.* If you were to ask the women in your church if they are a valued part of the household of God in these ways, what would they say? When outsiders to the faith look at your church, is this the image they see of the men and women there?

Although for contemporary Jewish women "the learning itself is considered blemished, an *un*necessary thing,"[11] Jesus says, *No, the learning, is* necessary, *because you are in my household, the church.* Although in the near future rabbis threaten to burn the words in the Torah before teaching them to women, Christ's Word will always remain. It does not go out void. Jesus doesn't end with saying one thing

---

11. Keren, "Torah Study" (emphasis).

is necessary and that Mary has chosen the good part. He adds, "It will not be taken away from her" (Luke 10:42). It's not going to happen. His kingdom values women.

Jesus didn't care about people whispering at the prospect of a rabbi entering the house of these two women. He didn't abide by Ben Sira or the ancient philosophers' teaching on male superiority and sex polarity. This man in their house is also the Creator of the universe and knows what these women were created for: eternal communion with the triune God and his people. There is no higher calling. There is no higher status. There is no freedom to be found in anything else. Reading between the lines, we understand Jesus's words as *Martha, I'm the one doing the serving right now. You didn't prevail on me to come in here. I prevailed on you and broke into your very heart and soul.* This can't be taken away!

Jesus values women. Women will travel with him, provide for him and his ministry, be healed by him, turn a whole town of enemies to him, and witness the gospel account of the crucifixion, burial, and resurrection. Women will be the first to share the gospel to the apostles and enter the upper room with them to pray. They will prophecy, plant the first churches with the apostles, help correct evangelists, colabor with the men in gospel work, host churches, and hand-deliver Scripture. This is what disciples do. This comes from sitting at Jesus's feet.

Because when we learn as Christ's disciples, we are responsible to live according to the truths we discover and teach them to others. That is what a disciple is supposed to do. Shall we bury and hide what the Lord gives us? It is necessary that women go to the feet of Jesus and learn from what he has revealed to us in his Word! He summons men and women every Sunday to gather with his people for worship and to receive his preached Word and sacraments. We don't come for the Moroccan fish; we come because this is the place and context in which we are promised to be blessed in Christ. Do we see Christ as the host on Sunday morning? We are fed by his Word, and we spiritually partake in a spiritual feast of his body and blood before we are sent back out into the world with a benediction. This is what brothers and sisters in Christ do when we come gather together in his household.

And yet even today we see people in the church trying to take this necessity away from women. Under the ostensible banner of "complementarianism" women are told they may learn alongside men but are to continuously be looking for, affirming, and nurturing male authority.[12] Many churches thus limit, in ways they do not limit for laymen, the capacity for laywomen to learn deeply and to teach. The consensus is that men are the necessary teachers in the church. While some give the nod for women to teach other women and children, they are sending the message that this is ancillary work to be done. Are the laywomen disciples in your church serving in the same capacity as the laymen?

NECESSARY ALLY

In chapter 4, I discussed man and woman as two ways to be human beings made in the image of God. This is the foundation from which we derive our primary value. We also have distinct value in our relationship to one another. Women have a particular value as *ezers*, or necessary allies to men. We hear the Lord God saying in Genesis 2:18 that "it is not good for the man to be alone. I will make a helper corresponding to him." I mentioned how the Hebrew word, *ezer*, translated "helper" in English, is a word used throughout the Old Testament often to describe God rescuing and saving Israel.[13] Professor John McKinley has therefore proposed that "necessary ally" would be a more accurate translation than helper, especially given the inferior connotations the word *helper* has in our language usage today:

> The issue in *ezer* is neither equality nor subordination, but distinction and relatedness. She is to be for the man as an ally to benefit him in the work they were given to do. Just as *ezer* tells of God's relatedness to Israel as the necessary support for survival and

---

12. See John Piper, "A Vision of Biblical Complementarity," in *Recovering Biblical Manhood and Womanhood*, ed. John Piper and Wayne Grudem (Wheaton, IL: Crossway, 2006), 35–36. All of these terms are capitalized in Piper's essay.

13. See Ex. 18:4; Deut. 33:7, 26, 29; Pss. 20:2; 33:20; 70:5; 89:17; 115:9–11; 121:1–2; 124:8; 146:5; Hos. 13:9.

military perils, the woman is the ally to the man, without which he cannot succeed or survive. Unlike helper, that could seem optional, and allow the man to think he's otherwise adequate for his task without the women, the distinction of ally marks the man's dependence upon her contribution. This dependence is plain when we consider Israel's need for God's contribution as her ally. . . .

What sort of ally is the woman to the man? She is a necessary ally, the sort without which he cannot fulfill humanity's mission. Certainly, the woman as a necessary ally is for the mission of family building. The pairing of the two terms *ezer* and *kenegdo* brings a meaning that is larger than gender complementarity and union for building a family. Necessary ally brings into view the joint mission for which the male and female are created to rule God's earthly kingdom.[14]

It's necessary for women to learn as Christ's disciples because women are necessary allies, not optional, subordinate assistants. Women are not only necessary allies to men in some things; we are a corresponding strength to men in the entire mission. The church can so easily frame service with men and women under a structure of authority and submission, with the notion that women constantly need to be led by men, that we end up focusing all our energy on squabbles about who gets what label, and we miss serving in God's mission together. We need one another. While we affirm the authority Christ gave to the apostles, he didn't leave all the important work to them. Likewise, while we have authoritative/authorized offices in the church, we also have a priesthood of believers, fellow workers ready to get their hands dirty.

THE CONSEQUENCES OF WOMEN AS NECESSARY ALLIES

We briefly looked at the consequences some of the more elite and powerful rabbis feared in teaching women the Torah. They didn't want

14. See John McKinley, "Necessary Allies: God as *Ezer*, Woman as *Ezer*" (paper presented at the Annual Meeting of the Evangelical Theological Society, Atlanta, GA, November 17, 2015), mp3 download, 38:35, www.wordmp3 .com/details.aspx?id=20759.

women involved in the public creative and intellectual life with the men. We read this reasoning now and see how ridiculous it is. But they are right that there are consequences to women learning God's Word. Paul knew this. In his writings, we even see women helping plant and host churches in their homes.

Women were even leaders of house churches:

PRISCA: "Give my greetings to Prisca and Aquila, my coworkers in Jesus Christ, who risked their own necks for my life. Not only do I thank them, but so do all the Gentile churches. Greet also the church that meets in their home." (Rom. 16:3–5)

CHLOE: "It has been reported to me about you, my brothers and sisters, by members of Chloe's people, that there is rivalry among you." (1 Cor. 1:11)

NYMPHA: "Give my greetings to the brothers and sisters in Laodicea, and to Nympha and the church in her home." (Col. 4:15)

APPHIA: "To Apphia our sister, to Archippus our fellow soldier, and to the church that meets in your home." (Philem. 1:2)

LYDIA: "After leaving the jail, they came to Lydia's house, where they saw and encouraged the brothers and sisters and departed." (Acts 16:40)

JUNIA: "Greet Andronicus and Junia, my fellow Jews who have been in prison with me. They are outstanding among the apostles, and they were in Christ before I was." (Rom. 16:7 NIV)

PHOEBE: "I commend to you our sister Phoebe, a deacon of the church in Cenchreae . . . for she has been the benefactor of many people, including me." (Rom. 16:1–2 NIV)

What do we do with these women? Were they merely opening their homes and making the communion bread? Or, since we see expressions such as "Chloe's people" and "the church in her home" and "risked their own necks for my life," do they have more of an active function with the body of believers meeting in their own homes?

We get several details regarding Lydia's conversion and church planting with Paul from Luke's description in Acts 16. We know that by the

Spirit's leading, Paul had a vision from a man pleading for him to come to Macedonia and help. But when he arrived in Philippi, one of the leading cities there, he found a small group of praying, God-fearing Gentile women. Paul didn't inquire about where all the manly men were for him to equip. He didn't move on, looking for that man he saw in his vision. He and Timothy sat down and spoke to the women who were there, fully hoping in the consequences of their actions. Lydia's heart was changed, and she prevailed on them to come to her house. Given her wealth and vocation, she probably became a patron or benefactor for them. And she seemed pretty eager to learn as a disciple of Christ. Lydia was a founding member of the Philippian church![15] Many have concluded, like Marg Mowczko, that "if Lydia didn't lead the fledgling church in Philippi, who did? Another member of her household? The unnamed jailer mentioned in Acts 16:22ff? Or a member of his household? Lydia is the only Philippian convert who is named in Acts, and we know that the Philippian church met in her home. So, she is the most likely person to have led and cared for the first congregation at Philippi."[16]

What do we do with that? Well, we know that Lydia and her household, which would include her servants, were baptized (Acts 16:15). Some time passed, and Paul healed a woman possessed with "a spirit of Python,"[17] leading to Paul and Silas's imprisonment. It's likely she was also converted. By the time they were released, we see that they saw and encouraged brothers and sisters meeting in Lydia's house (v. 40). Paul knew the consequences of sharing the gospel with a woman, as well as with his jailer and inmates. Kent Hughes elaborates: "*Some church!* Lydia the merchant princess, the ex-Pythoness, the Philippian jailer, and probably a few ex-inmates made up the first European church.

---

15. This is also confirmed in Phil. 1:5: "because of your partnership in the gospel from the first day until now."

16. Marg Mowczko, "Lydia of Thyatira: The Foreigner Who Became the Founding Member of the Philippian Church," *Marg Mowczko* (blog), November 30, 2017, https://margmowczko.com/lydia-of-thyatira-philippi/.

17. R. Kent Hughes, *Acts: The Church Afire* (Wheaton, IL: Crossway, 1996), 214. "According to myth, Python was a snake that guarded the Temple of Apollo and was eventually killed by Apollo. Later the word *python* came to mean a demon-possessed person through whom Python spoke" (214).

The rich and the poor, the slave and the free, male and female were all one in Christ."[18]

Isn't this a big contrast to the Jewish prayer from Paul's former teaching thanking God he was "not a Gentile, a slave, or a woman"?[19] Since Luke is the narrator of Acts, and he switches from the first to the third person narrative in describing Paul, Silas, and Timothy's departure, it is likely he stayed behind. So it doesn't look like Lydia, a new convert, was left on her own as a leader to care for the church. While it's clear that Lydia was a strong ally to Paul in starting this church, her initiative to plant with him was accompanied by his teaching, as well as by the continued care and teaching of Luke. Surely Lydia was active as a disciple and in caring for the church that met in her home, but she was not left alone to lead the church. Additionally, we see Paul traveling back through Macedonia in Acts 20:1. And we see that by the time Paul wrote his letter to the Philippians, overseers and deacons were in place.

Notice that Paul did not relegate these women to serving in a para-church group; they were planting churches. Also notice that they were not subjected to a subordinate "role," as he addressed them as the names associated with the church. Apphia is mentioned before Archippus. Prisca is mentioned before Aquila. That is significant, as both Jewish and Greco-Roman letters and inscriptions of the time reveal that the ordering indicates a higher status or even a greater influence and deeper involvement in the community. Congregants in the Corinthian church meeting at Chloe's house church are called "Chloe's people." They weren't addressed as dutiful wives, mothers, women's ministry leaders, or children's ministry leaders, either. We see no complaints from Paul fearing that the church will be too effeminate. He considered the consequences of witnessing to these women and got right to work with them. The church today needs to contemplate Paul's actions.

Likewise, Jesus considered the consequences when talking theology with a woman at the well and sharing his identity with her: "Now many Samaritans from that town believed in him because of what the

18. Hughes, *Acts*, 219.
19. Hughes, *Acts*, 213.

woman said when she testified" (John 4:39). Paul followed in the footsteps of Christ. Let's take a look inside these early houses of worship and see how men and women participated together.

SILENCE OF THE WOMEN?[20]

In the early church we see the gospel inaugurating a new creation, with the further inclusion of women and other outsiders. This new creation offer extends to all races, sexes, and statuses. We see women participating in Christ's earthly ministry as well as in fellowship and worship in the early church, not merely in their traditional roles as wife or mother. Some of the sections in Scripture that the conservative churches cite to keep women at arm's length in worship, such as 1 Corinthians 11 and 1 Corinthians 14, actually reveal the efforts to include the women's voice and contribution, even in the worship service. This is a fascinating contrast from the published material quoted above.

First Corinthians 11–14 gives us a glimpse of worship in the early church, along with some important directions on Christian worship from Paul. This doesn't exactly sound like the way our typical worship services look today. We would expect some differences, for cultural reasons, since many churches have exclusive worship sites now and no longer need to meet in personal homes, and due to the closing of the canon of Scripture. In these passages, we see the church in its infancy. But as it is preserved for us in God's Word, we also need to consider what lasting principles we can glean. What is the Holy Spirit saying to the church today through these passages? What do we learn about laypeople in worship from these passages? Many affirm that these passages teach a silence of the women in worship. In fact, a Biblicist reading of 1 Corinthians 14:34 can be pretty scary for women to read.

Before the creepy documentary thriller *The Blair Witch Project* launched Burkittsville, Maryland, into national fame, the small town

---

20. Material in this chapter is taken from my article "The Silence of the Women: Understanding Paul's Admonition in 1 Corinthians 14:33–35," *Modern Reformation*, August 2018, www.whitehorseinn.org/2018/08/the-mod-the-silence-of-the-women-understanding-pauls-admonition-in-1-corinthians-1433-35/. Used with permission.

was already well known to locals as a ghost story landmark. Teens looking for something to do on a Friday night drive the windy mountain back roads to Spook Hill, Burkittsville, and follow these directions: once you see the red barn on Gapland Road, drive to the bottom of the incline, put the car in neutral, feel the car drift *up*hill! How can this be? Three days before the Battle of Antietam, the Battle of Crampton's Gap took place at what is now Gapland Road. The story is that the ghosts of the Confederate soldiers are still going at it, pushing your car uphill, mistaking it for cannons and supplies. The tale has been embellished as thrill seekers have reported dusty handprints on the hoods of their cars, laughter coming from the woods, and the sound of boots on the pavement.

I can testify to the experience, as Spook Hill is just ten minutes from my house. It's definitely a creepy feeling to be in a car drifting uphill. Many have exposed the landmark (and the numerous other recognized "gravity hills" like it) as an optical illusion. Multiple factors are at work within the landscape that fool the eye, often with an obstructed horizon to really throw off visitors. Without a level, calculations of the elevation grade, or a know-it-all in your car, one is left only with what the eye can see. Without the greater perspective, ghost stories flourish. While I never bought into the ghost story, and I intellectually submit to the optical illusion argument, I still get confused and unsettled when I am actually in my car in neutral on Spook Hill. It looks and feels like an off-the-grid spot in the world that the laws of gravity somehow missed.

First Corinthians 14:34–35 can be a sort of Spook Hill in the back roads of the Bible. The landscape can be deceiving, and readers come at the verse with all kinds of obstructions in their horizons.

> The women are to keep silent in the churches; for they are not permitted to speak, but are to subject themselves, just as the Law also says. If they desire to learn anything, let them ask their own husbands at home; for it is improper for a woman to speak in church. (NASB)

At first glance, it seems like Paul was bucking against all the gravity of the gospel teaching applied to women, going back on his own words elsewhere. Some do interpret the text this way, haunting us with teachings barring women from the intellectual life of the church. So what is it that we are actually seeing in this passage? The more we look at it, the more questions we may have. When are women supposed to be silent? To what or whom are they to submit themselves? To what law was Paul referring?

One thing is certain, like the spooky landmark in Burkittsville, one cannot interpret the landscape of this text without stepping back and looking at the whole picture. As Silena Moore Holman argued to her male correspondents in 1896, "My friends, the point of view from which we consider has much to do, after all, with the manner in which we form our conclusions. Has it not?"[21] In reading this text, our own culture, presuppositions, and experiences may skew the horizon, so it's helpful to take a brief look at the time and place in which Paul was writing.

First, then, we need to back up and look at the whole context. Second, we need to use what we already know to be true of Scripture as proper guardrails to keep us on the right track. The laws of gravity prevent cars from drifting uphill; there aren't a bunch of confused Confederate ghosts hanging out in Burkittsville, and Paul didn't call for complete silence of women in worship.

Before tackling all the specific questions this text may raise, there are some basic questions that a skilled reader of Scripture can answer for clarity. What is the main thrust of the text we are looking at? As we zoom out from our Spook Hill, we can see that these two verses are part of the larger context, beginning in chapter 11, teaching the Corinthians about proper order in public worship. We can conclude with Stephen Um that "Paul is not leading with the subject of gender roles; he is responding to an occasion or development in the Corinthian church."[22] We need to be careful not to make a corrective response to a specific situation a blanket theological position about gender.[23]

21. Bobby Valentine, "Silena Moore Holeman: New Women & Exegetical Conscience of Churches of Christ," *Stoned-Campbell Disciple* (blog), January 28, 2016, http://stonedcampbell disciple.com/2016/01/28/silena-moore-holman/.

22. Stephen T. Um, *1 Corinthians: The Word of the Cross* (Wheaton: IL: Crossway, 2015), 247.

23. See Ben Witherington, *Women in the Earliest Churches* (New York: Cambridge University Press, 1988), 25.

As we consider this passage, we must ask what Paul's message was to the original recipients, as well as what God's Word is for us now. When we do that, we see a lasting principle in the text. Because "God is not a God of confusion but of peace" (1 Cor. 14:33 NASB), he provides an order within which we can freely function. As Kathy Keller says, "God gives unalterable commands, but he also gives us freedom to obey them in culturally diverse ways."[24] This proper order blesses both the God we are worshiping and our brothers and sisters in the faith, as we are told that our exercising of them should be driven by love (1 Cor. 13).

By taking a few steps back to look at the small chunk of landscape from chapters 11–14, we see a glimpse of the highway that guides us. Kenneth Bailey made some profitable and fascinating discoveries about the elevation grade of 1 Corinthians 11:2–14:40, the fourth of a five essay-collection in the epistle. The climax, or center of gravity, of this essay on men and women in worship is the foundational theological teaching by which the rest of the concentric circles around it should be interpreted. Viewed through the proper hermeneutical lens,[25] we see this is not subjugation or oppression, but love:

Men and Women *Leading in Worship*: Prophets and how they dress (11:2–16)
> Order in Worship: *Sacrament*—The Lord's Supper (11:17–34)
>> Gifts and the Nature of the Body (12:1–30)
>>> The Hymn to Love (12:31–14:1)
>> Spiritual Gifts and the Upbuilding of the Body (14:1–25)
> Order in Worship: *Word*—Prophets and Speakers in Tongues (14:26–33)

Women and Men *Worshiping*: No Chatting in Church (14:33–40)[26]

---

24. Kathy Keller, *Jesus, Justice, and Gender Roles* (Grand Rapids: Zondervan, 2012), loc. 99–104, Kindle.

25. In a chiastic literary structure, the center text highlights the main point, and the surrounding verses mirror one another as the sequence of ideas leading up to the main point are presented again in reverse order.

26. Kenneth E. Bailey, *Paul through Mediterranean Eyes: Cultural Studies in 1 Corinthians* (Downers Grove, IL: IVP Academic, 2011), 295 (emphases original).

We see that brothers and sisters both are to be sensitive to cultural symbols, are to feast together at the Lord's Table, and are called to discernment, maturity, and love in exercising spiritual gifts for the purpose of edifying the body of Christ. Even as we get closer to Spook Hill, we see that women as well as men are encouraged to prophesy and to speak in tongues during church meetings. The more I study these verses, the more fascinated I am by the efforts to include women in many facets of Christian worship. It makes me wonder about our debates in the church today about whether women are able to make announcements or even to pass out bulletins before the service.

But there is a time to speak and a time to be silent, so that chaos does not ensue and that everyone is properly built up in the word given. Men and women are to take turns speaking in tongues. If there is no interpreter, they are to be publicly silent (14:29). Brothers and sisters are called to prophesy, but as another has something to say, they are to submit their own turn in silence (v. 30). Others are called to weigh what is said, discerning whether it is from the Lord. It is within this evaluation-of-the-prophecies context that women are told to be silent (v. 34). But one still wonders, *why now?* And *why women specifically?* There may be both theological and cultural reasons behind this silence.

Some argue that the reasoning for this prohibition has to do with women who were overstepping into the authority of the elders' sole responsibility in weighing the prophecies. Um, for example, says, "Apparently there was a situation in Corinth where, when the prophecies were being weighed (presumably by male elders) certain women were interjecting, asking questions, perhaps even challenging the rulings."[27] Further, Ben Witherington adds, "If women were judging their husbands' prophecies and, by implication, questioning the veracity of their own husbands or other men in regard to prophesying, then they

---

27. Um, *1 Corinthians*, 251. Also see, Keller, *Jesus, Justice, and Gender Roles*, loc. 157–75.

were creating a situation where the Corinthian worship service might become a family feud."[28]

Nevertheless, there must be more to this landscape than the dynamic of church office, or else Paul would have cautioned laymen along with laywomen.[29] Were the women chatting and asking questions during this time of weighing the prophecies because they were trying to subvert authority? We must think about the cultural situation even more here—Paul mentions the women wanting to learn, not trying to take over. Women in the home were not often socialized the same as their husbands who were involved in commerce. They were not often equal participants in society and business, and therefore were not exposed to all the diverse languages and speech styles. We also need to consider the setting—as the early Christians gathered in house churches with shared fellowship meals, the women must have been distracted with hospitality, preparation, and tending the children.[30] "Multiple factors must be considered. Attention-span problems, limited knowledge of Greek, accent issues, language levels of Greek in use, lack of amplification for the speakers, along with chatting as a methodology for learning are all involved."[31] So Paul called for these women to act honorably, as with the other two times he called for silence when it led to disruption and disorder. And yet he also dealt kindly, encouraging these wives to go to their husbands after the service to get their questions answered or to learn what they might have missed.

This interpretation makes it more likely that the women were not so much needing to be told to submit to their husbands, but rather, as Witherington notes, to "the principle of order in the worship service, the principle of silence and respect shown when another person is speaking."[32] This also explains the "law" Paul referenced. "The Corinthians

---

28. Ben Witherington, *Women and the Genesis of Christianity* (New York: Cambridge University Press, 1990), 176.

29. And interestingly, we see Prisca correcting Apollos's teaching alongside of her husband in Acts 18:24–26.

30. See Cynthia Westfall, *Paul and Gender* (Grand Rapids: Baker Academic, 2016), 238–40.

31. Bailey, *Paul through Mediterranean Eyes*, 416.

32. Witherington, *Women in the Earliest Churches*, 102–3.

should know the OT speaks about a respectful silence when a word of counsel is spoken (Job 29.21)."[33]

Paul closed this essay with the verses of 1 Corinthians 14:37–40, beautifully summarizing and reminding us of the gravity of his rule for men and women in worship—the command to love. Again, Paul's strategic literary use of a chiastic structure shows us the main thrust he is communicating in the center of his essay, as we see the order needed in worshiping with our gifts in the surrounding verses, which mirror one another:[34]

[37]If anyone thinks that he is a *prophet*,	PROPHECY: Order Needed (1 Cor. 11)
or *spiritual*,	GIFTS: Order Needed (1 Cor. 12)
he should acknowledge that what I'm writing to you is a command of the Lord. [38]If any one does not recognize this, he is not recognized.	**THE COMMAND: Love (1 Cor. 13)**
[39] So, my [brothers and sisters], earnestly *desire to prophesy*, and do *not forbid speaking in tongues*;	GIFTS: Prophecy (1 Cor. 14:1–12) and Tongues (1 Cor. 14:13–25)
[40]but *all things* should be done in *decency and in order.*	ALL THINGS: In Order (1 Cor. 14:26–33)

This is not a back roads verse in the Bible that I want to avoid (nothing spooky to see here!). Upholding the proper order of worship, respecting the officers of the church, and refraining from noninspired

---

33. Witherington, *Women in the Earliest Churches*, 103. Also, "A survey of various uses of the Hebrew words for silence reveals that the only time silence is associated with submission in the OT is out of respect for God (Hab 2.20; cf. Isa 46.1; Zech 2.13), or one in position of authority (Jdgs 3.19), or wise men noted for their knowledge and counsel (Job 29.21), or it is a silence imposed by God on someone who speaks insolently to a righteous person (Ps. 31.17)" (102).

34. Bailey, *Paul through Mediterranean Eyes*, 417.

speech that disrupts worship all fall under the command of the Lord to love—the very thing Christians should be known for. And these are lasting principles for the church today.

THE CONSEQUENCES OF MEN AND WOMEN WORSHIPING TOGETHER

Men and women worshiping together this way was all very countercultural. Since the early church began assembling in personal households, I imagine how well they could resonate with the language we read in Scripture describing the church as the household of God. We are to treat household members with affection and respect. Unbelievers were very suspicious of these Christian assemblies. Marcus Minucius Felix, an early Latin Christian apologist, narrates popular accusations against the early Christians in his apologetic work called *Octavius*. In this dialogue on Christianity between a pagan and a Christian, the pagan Caecilius Natalis says to the Christian Octavius Januarius:

> And now, as wickeder things advance more fruitfully, and abandoned manners creep on day by day, those abominable shrines of an impious assembly are maturing themselves throughout the whole world. Assuredly this confederacy ought to be rooted out and execrated. They know one another by secret marks and insignia, and they love one another almost before they know one another. Everywhere there is mingled among them a certain religion of lust, and they call one another promiscuously brothers and sisters, that even a not unusual debauchery may by the intervention of that sacred name become incestuous.[35]

Here is the consequence of Jesus talking theology to a woman at a well in Samaria and telling sisters that they too can be disciples. Here are the consequences of Paul planting house churches with women,

---

35. Marcus Minucius Felix narrates these accusations in his apologetic work *Octavius* (published AD 150–210), trans. Robert Ernest Wallis, Early Christian Writings Book 1 (annotated) (Amazon Digital Services LLC, 2012), loc. 294–99, Kindle.

colaboring with them, and upholding the value of their participation in worship. The consequence isn't merely being misunderstood, but a whole argument being built against Christianity at such a vulnerable time as the early days of the church. Christians needed to meet in secret as they were under threat of persecution. "The Romans heard of their love feasts, which included wine, brother-sister language, and holy kisses, and let their imaginations run wild".[36]

> And of their banqueting it is well known all men speak of it everywhere. . . . On a solemn day they assemble at the feast, with all their children, sisters, mothers, people of every sex and of every age. There, after much feasting, when the fellowship has grown warm, and the fervor of incestuous lust has grown hot with drunkenness . . . the conscious light being overturned and extinguished in the shameless darkness.[37]

Didn't Jesus know these rumors were going to happen? Didn't he think about the consequences of teaching women? Of having them sit at his feet? Fall at his feet? Anoint him with oil? Of partaking of his hospitality back at Mary and Martha's, and then every Sunday after his ascension? Didn't he care about his reputation? And what about Paul? He already knew the lives of God's people were in danger. Why make it worse by giving the Romans more ammunition?

One thing I am always trying to teach my children is that doing the right thing often comes with painful consequences. We like to believe in a sort of prosperity gospel of decision making: if you do the right thing, blessings follow. Life will be the way you think you deserve. However, doing the right thing often comes with the pain of self-discipline, as well as consequences such as being left out, rejected, or as we see with the early church, persecuted. The rewards are not always fully attainable in this world, and yet we know that God is present even in our suffering, and through it he produces the "fruit of righteousness

---

36. Aimee Byrd, *Why Can't We Be Friends? Avoidance Is Not Purity* (Phillipsburg, NJ: P&R, 2018), 112.

37. Felix, *Octavius*, loc. 310–16.

to those who have been trained by it" (Heb. 12:11). Rather than cave to the Greco-Roman culture's expectations of gender, the early Christians loved one another as brothers and sisters. They saw their identity first as citizens of the heavenly kingdom, and just as they refused to participate in the expected sacrifices to the false gods, which led to their persecution, they also did not succumb to halting their exclusive religious practices or distancing themselves from one another for the sake of being an accepted religion in Rome. If their mission was to commune with the triune God and one another for eternity, it needed to show in their Christian worship and living. Almost two thousand years later we see how God has grown and preserved his church in this mission.

PEEL AND REVEAL

What consequences should we expect today? If Paul invested so much effort and care into the new freedom of women and other outsiders in the inaugurated new creation while upholding the timeless distinction of the sexes in worship according to the creation order, why are we, over two thousand years later, still debating who can pass the offering basket? Have we properly retrieved what the early church has passed down? How do we apply these lasting principles to our culture? And what will the next generation receive from us? Paul didn't merely "let" women participate in worship; their participation is vital to the *telos* of the church. Biblical manhood and womanhood isn't so biblical if women in the early church were able to contribute more than they may today.

After briefly surveying discipleship of women, as well as men and women in worship and fellowship in the early church, the question lingers: What does this all mean for us *now*? How are both men and women *participating in creative and spiritual life in the church*? How are both men and women *contributing literary expression and spiritual creativity*? How are both men and women *in the heart of existence*? How are both men and women vital to the important task of *passing on the heritage of the tradition to future generations*? How do both men and women *serve in roles that identify with knowledge of God's Word*? And how does this *inclusion affect our public image*?

Whatever our stance is on ordination, these are the questions we should be asking. And yet for some reason, even when we discuss the contributions of laypeople, the church is still stuck on this problem of women and where to draw the line. As one article published in *CBMW News* put it, "But What *Should* Women Do in the Church?"[38] I usually don't like to tell people they are asking the wrong questions, but maybe I can answer that question by asking the set of questions in the paragraph above. Wayne Grudem proposes that when considering what women should do, we need to weigh each contribution according to appropriate restrictions for women in three areas: "(1) governing authority, (2) Bible teaching, and (3) public recognition or visibility."[39] He makes three corresponding lists of service positions and explains, "In List 1, I proceed from areas of greater governing authority to areas of lesser authority. In List 2, I proceed from areas of greater teaching responsibility and influence on the beliefs of the church to areas of lesser teaching responsibility and lesser influence on the beliefs of the church. In List 3, I proceed from areas of greater public recognition and visibility to areas of lesser visibility."[40]

Grudem lists a total of eighty-three ministries. The idea is that a line must be drawn on each list, and women should not serve in any of the ministries above that line. He then offers guidelines of where those who signed the Danvers Statement would draw the lines for where it would be inappropriate for women to serve, followed by sharing his personal lines, which are stricter. He calls for us to use wisdom in drawing our own lines. The order given of greater teaching responsibility and influence is telling, as editing and writing a woman's study Bible is below writing a general book on biblical doctrines. Teaching a women's Sunday school class is below teaching a class of high schoolers.

Is this how we are to look at the contributions of service in the church—in hierarchies of authority and influence? Is the question of whether women are permitted to serve in each ministry always

---

38. Wayne Grudem, "But What *Should* Women Do in the Church?," *CBMW News* 1.2 (November 1995), http://cbmw.org/wp-content/uploads/2013/05/1-2.pdf.

39. Grudem, "But What *Should* Women Do?," 1.

40. Grudem, "But What *Should* Women Do?," 1.

looming over the church? Don't we see this in our own churches when we are looking for ushers, greeters, small group leaders, Sunday school teachers, and curriculum providers? In another article, CBMW tells us what they mean by authority: "We would define authority in general as the *right* (Matt. 8:9) and *power* (Mark 1:27; 1 Cor. 7:37) and *responsibility* (2 Cor. 10:8; 13:10) *to give direction to another.*"[41] This definition disqualifies a lot of women Jesus, Paul, and the other apostles served alongside in Scripture.

And this listing of ministries approach doesn't really speak to what a woman *should do*; it encourages lines to delimit what a woman is permitted to do. It seems to create "safe" areas for women as well—women's Sunday school and women's study Bibles—separating them from the intellectual and creative life of the whole body of believers. There isn't a list like this for lay*men*. While the article's ostensible aim is to help churches encourage women to serve in more places than what may be a traditional understanding, its very premise works against that.

PEELING BACK YELLOW FRACTIONS

Ironically, these lists promoting complementarian hierarchy also fall into the egalitarian error that they are trying to prevent—they fail to demonstrate what is distinctly valuable and meaningful about the woman's contribution. We see by the guidelines that wherever "the line" is drawn, the women's contribution cannot be in places with too high of influence. In the lower areas in which she is allowed to serve, or should serve, there doesn't appear to be any reason why she *should*, despite the title of the article.

While using the word *complementarity* as if it's positive, these lines do not promote communion through giving of the self through our differences, as discussed in chapter 4. Where is the reciprocity if the framework is always authority and submission between men and

---

41. John Piper and Wayne Grudem, "50 Crucial Questions: An Overview of Central Concerns about Manhood and Womanhood" (Wheaton, IL: Crossway, 1992), q. 36., p. 56; see https://document.desiringgod.org/50-crucial-questions-about-manhood-and-womanhood-en.pdf?ts=1471551126.

women? What "specific richness of [her] respective humanity" does the woman have to contribute?[42] And can our contributions divide so neatly along the line between masculine and feminine, or does each one of us also offer something unique in our personhood? This list in *CBMW News* is a showcase of fractional complementarity, broken down by tasks women may or may not be permitted to perform, and fails to address the dynamic of communion between the sexes or where we are headed. How do men and women coimplicate one another in the household of God with a future-oriented dynamism? How does my friend Anna's Ripstick[43] theology work within a list that starts out by questioning a woman's agency? Where is the beautiful mystery of likeness and nonlikeness between man and woman displayed? How can the men in the church grow in the teleological understanding of their humanness, as part of the collective bride of Christ, if they cannot learn from or be influenced by women? How do we gain mutual knowledge of one another if we separate women's teaching and writing for exclusive women's or children's ministries? How can we have integral, dynamic, synergetic, fruit-bearing complementarity in a model like this?

In contrast to these lists, we see something beautiful regarding the church as the bride of Christ in Revelation. She is radiant like her groom (Rev. 21:9–11, Heb. 1:3, see also Ps. 34:5). And she has a prophetic speaking function. In Revelation 22:17 we see that the church is to add her voice to the Spirit's, saying, "Come!" G. K. Beale connects this verse to Revelation 19:10, with "brothers and sisters hold[ing] firmly to the testimony of Jesus" as fellow servants with the angels in this prophetic work.[44] In the three calls to "come" in Revelation 22:17 we first see the prophetic leaders (19:10) calling the whole church collectively, and then all of us who hear join in, individually exhorting "other believers who are still dull of hearing."[45] I can't help but think of

---

42. Prudence Allen, *The Concept of Woman, Volume 3, The Search for Communion of Persons, 1500–2015* (Grand Rapids: Eerdmans, 2016), 460.

43. See p. 130 (end of chap. 4)

44. G. K. Beale with David H. Campbell, *Revelation: A Shorter Commentary* (Grand Rapids: Eerdmans, 2015), 407, 523.

45. Beale, *Revelation*, 523.

Mary Magdalene as the first picture of this, a typology of the church adding her voice to the Spirit (who revealed Christ to her), testifying to the apostles (her brothers), *Come! He is risen!* (John 20:11–18).

Beale also discusses how this call to come refers to "an entire life of faith," so it is more than an "open-ended 'invitation' to the world in general, but rather commands the people of God to persevere throughout the age and up until the final coming of Christ."[46] This is not only the responsibility of the ordained, but of laymen and laywomen as the bride of Christ, to hear and to speak the testimony of Jesus, spurring one another to wakefulness and perseverance.

PEEL AND REVEAL: REVEALING ESCHATOLOGICAL GLORY IN CREATION

Woman has a distinct contribution in this task. Her feminine voice is needed, as she reminds man of his *telos*, even teaching him something about it. And it is for his glory. Mark Garcia explains: "The LORD could have created man and woman at the same time, but he did not, and the creation of woman second, rather than being a sign of inferiority to the first, is in Scripture an eschatological marker: the second is the glory of the first. She is created to be his eschatological glory. Instead of reducing her, it elevates her."[47]

Woman is created second as man's glory, meaning, when Adam sees Eve, who was created from his side, he sees his *telos* as the bride of Christ—the church flowing out of Christ's wounded side. God creates Adam with the commission to expand God's temple/garden and therefore God's presence, with a promised reward for his obedience.[48] He then creates Eve from Adam, as both an *ezer*, corresponding strength and necessary ally in his mission, and a picture of his eschatological

---

46. Beale, *Revelation*, 523.

47. Mark Garcia, "Just Like a Woman, but What Is Woman?," *The Quarry* (blog), Greystone Institute, February 17, 2015, www.greystoneinstitute.org/quarry/2015/02/17/just-like-a-woman-but-what-is-a-woman.

48. See G. K. Beale, *The Temple and the Church's Mission: A Biblical Theology of the Dwelling Place of God*, ed. D. A. Carson, New Studies in Biblical Theology (Downers Grove, IL: IVP Academic, 2004).

glory. Woman is an embodiment of this glory, a typology of these waters of life[49] that we see the bride calling us to in Revelation 22:17.[50] Man's voice alone will not do. God's image is shown forth in two ways of being human, man and woman, which calls for communion and reciprocity, as his bride is the collective of all of those who hear his voice and testify of Jesus.

PEEL AND REVEAL: REVEALING THE STORY BEHIND THE STORY IN CREATION

We see the value of woman's contributing voice in the very beginning. Many of us have been taught that Eve added to the Word of God in her response to the serpent when she said, "But about the fruit of the tree in the middle of the garden, God said, 'You must not eat it or touch it, or you will die'" (Gen. 3:3). Some of us have learned from this that Eve was the first legalist by adding "or touch it" to God's prohibition. Numerous motives have been suggested for Eve's addition, as well as the possibility that Adam added these words when he told her about God's prohibition. Wayne Townsend proposes that these words of Eve tell us more of the story behind the story. Although Genesis is the beginning of the story, we need to think about the context in which it was received. "Genesis was written to a redeemed people of God. Genesis, as received, contains an apologetic for the origins of Israel as a distinct nation and its claim on the land of Canaan. Thus, Genesis assumes the history of exodus-conquest, in the midst of which Israel received the law-code of Sinai."[51] Townsend notes how the levirate marriage law code (Deut. 25:5–6) is assumed in the story of Judah and

---

49. See Richard Whitekettle, "Levitical Thought and the Feminine Reproductive Cycle: Wombs, Wellsprings, and the Primeval World," *Vestus Testamentum* 46.3 (1996): 376–91.

50. Another picture connecting these waters of life and the bride's call to come in Rev. 21:17 is the Samaritan woman whom Jesus invited to the well of living water, revealing himself as the Messiah to her. She responded by calling the people in the town to "come, see . . . the Messiah" (John 4:29).

51. P. Wayne Townsend, "Eve's Answer to the Serpent: An Alternative Paradigm for Sin and Some Implications in Theology," *Calvin Theological Journal* 33 (1998): 399–420, https://faculty.gordon.edu/hu/bi/ted_hildebrandt/otesources/01-genesis/text/articles-books/townsend_evesanswer_ctj.pdf.

Tamar, and how the flood is told with an assumed prior knowledge of clean and unclean animals in relation to sacrifice.

> While such concepts did predate the exodus, the post-exodus context of the first readers implies that these passages were intended to be read in the light of the law given at Sinai, including the cleanness code found in Leviticus. . . .
>
> In this context, the story of the Fall functions as a pretext for the exodus-conquest. Genesis 3 identifies the sources of evil that have led to the suffering of slavery. It also justifies the conquest by expanding the division between the woman and the Serpent to an ongoing struggle between their descendants (Gen. 3:15). All of this relies on a separation from, and over against, the rest of the nations—the very separation identified in the Levitical code (Lev. 18:24–30; 20:22–27).[52]

Given this context for Genesis and the writer's familiarity with Sinai law, we see that although "do not touch" is not part of the prohibition God spoke to Adam, Eve is expanding on the story:

> We find parallels to Eve's words in Leviticus 11 and Deuteronomy 14. Leviticus 11 defines food that is lawful for Israelites to eat. Concerning unclean land animals, verse 8 states, "You must not *eat* their meat or *touch* their carcasses; they are unclean for you" (emphasis added). The vocabulary and sentence structure of this verse strongly parallels Eve's words in Genesis 3:3: "You must not eat fruit . . . and you must not touch it."[53]

Original audiences, knowing the Levitical law, see what's coming after reading Eve's words, as touching anything unclean will make Adam and Eve unclean. The ramifications are fatal. Original hearers know that there must be a sacrifice and that Adam and Eve will be

---

52. Townsend, "Eve's Answer," 399–420.
53. Townsend, "Eve's Answer," 399–420.

cast out of the sanctuary of the garden-temple. Eve is giving us the story behind the story. She knows what accompanies God's Word. Garcia elaborates that Eve is "created as the liturgical responder to [Adam's] word. When she responds, she speaks the glorifying word which expounds, which elaborates, which fills out, even fructifies, the original word."[54] And yet the serpent is able to deceive her, disorienting her desires. "The woman saw that the tree was good for food and delightful to look at, and that it was desirable for obtaining wisdom" (Gen. 3:6). Such suspense! What will happen now? What will Adam do? Will he—*can he*—be the sacrifice?[55] Will he lay his life down for his wife? He participates with her and then blames her.

Now having full revelation given to us in God's Word, we have the testimony of Jesus, the One who suffered outside the gate with the unclean to sanctify us by his blood (Heb. 13:12), our Groom who is making us holy and "cleansing [us] with the washing of water by the word" (Eph. 5:26). And as this theme of uncleanliness, sin, and redemption plays out, we see this language in Revelation: "Blessed are those who wash their robes, so that they may have the right to the tree of life and may enter the city by the gates. Outside are the dogs, the sorcerers, the sexually immoral, the murderers, the idolaters, and everyone who loves and practices falsehood" (Rev. 22:14–15). We rejoice to see the bride of Christ calling "the one who desires" to take the "water of life" (Rev. 22:17). As the bride, "we are beholders of the Beholder's beholding of us."[56] Isn't that what we all long for?

Now let's return to CBMW's definition of authority as "the *right* (Matt. 8:9) and *power* (Mark 1:27; 1 Cor. 7:37) and *responsibility* (2 Cor. 10:8; 13:10) to *give direction to another.*" Is authorization an ontological right that belongs to a particular sex, a power bestowed on

---

54. Mark A. Garcia, Lecture 3.2, "Eve the Legalist? And Israel's Triumvirate," video lecture from Theological Anthropology course, Greystone Theological Institute.

55. See L. Michael Morales, *Who Shall Ascend the Mountain of the Lord? A Biblical Theology of the Book of Leviticus,* ed. D. A. Carson, New Studies in Biblical Theology (Downers Grove, IL: IVP Academic, 2015), 181–84.

56. Amy Brown Hughes, "Beholding the Beholder," in *Trinity without Hierarchy: Reclaiming Nicene Orthodoxy in Evangelical Theology,* ed. Michael Bird and Scott Harrower (Grand Rapids: Kregel, 2019), 131.

men to always have the say-so in all things? Don't we need to ask who is authorized and what each person is to do specifically with that authority? While church officers have a distinct authorization in teaching and ruling, brothers and sisters who hear the Word of our Groom are authorized as a priesthood under this ministry to testify Jesus to one another. As integral wholes, the voices of men and women together are fruitful and dynamic. What story behind the story might your church be missing by reducing a woman's contribution to a hierarchal list? What corresponding strength do your women have to offer? Rather than bury and hide what the Lord has given under an imaginary line on a hierarchal list, how can your church be counterculturally capable as opposed to some of the accepted teachings of so-called biblical manhood and womanhood in evangelicalism? Why is this necessary?

QUESTIONS FOR GROUP DISCUSSION

1. Consider the significance of Jesus saying that Mary is doing the one thing that is necessary. Do you urgently think this about women as disciples? How does it show in your church? Do you think of discipling women in any fractional capacity when compared to the contributions of male disciples? How so? How might the women in your church answer this question? Are they a whole, contributing part of the spiritual life of the church? Do they contribute literary expression and creativity? Are women in the heart of existence in your church? Are they vital to important tasks of passing on the heritage of the traditions to future generations? Do they serve in areas that identify with the knowledge of God's Word? Explain why or why not. How does this inclusion affect their public image?

2. Are there any services/ministries in the church that you think should be limited for only laymen or laywomen to serve in exclusively? Explain.

3. What would be the consequences in your church if the laywomen were invested in and serving in the same capacities as the laymen? What fears might you have here? Are they founded

on biblical truth? What contemporary expectations of gender might your church be catering to?

4. What extra efforts does Paul make to include a woman's voice and contribution in the worship service in 1 Corinthians 11 and 14? Do the officers in your church make such efforts? How? What principles of distinction of the sexes did Paul uphold in 1 Corinthians 11—authority and submission, or cultural markers of sexuality and availability?[57] If you hold cessationist convictions as I do, how do you think this detailed 1 Corinthians 11–14 description of a certain freedom under proper order in public worship applies to the church now, with the canon of Scripture complete, making the gifts of prophecy and tongues obsolete?

5. In considering the prophetic voice of the bride in Revelation 22 and even the first woman, Eve, expanding on Adam's words to reveal the story behind the story, how do you think the voice and contribution of women is distinctly meaningful and valuable in the church? How do you see it co-implicating the man's voice? What is dynamic about combining male and female voices and contributions?

---

57. For a helpful resource arguing the latter, see Philip B. Payne, "Wild Hair and Gender Equality," *Priscilla Papers* 20.3 (Summer 2006): 9–18, www.linguistsoftware.com/Payne2006 PP1Cor11_2-16.pdf.

CHAPTER 8

WHEN PAUL PASSES PHOEBE THE BATON

"I commend to you our sister Phoebe, a deacon of the church in Cenchreae" (Rom. 16:1 NIV). In chapter 5 we looked at how Phoebe was a sister, an agent or representative from Paul to deliver his epistle to the Romans, the first interpreter of that letter, and a benefactor or patron.[1] I'd like to come back to this passage now and further consider what it meant for Paul to commend Phoebe and to call her their sister.

Commending Phoebe to the Romans implies that she has a task that needs some outside authorization. It's interesting, as we see Paul commending Phoebe to them as his authorized deliverer of the letter, to observe how he uses that same word translated *commend* in 2 Corinthians 3:1–3. Here he tells the Corinthian church that they are Christ's letter, delivered by Paul and the apostles, that *commends* them for their ministry. In other words, the faith of the Corinthians was Paul's commendation letter from Christ, Paul's authorization as an apostle to continue to minister to them. This same word is used to commend Phoebe to the Romans.

Have you ever commended anyone for a mission? My house has reached that age when the original appliances are beginning to break

---

1. See pp. 148–51.

down. Our microwave was the first to go. After doing a ridiculous amount of research to find the best microwave for our price range, we discovered that it was a bit shorter than our last model and our backsplash tile came about a half inch short of meeting it. My husband, son, and I went to Lowe's and had some tile cut to fill in that space of exposed drywall. It took forever to get someone to cut it, so we ended up shopping for some more home improvement needs while we were waiting. Forever. My son was just standing around when Matt had the blessed opportunity to check out, so he put my son to work, telling him to grab some bags to take to the car. Finally, we were leaving, and we could get back to fixing our kitchen—or so I thought. My son dropped the flimsy plastic bag holding the perfectly cut tiles, and they broke into pieces once they hit the parking lot pavement.

This is the part where my husband and I both paused and processed whether we were going to act on how we really felt inside. I'm sure none of you parents have ever felt like unloading. But I did. There was no way we were going back in the store on that day—we were done. I took a breath and, as even-toned as I could, asked, "What happened? How did you drop the bag?" (Perhaps a bit of an exclamation mark should be added after the question mark. Maybe half.) My son replied, "Guys, I'm thirteen. Why did you give *me* the bag with the tile?" Now, a thirteen-year-old should be perfectly capable of carefully carrying a bag. But he also had a point. If we cared so dang much about how it was handled, was he really the best choice? I may commend to you some thirteen-year-olds to handle something fragile that you may need delivered, but not my son. At this stage in life, he didn't take the best care of things.

I've already discussed the fragility of the situation in which Phoebe is delivering this epistle. This is a group of house churches made up of Jews and Gentiles in an influential area that was not directly established by one of the twelve apostles. Paul cannot go to Rome himself to address the issues they are questioning or are divided on. He has the delicate task of trying to garner their support for his own apostolic missionary work, as well as uniting weaker and stronger siblings in the faith under a robust teaching of God and salvation. I wonder how long it took Paul to complete this epistle.[2] I wonder if when Paul finished, he thought to himself that the Holy Spirit had breathed out through him a masterpiece that theologians would be in awe of to this day. His heart must have been filled with gratitude, at the least, that the Lord would give him this profound and glorious teaching to share. I once heard Romans described as the diamond on the ring of the band that is the canon of Scripture. I imagine how Paul must have prayed over its reception by the Romans. No doubt, selecting the deliverer to get it there to communicate (make common) and commune (share, hold in common) with these churches was a big deal.

Think about all that is behind this commendation! Paul passes the baton to Phoebe. Donald Grey Barnhouse writes, "Never was there a greater burden carried by such tender hands. The theological history of the church through the centuries was in the manuscript which she brought with her. The Reformation was in that baggage. The blessing of multitudes in our day was carried in those parchments."[3] Paul authorizes a woman to communicate and make common "his greatest letter-essay, the most influential letter in the history of Western thought, and the singularly greatest piece of Christian theology"[4] with God's people. James Montgomery Boice notes that Phoebe likely had traveling companions, as it was unsafe for women, or anyone for that matter, to travel alone in the conditions of the ancient world.[5] But Paul makes sure Phoebe is known as the prominent one bearing the epistle on his behalf. It wasn't just because it needed to be delivered from point A to point B (like our kitchen tiles).

2. See E. Randolph Richards, *Paul and First-Century Letter Writing* (Downers Grove, IL: InterVarsity, 2004), for all the factors to consider in the process, such as rough drafts, editing, dictation, funds, copies for retention and dispatch, cost, and travel.

3. Donald Grey Barnhouse, *God's Glory: Exposition of Bible Doctrines, Taking the Epistle to the Romans as a Point of Departure, Vol. 10, Romans 14:13–16:27* (Grand Rapids: Eerdmans, 1964), 124.

4. Michael Bird, *Bourgeois Babes, Bossy Wives, and Bobby Haircuts: A Case for Gender Equality in Ministry* (Grand Rapids: Zondervan, 2012), 21.

5. James Montgomery Boice, *Romans*, 4 vols. (Grand Rapids: Baker, 1995), 4:1913.

SACRED SIBLINGSHIP[6]

The first thing Paul says about Phoebe in commending her to the Roman churches is that she is their sister. We can easily overlook the significance of this status, as we often use this expression as a casual term of endearment. But there is both an affection and a theology behind Paul introducing Phoebe as not only his sister but theirs in common.[7]

And this isn't a status that Paul reserves just for his favored colaborers or leaders. Reidar Aasgaard, professor of intellectual history at the University of Oslo, wrote extensively on the meaning of Christian siblingship in Paul's writing, noting that this is his most frequent way of describing the church. Aasgaard studied the epistles to the Romans, 1 and 2 Corinthians, Galatians, Philippians, 1 Thessalonians, and Philemon to discover that Paul used the Greek root for siblings 122 times, and only 2 of those instances refer to biological siblings. Comparatively, Paul describes his fellow Christians as "church" 45 times, "holy" 25 times, "called" 5 times, and "body of Christ" 3 to 4 times.[8] In communicating this way, Paul "says something about Christian relationships, what they are like, and what they should be like: in fact, he here appears to disclose elements of his ecclesiological and ethical thinking."[9]

Aasgaard explains how Paul is drawing on the notions his hearers have regarding siblingship, one of the most powerful ancient social institutions in antiquity, to teach Christians about how their affection toward one another should be oriented, and what rights and obligations they have as siblings. It's an influential term "to appeal to them, criticize them, strengthen them, or make them change."[10] Paul is introducing some novel kinship applications for Christians as he draws from

---

6. I first saw this term used in Sue Edwards, Kelley Matthews, and Henry J. Rogers, *Mixed Ministry: Working Together as Brothers and Sisters in an Oversexed Society* (Grand Rapids: Kregel, 2008).

7. See Aimee Byrd, *Why Can't We Be Friends? Avoidance Is Not Purity* (Phillipsburg, NJ: P&R, 2018), 11–127.

8. Reidar Aasgaard, *"My Beloved Brothers and Sisters!" Christian Siblingship in Paul* (New York: T&T Clark, 2004), 3.

9. Aasgaard, *Christian Siblingship*, 3

10. Aasgaard, *Christian Siblingship*, 5.

the Jewish, Hellenistic, and Roman cultural concepts to which the church in that context could relate.[11]

The average household size in ancient times was smaller than you might expect. Women had a life expectancy of only sixty years old if they weren't among the many who died giving birth. Men weren't expected to live past forty-five. Thus it was common for children to grow up without both parents. "Only about 20 per cent were born with a (paternal) grandfather."[12] Child mortality rates were also high. "On average, every female had to bear five children for two of them to reach adulthood, and thus be able to marry and secure succession."[13] By ten years old, one typically had about two siblings, and by thirty-five, the demographic dropped to around one and a half. Given these statistics, you can imagine how meaningful siblings were to one another and how much they depended on one another. The household responsibilities were enormous for the mission of the family name, including the family faith, and the household was the center of economic production, education, religious and judicial functions, social security, emotional support, and social contact.[14] "While deaths changed the head of the household and shook up the siblings' responsibilities, the relationships between surviving siblings were an anchor to their family history and identity. . . . By using the metaphor of natural siblings in ancient households, he draws on the common knowledge that Christians should honor one another in this valued relationship, promote unity, and live in harmony, which was 'a fundamental condition for a successful family life.'"[15]

Joseph Hellerman picks up on this kinship language in Scripture as well, describing the early church as a "surrogate kinship group" which functioned in similar kinship norm behavior as Mediterranean families.[16] "These ideals became more focused between the first century

---

11. Aasgaard, *Christian Siblingship*, 35.

12. Aasgaard, *Christian Siblingship*, 37; see also for above percentages referenced.

13. Aasgaard, *Christian Siblingship*, 38; see also for below percentages on sibling mortality. Aasgaard does note that Jewish families were thought to have more children, but there is no reliable documentation to attest to this.

14. Aasgaard, *Christian Siblingship*, 45–48.

15. Aasgaard, *Christian Siblingship*, 54.

16. Joseph Hellerman, *The Ancient Church as Family* (Minneapolis: Fortress, 2001), 21, noting the picture of this we have in Acts.

BC and the first century AD, as smaller households of immediate family members became prominent over the larger *familia*, in which extended family, freedmen, and slaves lived together. The smaller household model fostered more gender balance than the strictly patri-archal *familia* model. People traced their family lines through both the mother and the father, rather than exclusively through the men. This can be seen in Matthew's genealogy of Jesus, which includes Tamar, Rahab, Ruth, and Bathsheba (see Matt. 1:3, 5–6)."[17]

Aasgaard speaks of sibling obligations as distinctive yet much more fluid than we would expect.[18] Many in the church today tend to view relationships through either a lens of authority and submission or of full equality, but the mutuality in these relationships came with distinctive rights and obligations, even as the "sibling relationship seems to have involved more latitude than many, or most, other social relations."[19] Factors such as age, gender, skill, and birth order all contributed to authority and responsibility both in the household and public spheres. As far as the dynamic between the sexes, brothers were to respect their sisters, protect their honor, defend them, even take their side if they were in a marital dispute. Sisters had strong devotion to their brothers, valuing their relationships with their brothers even over their own husbands.[20] It was common for sisters to arbitrate when there were tensions between their brother and their father. Considering the obligations siblings had to one another in the household, the mortality rate, and the ways they must have depended on one another for stability, relationship, family unity, and harmony, it's easy to imagine just how much they were valued. Siblingship is the longest-lasting relationship many had. Siblings were expected to have a "natural affection toward one another that bore fruit in their actions" and was "distinguished from all other loves throughout a lifetime."[21]

---

17. Byrd, *Why Can't We Be Friends?*, 116, see also Aasgaard, *Brothers and Sisters*, 41, 60.

18. Aasgaard, *Christian Siblingship*, 63. This paragraph is a paraphrase of his findings on pp. 62–70.

19. Aasgaard, *Christian Siblingship*, 70.

20. Aasgaard quotes from Sophocles's play *Antigone* as an example. When she risks her own life to ensure a proper burial for her brother, Antigone "exclaims: 'If my husband had died, I could have another, and a child by another man, if I had lost the first, but with my mother and father in Hades below, I could never have another brother.'" Aasgaard, *Christian Siblingship*, 64–65, quoting Sophocles, *Ant.* 909–12.

21. Byrd, *Why Can't We Be Friends?*, 118.

This is just a small overview of the notions Paul is drawing from when he calls Christians brothers and sisters. Therefore, we really do zoom past significant context if we don't allow this sibling title to inform our attitudes.[22] He is not merely using siblingship as a metaphor for the church. This is our new reality, our new status in Christ, who is our Elder Brother.[23] And this new status has precedence even over biological siblings. Jesus presses this truth when he is interrupted from his teaching by someone saying, "Look, your mother and your brothers are standing outside, wanting to speak to you" (Matt. 12:47). He doesn't reply, *Oh, this must be important; excuse me for a second.* He doesn't even reply, *Okay, let them know I'll talk to them when I'm done speaking to the crowds.* No, quite shockingly he says, "'Who is my mother and who are my brothers?' Stretching out his hand toward his disciples, he said, 'Here are my mother and my brothers! For whoever does the will of my Father in heaven is my brother and sister and mother'" (vv. 48–50). While we know Christ loved and cared for his biological family and Scripture exhorts us to do the same,[24] we see that Christ now views those spiritually united to him as siblings in an even truer sense! "By faith, we are new creations with exclusive family ties to Christ. We have an unremitting advocate who is now seated at the right hand of the Father (see Ps. 110:1, 5; Rom. 8:34; Heb. 7:25)."[25]

So, even as we see Paul commending Phoebe as a deacon and a *prostasis*, her highest honor and title is as our sister in Christ. Paul is saying that she is one of us. And that means that she too has rights and obligations as a sister. Repeating Cohick, "As a sister in the household of God, Phoebe would be expected to use her resources to better the lives of her brothers and sisters."[26] Paul is commending a sister who is going to use her resources, the knowledge of Paul's instruction as well as any means by which she may be able to assist through her social status,

---

22. Thanks to Dave Myers for adding this additional thought.
23. See David B. Garner, *Sons in the Son: The Riches and Reach of Adoption in Christ* (Phillipsburg, NJ: P&R, 2016).
24. See Ex. 20:12; Prov. 1:8–9; John 19:26–27; Eph. 6:1–4; 1 Tim. 5:8.
25. Byrd, *Why Can't We Be Friends?*, 120.
26. Lynn H. Cohick, *Women in the World of the Earliest Christians* (Grand Rapids: Baker Academic, 2009), 304.

and he asks for the siblings in Rome to provide for Phoebe through their hospitality.

Do we commend sisters in the church this way now? Obviously, Paul has invested in Phoebe. There is reciprocity in the relationship. He was happy to be helped by her benefaction, but he also must have picked up on her theological vigor and poured into her, equipping her well to answer the questions the Roman church was sure to have regarding the epistle. In a day with Google and cell phone accessibility, we can easily miss the value of the deliverer. Paul wasn't traveling to Rome yet, he couldn't be reached via FaceTime, and these churches were not even established by him or Peter. There was no backup drive, just a painstakingly written thirteen-foot-long scroll. He sends Phoebe. With the letter to the Romans. Let that sink in! This is what a sister can do!

A CAPPADOCIAN SISTER

Earlier I mentioned the significance of the early church creeds in helping us to interpret Scripture. The works of the Cappadocian fathers Gregory of Nazianzus, Basil the Great, and Gregory of Nyssa are pivotal to upholding an orthodox confession of the church, particularly in their work on the Trinity, which led to the revised version of the Nicene Creed finalized at the First Council of Constantinople in 381. But as Lynn Cohick and Amy Brown Hughes point out, there is much theological work underneath these creedal statements and councils. "Especially in regard to the central discussions on the Trinity and Christology in early Christianity, core work on these subjects was happening in imaginative rewritings of Plato, the construction of the Christian historical narrative, letters between friends, dialogues in the middle of the night, the establishing of monastic communities in homes and in the desert, pilgrimages to the Holy Land, reception of the martyr tradition, and the ascetic negotiation with the body."[27]

---

27. Lynne Cohick and Amy Brown Hughes, *Christian Women in the Patristic World: Their Influence, Authority, and Legacy in the Second through Fifth Centuries* (Grand Rapids: Baker, 2017), xxvii.

I'd like to highlight one woman who unquestionably made a profound impact on the work of two of these Cappadocian fathers—Basil and Gregory of Nyssa's older sister, Macrina.

Gregory of Nyssa wrote quite a bit about his sister and how she shaped his learning in *The Life of St. Macrina*, his tribute to her after her death, and *On the Soul and the Resurrection*, where he portrays a conversation with his sister on her deathbed in the philosophical, Socratic style of a pupil-teacher dialogue. In this deep metaphysical and theological conversation on the nature of the soul, virtue, the resurrection, and beatific vision, Gregory is the student asking provocative questions, and Macrina is "the Teacher"[28] imparting her great wisdom. In this genre of writing, the reader isn't expected to believe this was the literal account of their conversation. But Gregory is sharing something about the impact and teaching in which his sister shaped his own life and theology.[29] Perhaps, even in this idealistic portrayal of her voice, Gregory is like the African lover in *The Wall of the Plague*, telling the story behind the story of the Niceno–Constantinopolitan Creed and the female voice that lurks behind it. By taking on his sister's voice, Gregory is showing us more of the picture. "Thus we hear Macrina's voice in Gregory's theologically attuned writings and instructions on the monastic and ascetic ideal."[30] He does describe this conversation with Macrina in her painful condition, awaiting the meeting of her Bridegroom, in *The Life of St. Macrina*:

> My soul seemed to be almost outside of human nature, uplifted as it was by her words and set down inside the heavenly sanctuaries by the guidance of her discourse. . . .
>
> And were it not that my narrative was stretching out to infinity, I would record everything in the order and way it happened: how she was lifted up by her discourse and spoke to me of her

28. See Gregory of Nyssa, *On the Soul and Resurrection*, in *The Complete Ante-Nicene & Nicene and Post-Nicene Church Fathers Collection*, ed. Philip Schaff (London: Catholic Way, 2014), loc. 523106, 523111, Kindle.

29. See Cohick and Hughes, *Christian Women*, 171.

30. Cohick and Hughes, *Christian Women*, 160.

philosophy of the soul; how she explained the reason for life in the flesh, for what purpose man exists, how he is mortal, what is the source of death and what release there is from death back to life again. On all of these subjects, as if inspired by the Holy Spirit, she explained everything clearly and logically, her speech flowing on with complete ease as water is borne from some fountain-head downhill without anything to get in its way.[31]

Possibly the oldest of ten siblings, four of which are well known, Macrina devoted herself to the Lord in a life of celibacy and to her family as they suffered through the tragedy of their father's death, as well as the death of their esteemed brother, Naucratios. "She became the spiritual mentor of the household, educating, comforting, and developing a devoted community."[32] Although Macrina was content to modestly serve the Lord within the ascetic community she established, Gregory wanted the world to know about her great character, love of God's Word, and teaching, which affected the future of Christ's church. He presents Macrina as a strong woman, comparing his sister to an athlete as her character is tested with the death of each of their loved ones, "first by the death of her other brother, Naucratios, after this by the separation from her mother and third when Basil, the common honour of our family, departed from human life. So she stood her ground like an undefeated athlete, who does not cringe at any point before the onslaught of misfortune."[33] Her strength and resolve contributed to the work of her brothers. We see from Gregory's writings that "woman's theologizing is fundamental to the development of Christian thought and should not be relegated to the fringe or regarded as a concession prize at best."[34]

This is what a sister can do! Macrina is a tradent of the faith, communicating God's Word and sharing communion in it. To her brothers she is "the teacher,"[35] while Gregory makes her contribution visible to

31. Gregory, Bishop of Nyssa, *The Life of Saint Macrina*, trans. Kevin Corrigan (Eugene, OR: Wipf & Stock, 2005), 35–36.
32. Cohick and Hughes, *Christian Women*, 163.
33. Gregory, *Life of Saint Macrina*, 33.
34. Cohick and Hughes, *Christian Women*, xxviii.
35. Gregory, *Life of Saint Macrina*, 36.

the church, revealing the story behind the story with her voice. Because Macrina is not only the biological sister of Gregory of Nyssa and Basil the Great, she is our sister as well, a sister in Christ retrieving the baton of God's Word, beholding it (and beholding him by it), offering a reciprocal and even teaching voice to her brothers' voices, getting her fingerprints all over it, simultaneously holding on and passing it not only to her brothers but to all who were influenced through their work—us!

A MYSTERIOUS SISTER

I'm not going to spend too much time here, as we are now entering the realm of what Richard Bauckham calls "historical imagination."[36] But apostles were major baton passers, and some parts of Scripture just about dare us to imagine (responsibly imagine, of course). The greetings Paul sends in Romans 16 provoke the imagination. Who are all these people Paul holds in such high regard? One of the more notorious sisters in Christ to whom some historical imaginers tried to give a sex change is Junia. "Greet Andronicus and Junia, my fellow Jews who have been in prison with me. They are outstanding among the apostles, and they were in Christ before I was" (Rom. 16:7 NIV). Some translators, relying on the assumption that Paul could never refer to a woman as an apostle, changed the feminine "Junia" to the masculine "Junias." Given the fact that there are plenty of instances where the name Junia is referenced in ancient documents, there are no records of the name Junias, the ancient manuscripts say Junia,[37] and most of the patristic writers understood Junia to be a woman, most scholars today agree that Paul is referring to a woman named Junia. We can safely affirm this, no historical imagination here.

But affirming that Junia is a sister, she is still mysterious. We see her

---

36. Richard Bauckham, *Gospel Women: Studies of the Named Women in the Gospels* (Grand Rapids: Eerdmans, 2002), 194.

37. "The first noticeable shift from Junia to Junias was apparently made by Faber Stapulensis, writing in Paris in 1512. His work subsequently influenced Luther's commentary on Romans." Kenneth Bailey, "Women in the New Testament: A Middle Eastern Cultural View," *Theology Matters* 6.1 (January–February 2000): 4, https://godswordtowomen.org/women_new_testament.pdf.

nowhere else in Scripture, and yet Paul says that she and Andronicus are outstanding among the apostles. Some translations interpret this as "they are well known to the apostles" (Rom. 16:7 ESV) or "they are noteworthy in the eyes of the apostles (CSB). This translation removes the vocation of apostleship from the two (spouses? siblings? colaborers?). In doing this, it really doesn't add anything meaningful to their description—why would Paul mention that they are well known to the apostles? For what? The early church regarded them as apostles, as John Chrysostom indicates in his thirty-first homily on Romans: "And indeed to be apostles at all is a great thing. But to be even among these of note, just consider what a great encomium this is! But they were of note owing to their works, to their achievements. Oh! How great is the devotion (*philosophia*) of this woman, that she should be even counted worthy of the appellation of apostle!"[38]

Surely they were not one of the original Twelve. But we see others in Scripture, such as Paul and Barnabas (Acts 14:14), Apollos (1 Cor. 4:6–9), James (Gal. 1:19), Epaphroditus (Phil. 2:25), Timothy and Silvanus (1 Thess. 1:1; 2:7), as well as two unnamed people (2 Cor. 8:23) and Jesus himself (Heb. 3:1) referred to as apostles. What does Paul mean by apostle here? Kenneth Bailey concludes, "The title is best understood to have maintained its original meaning, which was an eyewitness to Jesus who had received a direct commission from him."[39] This would make a lot more sense in Paul's description of Andronicus and Junia—they are outstanding among those commissioned by Jesus, giving testimony to his life, his lordship, and his gospel in planting churches. In addition, he also mentions that they are fellow Jews and prisoners who have been in Christ even before him (Rom. 16:7).[40]

So far we haven't had to use much historical imagination for this sister, as we've just been looking at the vocabulary in Scripture. But there is still this mystery that Junia is such a prominent apostle and we do not see her

---

38. Chrysostom, "Homilies on the Epistle to the Romans," Homily xxxi, in *The Complete Ante-Nicene & Nicene and Post-Nicene Church Fathers Collection*, ed. Philip Schaff (London: Catholic Way, 2014), loc. 392100–392104, Kindle.

39. Bailey, "Women in the New Testament," 4. See Acts 22:14–15; 1 Cor. 9:1.

40. Which would make sense: if they were eyewitnesses to Jesus's earthly ministry, they would have had to been Judean Jews and Christians before Paul.

name anywhere except in these greetings by Paul at the end of his epistle. Really considering each person he mentions in this active snapshot of the church is exciting. And it's not a stretch of the historical imagination to think of the outstanding work involved in planting churches and spreading the gospel to both Jews and Gentiles in Rome and connecting that to Paul's affirmation of their great work in his greeting.

But Bauckham has stretched the historical imagination even further, proposing that maybe we have record of Junia's time with Jesus that further qualifies her testimony.[41] Luke names some women among Jesus's disciples who traveled with him for at least two years, straight to the cross, and were the first to discover the stone rolled away at his empty grave. He names Mary Magdalene; Joanna, the wife of Herod's steward Chuza; and Susanna among the women who were with Jesus and the Twelve from the beginning of his public ministry in Galilee (Luke 8:1–3; 23:49, 55–24:11). We are going to focus on Joanna.

Bauckham suggests that Joanna, from a prominent Jewish family of Galilee, was arranged to be married to the Nabatean nobleman Chuza, his wife's Jewish religion being an advantage for him in Herod's administration. Joanna had a healing encounter with Jesus that changed her life. Rather than merely being a sympathizer to Jesus's ministry, she joined in as a disciple, leaving her own household to follow him. "Sometimes as many as a hundred were traveling with him, sometimes far fewer, but Joanna, with the other women and the twelve men, belonged to the inner circle of those in constant attendance."[42] She was a patron to Jesus and the disciples, as well as one that could assist in his ministry in creative ways in reaching out to other women among their daily activities or who were looking for healing. Like Jesus, she was a model of "'the patron who serves' ([Luke] 22:27). . . . The usual pattern of patronage with its unequal relationship of patron and client is now put within the structure of the new community and transformed."[43]

---

41. The following three paragraphs paraphrase some of Bauckham's findings in *Gospel Women*, 109–99.

42. Bauckham, *Gospel Women*, 197.

43. Bauckham, *Gospel Women*, 165, quoting H. Moxnes, "Patron-Client Relations and the New Community in Luke-Acts," in *The Social World of Luke-Acts*, ed. J. H. Neyrey (Peabody, MA: Hendrickson, 1991), 263.

Given her contacts in the Herodian court, she would have been one of the first to hear about Jesus's sentencing to crucifixion once they were in Jerusalem. Unlike the male disciples who fled, she witnessed the death of her Savior, was one of those who returned to his tomb with spices and ointments to care for his dead body, and was first to hear the good news of the resurrection. She was one of the few who first told the gospel to the eleven apostles (Luke 24:10). How about that for a commissioning?

Given that, as courtiers, she and her husband likely had connections in Rome, it is highly conceivable that they were missionaries from Jerusalem, as Joanna had eyewitness details of the gospel and was discipled under Jesus (able to communicate his teaching, leading to covenantal communal fellowship in it with new churches of believers), and eventually sent to Rome to help establish the churches as the gospel reached the Jewish community there. You see, Bauckham suggests that Joanna *is* Junia.[44] While it wasn't common for Palestinian Jews to take on a Latin name, as they did not want to appear under allegiance to Rome, it would be beneficial for Joanna to do so within the Romanized Herodian court of Tiberias. And it would be a natural selection semantically for Joanna to take on the additional Latin name Junia. That both Joanna and Junia "were founding members of the Jerusalem church gives this suggestion considerable plausibility."[45] Boom. Well, an unverifiable but incredibly fascinating and plausible boom.

What kind of takeaway can we get from historical imagination? Well, true or not, we have here a very mysterious sister(s) who had major influence on the formation of the early church, tasked with communicating and communing, which always go together. Michael Bird gets practical in application regarding Paul's greeting to Junia, "When it comes to developing ministry teams, especially in church planting, we would be wise to follow Paul's example and incorporate women into key roles, especially when our field of ministry is either highly difficult

---

44. And perhaps Chuza was Andronicus, although Junia could have been widowed and remarried; or Andronicus could have been her brother or another colaborer.

45. Bauckham, *Gospel Women*, 184.

or boldly ambitious."[46] Perhaps Jesus and Paul both incorporated this sister in her key vocations. Having a coed team of apostles in Rome sounds wisely strategic in reaching the diverse men and women to whom they hoped to minister.

The difficult part to wrestle with for complementarian churches, and for the first time in this book, is that we are moving a little further past lay work here. Apostle is a fairly big title. What do we do with this now? We no longer have apostles in the church, but how does this presentation of Junia translate into contemporary ministry? Churches may not all come to the same conclusions, but this is something that we all need to wrestle with. What principles do we find here, and what is the Holy Spirit saying through his Word here to our churches?

PEEL AND REVEAL

This last peel and reveal focuses less on the movement of biblical manhood and womanhood that I've been interacting with and more on its effect in your local body of believers. Look at these questions as an opportunity to self-evaluate. They are peeling-and-revealing questions. Have you ever heard of being clutter blind? It's when you are so used to the clutter in your house that you no longer notice it. Or similarly, when we have small children, we can be so busy with the regular daily chores of cooking, tidying up, brushing teeth, and doing dishes, that we fail to notice all the fingerprints on our walls. We see them every day and they have now become part of the landscape. It's not until we are ready to repaint that we see the grime for what it is. Then we want to be champion wall wipers.

Here I am asking you to look for yellow wallpaper that has been left behind in your church. Maybe it's been there so long that you have learned to live with it. In fact, you may not even notice it anymore. Or perhaps you do—it's been nagging at you with all its confusing lines—but you know how hard it is to peel away old wallpaper. And you don't want to

---

46. Michael F. Bird, *Romans*, Story of God Bible Commentary, ed. Tremper Longman III and Scot McKnight (Grand Rapids: Zondervan, 2016), 528.

lose church members over it. Heck, you don't want to lose your own job over it. As one man said, "It is difficult to get a man to understand something when his salary depends upon his not understanding it!"[47]

What is the culture like in your church? Churches that uphold male-only ordination especially need to consider whether the male officers in the church are fostering a male culture in the church. This can especially be a blind spot if they were trained in seminaries that had little to no female presence or contribution.

What responsibilities do your laywomen and laymen feel they have toward their other household members? Scripture has about sixty "one another" passages to help direct us. They are not gendered. I've categorized them under seven[48] different headings:

- Loving one another: John 13:14, 33–34; 15:12, 17; Romans 13:8; 1 Corinthians 12:25; Galatians 5:13; 1 Thessalonians 3:12; 4:9; 1 Peter 3:8; 4:8; 1 John 3:11, 23; 4:7, 11, 12; and 2 John 5, and my favorite, "Love *one another* deeply as brothers and sisters. Outdo *one another* in showing honor" (Rom. 12:10, italics added).
- Promoting peace and harmony with one another: Mark 9:50; Romans 12:16; 14:13; 15:7.
- Being teachable while teaching and admonishing one another: Romans 15:14; Ephesians 5:19, 21; Colossians 3:16.
- Greeting and welcoming one another "with a holy kiss": Romans 16:16; 1 Corinthians 16:20; 2 Corinthians 13:12; 1 Peter 5:14. Others: 1 Corinthians 11:33; 1 Peter 4:9.
- What not to do to one another: Galatians 5:15, 26; Colossians 3:9; James 4:11; 5:9.
- Bearing with one another: Galatians 6:2; Ephesians 4:2, 32; Philippians 2:3; Colossians 3:13; 1 Peter 5:5.
- Encouraging one another: 1 Thessalonians 4:18; 5:11; Hebrews 3:13; 10:24–25; James 5:16.

---

47. Upton Sinclair, *I, Candidate for Governor: And How I Got Licked* (1935; repr., Berkeley: University of California Press, 1994), 109.

48. See Byrd, *Why Can't We Be Friends?*, 150–55.

Do the laypeople in your church have the agency to fulfill their obligations toward one another, including toward the church officers? What are the relationships like in your church? Are they ones that express godly affection in all purity and promote holiness in one another? These are important questions because we are handing down more than an orthodox confession of the faith. God's people hand down the longest-lasting relationships God gives us: siblingship. This is a different dynamic than the gender tropes of biblical manhood and womanhood that keep us trapped in the yellow wallpaper.

And it helps us maintain unity and harmony in God's household. Siblingship is the very framework that will help us to uphold distinction without reduction. We have unique responsibilities and contributions to our sexes because women will never be brothers and men will never be sisters. The plethora of sibling language in the New Testament teaches us about the realities of being summed up into Christ's household and how that shapes our communion with one another. As Christine Pohl says, "The best testimony to the truth of the gospel is the quality of our life together."[49] The church cannot give a credible testimony to the power of the gospel if we do not model the covenantal and relational fruit of it now as new creations.

How do you see the men and women in your church serving together under the common mission of handing down the faith to the next generation and the active traditioning that involves? Is it dynamic and fructifying? What if the traditioning that your church is handing down is wrong? Or what if the good stuff is hindered because of the yellow wallpaper slapped over it? How do you address that? Or how can you even identify that? Here is a discerning distinction offered by Jaroslov Pelikan: "Tradition is the living faith of the dead, traditionalism is the dead faith of the living. And, I suppose I should add, it is traditionalism that gives tradition such a bad name."[50] Is your church handing down the living faith of the dead, holding fast to our confession of hope (Heb. 10:23)

---

49. Christine D. Pohl, *Living into Community: Cultivating Practices That Sustain Us* (Grand Rapids: Eerdmans, 2012), 2.

50. Jaroslav Pelikan, *The Vindication of Tradition* (New Haven, CT: Yale University Press, 1984), 65.

together as a covenant family, or inadvertently handing down traditional stereotypes that Christ's kingdom has already turned on their heads?

REVEALING THE BEAUTY OF SUBMISSION— FOR MEN AND WOMEN

Here's a yellow-wallpaper-spotting question: Are the women in your church the only ones learning about submission? Or is submission taught, as Andrew Bartlett has helpfully defined it, as "the heart of Christ-centered gospel living. . . . To be imitators of Christ (Eph. 5:1– 2), believers are called not to rule over other people but to be the 'slave' of all. This is what Jesus taught and lived, both in his ministry and supremely at the cross (Mark 10:42–45; John 13:1–17; 15:12–17; Phil. 2:5–8). Submission, in the sense of humbly ranking others as more important than oneself, is a vital element of godliness."[51] Along with this, when women are trying to contribute as necessary allies or in the "one another" categories commanded in Scripture, are they viewed as trying to usurp authority from men? Do the women in your church feel suspect in that way when they have a correcting voice to offer, something to teach, or even when they step in to help bear a burden? Have they been asked this question? And will they feel secure enough to give the honest answer? Are you willing to hear their honest answer even, or especially, if it is not what you want to hear? What will you do with that? One of my favorite women in Reformation history, Katherine Zell, responded to charges like this rather boldly, saying, "I do not pretend to be like John the Baptist rebuking the Pharisees. I do not claim to be Nathan upbraiding David. I aspire only to be Balaam's ass, castigating his master."[52]

What messages does your church send about sexuality? Do the men feel reduced to trying to avoid so-called animalistic impulses, always on the brink of having an affair? Do the women feel like threats to the

---

51. Andrew Bartlett, *Men and Women in Christ: Fresh Light from the Biblical Texts* (London: Inter-Varsity Press, 2019), 340.

52. Roland H. Bainton, *Women of the Reformation in Germany and Italy* (Boston: Beacon, 1974), 55.

men's purity or reputation? Or is there healthy sibling interaction in an environment where household members view one another holistically and can grow in discernment and wisdom? Does your church witness to the fact that "relationships in the church are shaped by the new creation," where "created gender distinctions remain in existence, but are also transcended"?[53]

REVEALING THE RECIPROCITY

What plans are in place at your church to make disciples? Are you intentional about investing in and training the women in the church the same as the men? Do the women have the same agency as the men as disciples? Do they get to carry the baton? How does the female voice function in your congregation? Is it present at all in worship? I was asked an excellent question at a conference where I was speaking just last weekend. This was at a church that held to male-only ordination. I was asked about the connection between the worship service and the culture of the church: "What message does a first-time visitor get about the dynamic between the brothers and sisters in your congregation and the leadership of worship? Do they see any reciprocity there? Then why would they expect to see it in the life of the church?" I offered several layers of suggestions to answer these questions.

First and foremost, a visitor to our church should notice a different dynamic in corporate worship from the rest of the activity of church life: God has summoned us to come and receive Christ and all his blessings. The prominent voice we should be hearing, which is spoken through the preached Word, is Christ's. Our voices in worship are responsive to his. This is part of the apologetic in churches that hold to male-only ordination—Christ, our Bridegroom, would be best represented by a man.

And yet we see in 1 Corinthians 11–14 that there is more to worship than preaching. We see the fruit of that in the dynamic of both men and women prophesying, speaking in tongues, and praying. As a

---

53. Bartlett, *Men and Women in Christ*, 343.

cessationist, I must ask how this translates into the life and worship of the church now. I see the public reading of Scripture and leading of corporate prayers as two ways both laymen and laywomen should contribute in corporate worship in line with the principles of worship in 1 Corinthians.[54] Some denominations and churches that hold to male-only ordination also think the reading of Scripture and prayers in corporate worship should be led by the ordained elders only. This means that not only laywomen, but laymen, will not participate in this way.

I also spoke with a woman who loves to be a part of the music group that leads the singing. However, she is not allowed to have any speaking parts in her church because the leadership thinks that is too authoritative for a woman in worship. But even in the Old Testament, we see Miriam leading with song and tambourine in worshiping the Lord for parting the Red Sea for the Israelites' rescue. It's not exactly the same as a worship service, but it's quite a mighty moment of corporate worship where women are telling the Israelites to join them in worshiping the Lord for a major redemptive-historical event. And if we sing songs that are written by women in worship, whether hymns or contemporary, or if we burst into singing the words from Mary's Magnificat, why can't a woman say something to lead us to the next song? Ultimately, I look at the pastor as leading worship as a whole, but these are all responsive, reciprocal voices to the call to worship.

One thing my pastor does to help us prepare our minds and hearts for worship is to write a couple reflections in the bulletin that are related to the Scripture passages that he will be preaching on. They are usually quotes from a book. I was "that person" who emailed him to let him know how much it stuck out to me when I first saw a woman author quoted in this section. I don't want to be counting the times in comparison to male quotes or anything like that, but it was noticeable to me that he directed us to a sister's meditation and wisdom. I also notice this when women are quoted from the pulpit alongside of men or used in sermon illustrations that break through cultural stereotypes.

---

54. Although I do concur that the pastor should pray for the main, congregational prayer as a shepherd.

We can even back it up a bit. Do you have only men handing out bulletins, helping visitors to find a seat, and passing the offering basket? Why? What message might that be sending? If Phoebe can deliver the epistle to the Romans, a sister should be able to handle delivering an offering basket.[55] Backing it up a little more, are laypeople teaching adult Sunday school in your church? If so, are both laymen and laywomen being equipped to do that? If Junia can be sent as an apostle with Andronicus to establish churches throughout Rome, then you should at least value coeducational teaching teams in Sunday school. Do the men in your church learn from the women's theological contributions? If the Cappadocian father Gregory of Nyssa can call Macrina "the Teacher," showing just how dependent his theological understanding of the Scriptures was on his sister, then the men in your church can learn from their sisters as well. Sisters make great adult Sunday school teachers when invested in well, as well as excellent contributors in class discussion as learners. They could also contribute theologically in written resources the church offers. And helpful women authors should be recommended as church resources. Like Macrina, they may even excel in training other theological leaders. That should all be seen in the dynamics of a typical Sunday in your church, whether you hold to male-only ordination or not—men and women colaborers serving under the fruit of the ministry with reciprocal voices and dynamic exchange, the house of God as a Ripstick!

Like Mary, and like Joanna, we all have now been brought into Christ's inner circle. We are to learn from the Good Teacher. Sisters are necessary allies to our brothers. We all are called to sibling solidarity, to learn as Christ's disciples, and to serve in his household as colaborers in the gospel. Jesus Christ himself said these things will not be taken away from women. Right now we are being prepared for eternal communion with the triune God and one another. So we all need to be active participants in God's household. As disciples, sisters in his family, we are to stimulate our brothers and sisters to holiness and pass down the faith given to us.

---

55. I have had it explained to me that this is a service to the women so that they may stay seated throughout the whole worship service.

Let me repeat: this is the one necessary thing. We need to know Jesus. We need to sit at his feet, that is, do the things disciples do: *participate in creative and spiritual life in the church, contribute literary expression and spiritual creativity*, in the *heart of existence*. We are all called to the important task of *passing on the heritage of the tradition to future generations*. We are to *serve in roles that identify with knowledge of God's Word*. And this inclusion will *affect the public image* of God's household. It will model the communion Christ's brothers and sisters have with him, where we are headed, and what we expect for eternity.

Like Phoebe, men and women all hold a treasure in our hands, and we play a vital role in spreading the good news. Phoebe served as Paul's intermediary to *make common* his teaching, to further communicate Paul's message for understanding, and to *share communion* through Christ. She was trusted to communicate Paul's teaching in the epistle to the Romans. But we each have several copies of the sixty-six books that make up the complete canon of God's Word. Or in an instant we can click on a handy Bible app.

What I'm getting at here is that while women may not be in the ordained ministry of your church or denomination, and while women are gifted to serve in differing ways, men and women are all called to communicate well. Laypeople have honorable work to do. We are to read God's Word for understanding, as that knowledge fills our hearts and directs our actions. As part of this life-giving covenant community, we all are active traditioners, retrievers, and reformers, receiving God's Word as it has been historically confessed through his Spirit and making it common to others.

What Phoebe held in her hands, we hold in ours! All of us!

QUESTIONS FOR GROUP DISCUSSION

1. Paul's most frequent way of describing the church is as siblings. What does this disclose about his ecclesiological and ethical thinking? One common argument that I hear when promoting the equipping of laywomen to serve as tradents in the church is that of the slippery slope: complementarian churches fear that

this will lead to women's ordination. Another slippery slope fear is that gender "roles" will be reversed, and the next thing you know we will be sanctifying homosexual relationships. How does a biblical understanding of sibling relationships in the household of God combat this slippery slope argument—particularly teaching us how to value our relationships, defining what our rights and obligations are to one another, identifying distinctiveness between the sexes, and maintaining unity and harmony in God's household?

2. How does this understanding of siblingship affect the relationships between the clergy and the laypeople?

3. Does your church value women's theologizing as fundamental to the development of Christian thought? Why or why not? If your church upholds male-only ordination, does that squelch or promote the sisters in your congregation in communicating and communing in key responsibilities?

4. What do we do with this Junia/apostle passage now as a church in the twenty-first century? How does this designation of "apostle" translate for us—what principles can we take from it and apply to our churches?

5. Do you see any yellow wallpaper in your church? Where? I once read a study that revealed men answer much more positively about the condition of their marriage than women do, when asked. Make sure to ask the women in your church if they see any yellow wallpaper. Imagine you are a visitor to your church in answering this question: How does the female voice function in this congregation? What consequences do you foresee in peeling off the wallpaper?

6. Bonus question for complementarian churches: If there are no female teaching voices in seminary, how do we expect the pastors graduating *not* to shepherd a church with a distinctly male culture? If men and women are distinct sexes, how do we train pastors to preach for and shepherd both men *and* women in their congregations? How do we expect them to value the female voice if they are told they should not learn from them in seminary?